ROUTL
LITER

Volume 4

PERFORMING LA MESTIZA

PERFORMING LA MESTIZA
Textual Representations of Lesbians of Color and the Negotiation of Identities

ELLEN M. GIL-GOMEZ

LONDON AND NEW YORK

First published in 2000 by Garland Publishing, Inc.

This edition first published in 2017
by Routledge
2 Park Square, Milton Park, Abingdon, Oxon OX14 4RN

and by Routledge
711 Third Avenue, New York, NY 10017

Routledge is an imprint of the Taylor & Francis Group, an informa business

© 2000 Ellen M. Gil-Gomez

All rights reserved. No part of this book may be reprinted or reproduced or utilised in any form or by any electronic, mechanical, or other means, now known or hereafter invented, including photocopying and recording, or in any information storage or retrieval system, without permission in writing from the publishers.

Trademark notice: Product or corporate names may be trademarks or registered trademarks, and are used only for identification and explanation without intent to infringe.

British Library Cataloguing in Publication Data
A catalogue record for this book is available from the British Library

ISBN: 978-0-415-78487-0 (Set)
ISBN: 978-1-315-21275-3 (Set) (ebk)
ISBN: 978-0-415-78956-1 (Volume 4) (hbk)
ISBN: 978-0-415-78975-2 (Volume 4) (pbk)
ISBN: 978-1-315-21372-9 (Volume 4) (ebk)

Publisher's Note
The publisher has gone to great lengths to ensure the quality of this reprint but points out that some imperfections in the original copies may be apparent.

Disclaimer
The publisher has made every effort to trace copyright holders and would welcome correspondence from those they have been unable to trace.

Performing La Mestiza

Textual Representations of Lesbians of Color and the Negotiation of Identities

Ellen M. Gil-Gomez

Garland Publishing, Inc.
A member of the Taylor & Francis Group
New York and London
2000

Published in 2000 by
Garland Publishing Inc
A Member of the Taylor & Francis Group
19 Union Square West
New York, NY 10003

Copyright © 2000 by Ellen M Gil-Gomez

All rights reserved. No part of this book may be reprinted or reproduced or utilized in any form or by any electronic, mechanical, or other means, now known or hereafter invented, including photocopying and recording, or in any information storage or retrieval system, without permission in writing from the publishers

10 9 8 7 6 5 4 3 2 1

Library of Congress Cataloging-in-Publication Data
Gil-Gomes, Ellen M
    Performing la mestiza textual representations of lesbians of color and the negotiation of identities / Ellen M. Gil-Gomez
      p. cm — (Literary criticism and cultural theory)
    "A Garland series"
    Includes bibliographical references and index
    ISBN 0-8153-3647-0

    1 Lesbians' writings, American—History and criticism 2. Feminism and literature—United States—History—20th century 3 American literature—Minority authors—History and criticism 4 Women and literature—United States—History—20th century. 5. American literature—Women authors—History and criticism 6 Identity (Psychology) in literature 7 Minority women in literature 8 Group identity in literature 9 Ethnic groups in literature. 10. Minorities in literature. 11. Lesbians in literature. 12. Race in literature. I. Title. II. Series.
PS153 L46 G55 2000
810 9'9206643—dc21
                                                                                 99-055077

Printed on acid-free, 250-year-life paper
Manufactured in the United States of America

Contents

Acknowledgments	vii
Preface	ix
Introduction	xv
1. Rethinking Identity Construction: Placing the Lesbian of Color	3
2. Naming the Enemies: Multiple Threats to the Existence of the Lesbian of Color	39
3. Strategies of Survival: The Limits and the Consequences	91
4. The Path To Survival: Rewriting Cultural Traditions and Creating Living Theories	135
Conclusion	167
Endnotes	177
Bibliography	193
Index	203

Acknowledgements

In many ways this book began in 1991 when I began my doctoral study knowing that women of color are trained to be silent, though missing the tools to understand and articulate how and why. I most credit Dr. Carol Siegel for nurturing this project at every stage, by giving me the tools to begin and the support to continue this many times disrespected and neglected research. She has helped me realize that theorizing can produce personal and community strength. I also wish to thank Dr. William Cain, Damon Zucca, and James Morgan from Garland for their enthusiastic support of, and suggestions for, this project.

I most appreciate my family for giving me everything. They have pushed me through and forgiven me the work that has sometimes driven me crazy and sometimes made me jubilant. I give these pages to my parents Alvaro and Marilouise, who are always there, to Kelly, who holds me up and has given so much, and to my daughters Hannah and Selina who hold the future. I dedicate this book to them and to all women and girls of color who have the determination to survive on their own terms and against all odds.

Preface

The impetus for this project developed with my realization that there had been little study of women of color's view of gender. Indeed, much of the canonical feminist theory produced by women of color had been primarily positioned as work that focused on "difference" or race or ethnicity. I was troubled that even with the huge influx of work by feminists of color in the 1980s, the study of ethnic and/or racial identity was still seen as secondary to the study of gender and only tangenital to the larger category of "women" in the mid 1990s.

This struck me very plainly as a graduate student studying feminist theory from the seminal collection from Warhol and Herndl called *Feminisms*. The overwhelming majority of works that were by women of color were put into the "Ethnicity" category with only a small number of essays addressing other topics. While lesbian authors and lesbian topics did appear in various categories of the text, I was surprised that lesbian identity/lesbian theory was not considered enough to be given a category in the text. In the early 1990s, it was the work of queer theorists like Judith Butler and Diana Fuss that held the biggest possiblities for feminist theory and yet this work was totally unrepresented in the collection. While I was intrigued by the work of these queer theorists and could see the potential for change that their ideas brought, I was again disappointed that women of color were still primarily silent in this dialogue.

This project then was my attempt to consider the history of gender studies and to analyze how the natural consequence of academic white supremacy, homophobia, and ethnocentrism was to marginalize women of color in these debates. I wanted to focus my study not only on works of literature by lesbians of color but also to foreground the consequences of academic ethnocentrism in the devaluation or nonrecognition of these authors' theoretical works. This point is not a new one, for example Barbara Christian discussed it at length in her 1989 essay "The Race for Theory". But, the fact remains that theory by women of color still remains primarily outside the traditionally defined scope of gender studies.

Even though my manuscript was complete in 1995 and was focused on the material available at that time, for better or for worse, it retains its importance for the present situation of gender and identity studies. I would like to highlight some important work that has been published since my own was completed in order to further contextualize the material that follows, and in order to connect my own conclusions with other recently published works by scholars in this field.

A particularly noteworthy change since my original research is the revised edition of *Feminisms* from 1997. In the new edition many different women of color are represented in categories beyond ethnicity and many lesbian topics and approaches are newly included as well. In their opening notes the editors address these changes. While their remarks are primarily true—the original collection did do something to redress the narrow focus of feminism on straight, white, middle-class women—I feel the editors don't adequately explore the bias to which their volume contributed, and therefore I feel they brush by an important time in the history of feminism. That is, that feminists of color were, and still mainly are, contained to specific and separate topics. This implies of course, that issues of race or ethnicity are not primary concerns in all areas of feminist study. The editors of *Feminisms* mention that their new choices reflect "a widening acknowledgement" (xi) that the visions of feminism were dominated by white straight women. Since the visions of women of color and lesbians (and lesbians of color) have appeared in print since the early 1980s[1] what Warhol and Herndl should have written is that their choices reflect that more white women are finally listening to what women of color have been saying for almost two decades. The change that I acknowledge here then is that canonical literature is beginning to reflect what women of color have been shouting out for too long: that "race, sexual orientation, and class always inflect understandings of gender." (xi) While charting the changes in one particular anthology is fruitful and revealing I would like to mention some books that have recently been published that analyze the intersections of ethnic/racial identity,

Preface xi

gender, and sexuality or that focus on general theories of multiple identities.

Many of the theorists that I depended on in my project are Chicanas or Latinas and many women in this community of scholars broke the ground in women of color lesbian studies (if there is, yet, such a thing!) Happily there are now routinely more than just two or three Latina scholars who are vocal on these topics. In recent years there have been a number of volumes focused on Latina scholarship, writers, contributions and communities. There have been a number of texts specifically on Chicana experience and vision and some do include issues important to Chicana lesbians. Some of these volumes include *Building with Our Hands, Chicana Feminist Thought, Home Girls, Living Chicana Theory, Migrant Song* and *Women Singing in the Snow*. All of these texts complicate earlier notions of Chicana lives and experiences and their relationship to feminism as well as the study of American culture and literature. One new book, *Show & Tell: Identity as Performance in U.S. Latina/o Fiction*, focuses on Latino/a literature and identity. It argues that this fiction is strongly performative in that it recreates self, ethnic and cultural identities within its pages. Though I don't agree with all of Christian's arguments or conclusions her approach is very similar to my own. I find her vision of the anti-essentialist nature of Latina/o fiction a helpful one when I consider the ramifications of embracing multiple performative identities.

During my own research the field of Asian American Studies was mainly silent on the questions that interested me in this project. Therefore, of major importance in my view is Leong's 1996 volume *Asian American Sexualities: Dimensions of the Gay and Lesbian Experience* because it includes multi-disciplinary theories and expressions of Asian American Gay and Lesbian identities. This is a foundational text in the field and the first extended analysis of the intersections of Asian American and Gay and Lesbian communities; it is the first volume to accomplish this. The edition showcases authors, performers, artists and critics that were previously unavailable or only to be found in chapbooks, out of print books from local presses, and in little circulated journals. These people were almost impossible to find at the time of my own research.

Another important anthology I'd like to mention here is *Other Sisterhoods: Literary Theory and U.S. Women of Color* because it includes many different theoretical approaches to women of color scholarship. It also includes a substantial introduction that provides a nice general history of women of color feminism, theory and experiences in the academy. It explores important contextual concerns like labeling, community identification, redefinitions of theory, appropriation, activism and publishing. Of prime importance here is the emphasis on theory. The three sections intend to examine the ways that theory is discussed in this arena: how "the race for theory" affects women writers of color, how these writers deal with various social issues, and how they recategorize theory through their own visions. To me, the use of these categories is telling of the importance and value (still primarily untapped, as I have argued) of these women. Not only does it reflect what issues are relevant to them but also highlighted is what potential importance these authors have for the larger academic and social communities.

The final piece of scholarship that I want to mention here is Aida Hurtado's *The Color of Privilege* wherein she articulates what she calls her three blasphemies. She attempts to formulate the connections between feminism and critical race theories in a way that is beneficial for all involved. She focuses her study then partially on the arena that I outline in my own book: the history and consequences of racism in feminist studies. She argues for all people to consider their own privilege and to analyze the framework that is inherent in privileging, in order to dismantle the burdens of identity politics and thus to unleash the full power of feminism to attack social and financial inequalities for all women. What I find particularly fruitful in Hurtado's argument is her belief that a theory must have within it the potential for its own demise in order for it to be truly revolutionary. (xii) Her insights will provide much to anyone studying feminism and any critical identity theory.

The other area of change that I'd like to address is the existence of some new and important primary sources by/about lesbians of color. There has not been a "boom" by any means, but I do feel that the growing respect for the voices of these authors has encouraged new authors and made new publications possible. Ana Castillo continues to write creatively about Latina sexuality in her collection of short stories *Loverboys* and her most recent novel *Peel My Love Like an Onion*. There are also works by new authors, most notably Larissa Lai and Erika Lopez. They have written *When Fox is a Thousand* and *Flaming Iguanas* respectively; these novels are experimental works of fiction that include popular culture, ancient history, and creative visions of lesbian lives. One important new anthology is *Afrekete: An Anthology of Black Lesbian Writing* which contains fiction, nonfiction and poetry and wishes to document and explore the history of black lesbian creativity. Another important collection is Rosamund Elwin's volume *Tongues on Fire: Caribbean Lesbian Lives and Stories* where she includes both fiction and life stories in order to document zami experience and history[2]. I single out these volumes because of their experimentalism, focus, and the impact I feel they will have on various fields of identity studies.

I want to thank all the women of color who directly or indirectly influenced this project. I hope that my own project will be considered with those of the past, present and future that complicate the place that lesbians of color have in academic and social communities. It is by no means the last word on lesbian of color studies; I hope it will be taken as another avenue for change and a step towards destabilizing those identities which are most entrenched. On the cusp of a new millenium perhaps we can do more than imagine the world as mestiza: "Let's try it our way, the mestiza way, the Chicana way, the woman way" (Anzaldúa, *Borderlands* 88).

July 1999

Introduction

The women's movement of the 1970s arguably led to a new awareness of the politics of gender difference within the academic literary community as well as society at large. Because this commentary on the politics of gender difference was conceived of within the terms of the dominant racial group, many literary critics of color soon voiced their concerns about how feminists were employing a white supremacist agenda by implying all "women" were white by default.[3] Soon after, the relation of many other concepts of difference to feminism began to be discussed; however, it seemed that all of the varying articulations of self were conceived of as dichotomous.[4] Each of these various differences (gender, race, ethnicity, or homosexuality) is primarily seen as the "Other" of something else, and only important because each was seen as completely embodying difference.

This difference was interpreted as something with which to amend the primary discussions; like a footnote to the general discussion. This had the negative consequence of creating a kind of ranking system of oppression whereby a Black woman was seen as doubly oppressed, a Black lesbian triply oppressed, etc. And thus, it created an atmosphere whereby the more oppressed one was (and the more "Other" one became) the more of a right one had to speak one's very specific, and therefore authentic, experience within the academy. As Cherríe Moraga states "The danger lies in ranking the oppressions. *The danger lies in failing to acknowledge the specificity of the oppression*" (*Loving* 29). In many ways, these voices have been more silenced, of course, and yet they are also given a space to speak although it is only within a limited space provided and defined by the larger academy. Therefore, either path constructed for this "Other" is laden with dangerous consequences for her subjectivity.

I am specifically concerned with constructions of selves, and subjectivities, that are exemplified and implied within contemporary literary criticism and am not as interested in theories that lay outside of the literary field. This study then will reflect this tendency as I focus on how editors of literary and critical texts and authors construct individual or group identities. It is principally within this framework that I read current group identified theories, by providing close readings of critical texts. Within the larger literary community, the theoretical construction of identity has remained primarily a binary one and as such it rests on the notion that some aspect of one's identity has precedence over another. Now, this use of theory might work when one is focusing on white women for example (when assuming that whiteness is not a race) but when one considers the identity of the lesbian of color[5] how does one conceive of her?[6] For the most part the articulations of selves that originate in feminist theory, lesbian theory, or racial/ethnic theory, cannot individually and adequately account for her.[7] Neither has there been much interest in exploring the intersections of these theories or the consequences that this kind of exploration would have on constructs of identity.

To consider the subject who forces these intersections is to revise the idea of identity as one, constant, essential element of selfhood which is frequently the assumption of much current literary studies and literary criticism. Yvonne Yarbro-Bejarano finds this the central problem with identity-based theories and views this problem and its consequences thusly:

> At the root of these problems is the focus on one issue, whether it be gender, race, class, or sexuality, as if it existed separately from the others. The insistence on keeping these analytic categories discrete indicates white people's resistance to perceiving their own gender or sexuality as racially constructed and their tendency to assign the category of race exclusively to people of color, as well as the resistance of people of color to perceiving their own gender or heterosexual privilege. ("Expanding" 127)

In order to remedy this situation and thus make identity-based theories more useful these blind spots must be illuminated.

Introduction

This problem of focusing on one identity issue, that dominates the academy, is the key backdrop for this book. A useful place to begin this study then is with an exploration of the articulations of self that the theories I have named construct in order to understand how they create a subject and then construct a theory around it. There are both benefits and negative consequences to this subject creation. For example, Judith Butler refutes the previously assumed necessity of a definitive subject called "woman" for feminist study to rally around. For example, she states that:

> For the most part, feminist theory has assumed that there is some existing identity, understood through the category of women, who not only initiates feminist interests and goals within discourse, but constitutes the subject for whom political representation is pursued. (*Gender* 1)

Butler believes that while this subject is important for political reasons "there might not be a subject" who is "awaiting representation" (2). Because various identity theories, as presented within the realm of the literary, have articulated (or at least posited the need for) a static subject "awaiting representation," this subject has generally been defined as it existed *only* within the parameters specific to each theory. For example, if one is racially marked, one is neutral in terms of gender (in other words male) and so on. Therefore, it should be clear that a subject whose identity exists simultaneously within different theoretical models finds no permanent home. This is indeed the case for lesbians of color; they have been tokenized by all three camps.

The goal of this project, then, is to account for the lesbian of color as subject and consider the affect that theorizing her identity has on the identity theory that prevails within literary criticism[8] as well as within canon formation, and the development of identity-based studies.

Judith Butler's performance theory has lately been seen as the most useful articulation of lesbian subjectivity, and therefore I begin with a consideration of the performance theory that she develops in *Gender Trouble*. Butler specifically addresses gender as an identity issue, by way of a Foucaldian genealogy. She claims that:

> a genealogical critique refuses to search for the origins of gender, the inner truth of female desire, a genuine or authentic sexual identity

that repression has kept from view; rather, genealogy investigates the political stakes in designating as an *origin* and *cause* those identity categories that in fact the *effects* of institutions, practices, discourses with multiple and diffuse points of origin. The task of this inquiry is to center on—and decenter—such defining institutions: phallogocentrism and compulsory heterosexuality. (*Gender* viii-ix)

As a result of this genealogy she ultimately envisions gender as performative. Butler summarizes:

As a strategy to denaturalize and resignify bodily categories, I describe and propose a set of parodic practices based in a performative theory of gender acts that disrupt the categories of the body, sex, gender, and sexuality to occasion their subversive resignification and proliferation beyond the binary frame. (*Gender* x)

This concept of "subversive resignification" can also be seen as the definition that Butler gives to "gender trouble" because she sees that within gender "trouble is inevitable and the task, how best to make it, what best way to be in it" (vii). Butler sees the subversiveness of parody as the best way to make or be in "gender trouble."

This application of performance theory to the discussion of gender and lesbian identity obviously has merit. However, I am concerned with how this notion of performing identities can be related to women of color, specifically, with how it relates to lesbians of color. As Yarbro-Bejarano also points out:

[Butler's] interpretation of gender as a "stylized repetition of acts," assumed through a structure of impersonation or imitation for which there is no original, does not actively factor in how racial formations shape the "performance" of gender and sexual identity" ("Expanding" 129).

Butler does not discuss this issue in depth, and therefore she implies that no other elements of identity outside of lesbianism alone might affect the subject's subversive performance.

I would posit that Butler's arguments themselves are of little use when considering lesbians of color simply because she does not adequately account for the many cultural contexts that exert force upon them. But I do think her theory of performative gender identity has

Introduction

many possibilities for articulating queer (or straight) racial and ethnic identities. Clearly there are elements of performance in all identity formations and constructions whether they exist for subversive or strategic means or not. Butler's lack of concern with other elements of identity makes her performance theory difficult to apply to lesbians of color. As I will show in Chapter Three, the gender trouble that Butler advocates can easily become gender danger for lesbians of color; danger that affects them financially, emotionally, spiritually and physically. So though her concept of performing identities does give the lesbian of color the potential to subvert prescriptions on her articulation of subjectivity, ultimately it does not adequately account for the devastating affects that "trouble" can cause.

This is true not only for lesbians of color, although the potential affects are the most devastating to those who are the most disenfranchised from hegemonic society, but for white subjects as well. Though because white subjects are also in jeopardy from "trouble making" it shows how truly threatening the gender danger can be. I do not intend to "justify" the existence of gender danger, or the experiences of lesbians of color, by focusing on white lesbian experience rather, I find it useful to make it clear that even privileged subjects are placed in jeopardy by enacting Butler's theory. I hope this will clearly show that a consideration of lesbians of color cannot be pushed into the margins as a highly specialized pursuit but that it greatly affects "dominant" issues as well.

To illustrate this point I'd like to briefly consider Lois Gould's novel *A Sea-Change* which concerns a number of privileged white characters. Even for these subjects in this position (holding many of the markers of success: wealth, class, whiteness) enacting gender trouble can have damaging effects. Interestingly, the novel begins with both a scientific and literary allusion when describing transformation. The scientific allusion relates to a fish that is able to change it's sex when necessary for the group's procreative survival. Whereas the literary allusion comes from Shakespeare's play *The Tempest*:

> Full fathom five thy father lies;
> Of his bones are coral made;
> Those are pearls that were his eyes:
> Nothing of him that doth fade
> But doth suffer a sea-change
> Into something rich and strange.(n.p.)

It's with these "sea-changes" that the novel is framed, showing in a microcosm the extreme traditions, from the scientific to the lyrical, of identity construction and encouraging the reader to take note of where the rest of the novel will travel within this debate.

The novel mainly focuses on Jessie Waterman, who epitomizes the fantasy of female whiteness. She's a beautiful, blonde, blue-eyed model who is completely defined by her husband:

> Jessie, of course, answered both of [her husband's] instinctive needs. Being beautiful, she satisfied his inordinate longing for perfection in the natural order of things. Being his wife, she confirmed his manly power. Other men envied him. That too was beautiful. And that too was natural. (27)

After Jessie is robbed, tied up, and sexually threatened by a black gunman whom she nicknames "B.G." they decide to move away from New York and onto a reclusive island.

It is with this move that Jessie begins to change; first emotionally, as she reevaluates her life in terms of her musings on the nature of femaleness, and then physically, through her costume and physique. Jessie also begins a lesbian affair with her friend Kate, who herself is having an affair with Jessie's husband. The women's relationship accentuates the gender role-play as they both ruminate on the meaning of the other's behavior.[9] From the beginning of the novel Jessie is presented as someone who can manipulate appearances, and of course her occupation as a model highlights that as well. She apparently wills a new appearance into being and begins to see herself becoming a different creature with the "old" Jessie as a smaller and smaller part of herself:

> One day I may even forget to look for *her*. In the meantime, though, she till saw traces. Have to keep erasing, she thought, frowning at herself as though that would do it. As though she were covering up for some secret crime, some shameful mark of conscience. That would have been so much simpler. She would have to be patient. There was no way to eradicate the source of her pain, or the elaborate web of memories and reflexes that inflamed it. (72)

An incredibly complex web of gender confusion grows, in Jessie's husband's absence, between Jessie, Kate, and Jessie's two daughters.

However, the focus here is on Jessie's evolution. It is clearly problematic that it is "B.G." who is the spark that ignites Jessie's transformation as he embodies the ultimate male violence against white womanhood. Jessie keeps seeing her femaleness in relation to him:

> B.G.—her black gunman. Jessie never ceased to think about B.G. He had touched her here—and also here. B.G., caressing her breasts with his gun. Her breasts; inviolate whitegold treasures that she permitted no one to touch in love. How fitting it was, his gun as *her* symbol, as trigger mechanism for the implosion of hate inside her. (60)

Ultimately Jessie *becomes* B.G., whether in reality or in fantasy is unclear, and forces herself on Kate, as the real gunman originally did to Jessie. "After this," Jessie fantasizes (and apparently narrates) "no one could say he wasn't a man" (130).

This entire novel seems to epitomize gender trouble, but at what cost? Clearly it is problematic that a racist construction of the Black male is responsible for turning Jessie into a monster. Yes, she undergoes a sea-change, but into what? Even though her husband does not recognize "her" when he is introduced to B.G. Kilroy, the identity she creates for herself, we never know the extent of her change. However, this change does not subvert institutions of power, white supremacy and misogyny, but rather it reifies them. Jessie's transformation occurred within the tenets of the dominant society as she was not able to erase the external discourses from her mind, and so she merely duplicates their destructive power. Even with all of the opportunities of privilege on her side Jessie is destroyed in order to become powerful through violence and as someone who "feel[s] like a new man" because he's living with "his woman" (161).

This novel is a fantastic one which perhaps is reflective of the necessity of fantasy in order to have gender transformation because external pressures can be partially ignored. There is no real transformation though, only different people in different gender roles. Therefore, even when the subject is privileged a performance theory conceived without meaningful attention paid to context, ideology, and historical tradition, ultimately fails to transform.

After reflecting on varying critiques of her performance theory Butler's work has increasingly been focused on a psychoanalytic study of language. She is quickly traveling in a direction that points away from material experience. I find this work to be even less relevant to the women I study here; in my view she is moving much too far into the realm of word games as opposed to things relevant to the subjects of which she speaks. As a critic I have moved from her theory of performance farther into cultural criticism, because I feel that there has been an appalling lack of focus on cultural and historical contexts within literary study.

In the absence of a theory of identity that fully accounts for lesbians of color I must turn to their own writing, because the best way to consider the problems that lesbians of color face, as well as the strategies and solutions they create, is to read the words they write. Therefore, as I do close readings of these texts, I also focus on how these creative texts theorize, in full or in part, their own identity theories. I explore literature and theories written by lesbians of color, and also consider literary characters who are lesbians of color.[10] I have chosen to focus on texts that include one or more of the following elements because I see them as most relevant to my discussion. They are texts in which:

> **1.** the articulation of a lesbian self[11] is impossible for a character because of the limits her culture places on her, **2.** an articulation of identity requires a critique of the author's or character's own hostile culture, and **3.** there are articulations that require an author or character to rewrite her own culture in order to escape its limitations.

Many of these elements are present in one text at different times and for different reasons, highlighting that these elements are important when reading the "journey" that many of these lesbians undertake to construct their identities. These characteristics are not meant to be placed as monolithic descriptions of "the" lesbian experience, and indeed the authors don't present them as such, but rather they are parts of a discussion of how some lesbians of color accommodate life on multiple borders. Therefore, in the chapters that follow I examine primary texts in order to illustrate differing strategies that lesbians of color employ (as author, narrator, and through character) in order to survive and ultimately what these strategies mean for identity construction.

In the first chapter, I delve into how subjects are constructed within feminist, lesbian, and racial/ethnic theories and show that these constructions are based on specific goals in order to illustrate what I see as the present atmosphere of exclusionary studies. Throughout this text, I conflate the terms racial and ethnic when related to a theoretical approach. I do so not to oversimplify many complex issues but rather to reflect the variety of titles for this framework that are currently in use. It is not meant to separate out race from ethnicity or vice-versa. After this consideration, it is apparent why lesbians of color, for the most part, have been left out of these theoretical discussions. It is mainly because the political aims of these theorists require the creation of a subject that clearly stands to benefit from the theory. In other words, many of these critics use "strategic essentialism" in order to further their political interests. Although this strategy can definitely be a useful one, to a certain extent, because lesbians of color disrupt the fiction of an essential self they limit the usefulness of this political exercise, and, I believe, illustrate the need for a different way of politicizing identity.

Because there has not been much attention paid to societal contexts within lesbian theory, in the second chapter, I show the specific cultural and societal hostilities that lesbians of color face and I read relevant primary texts to show how the hostility is constructed. I am concerned here with close readings of literary texts, primarily identity-based anthologies, that posit themselves as speaking the histories of various groups, and focus on how they construct the specific subject, as well as its history, for political change. Even though these sources are, therefore, limited in their historical scope, they are very useful in determining how each group describes the forces that exert pressure upon their subjectivities. Within all of the texts I explore in this chapter, the authors focus on the many communities that exclude them as well as the specific hostilities they face because of their multiple identities. These articulations are accomplished through various genres and through the development of characters, from autobiographical narrators, and through literary devices. I look at such texts as Audre Lorde's *Zami: A New Spelling of My Name* (1982), Paula Gunn Allen's *The Woman Who Owned the Shadows* (1983), Gayl Jones's *Corregidora* (1975) and *Eva's Man* (1976) as well as Cherríe Moraga's *Loving in the War Years* (1982), Kitty Tsui's *The Words of a Woman Who Breathes Fire* (1983) and Ana Castillo's *The Mixquiahuala Letters* (1986). The hostilities illustrated in these texts make it treacherous, and sometimes impossible, for individual lesbians of color to exist as they choose. The importance of exploring these oppositions is that they illustrate the need for a deeper inquiry into the dangers inherent in the lesbian of color's interaction with the social world. The full force of these dangers must be accounted for within any theory of subjectivity.

Chapter Three shows the very real dangers involved in negotiating these hostilities. If lesbians of color are able to articulate a lesbian self, then they must critique their own culture, which also poses certain problems. Therefore, by considering such texts as Beth Brant's *Mohawk Trail* (1985), Gloria Naylor's *The Women of Brewster Place* (1980), Ann Allen Shockley's *Say Jesus and Come to Me* (1987) and Barbara Noda's *Strawberries* (1979) I show what ideologies and discourses in each culture must be rejected in order for lesbians of color to survive. I also discuss the very dire consequences that lesbians of color may face if they do reject parts of their cultures. The most dire consequence is that the gender trouble that they may wish to enact in order to be free from cultural limitation can easily become gender danger threatening to destroy them at any turn. In order to elucidate this point, which is lacking within a Butlerian consideration of identity construction, I explore this danger, which encompasses spiritual, financial, emotional, and physical jeopardy, within the primary texts.

In the fourth chapter I focus on how some lesbians of color have successfully articulated their identities within the boundaries of their own cultures. I show how these women of color actually "rewrite" cultural traditions in some way in order to survive as "out" lesbians. I discuss texts including Ann Allen Shockley's *Say Jesus and Come to Me*, Beth Brant's *Mohawk Trail*, and Audre Lorde's *Zami*. Anzaldúa's theory of mestiza consciousness becomes most important here as a different mode of identity construction than Butler's. Clearly Anzaldúa's theory of la mestiza touches on feminism, lesbian feminism and race and ethnicity and her awareness of the overlap amongst these identities and consciousnesses makes her indispensable for this project.[12]

Even though Anzaldúa centers her text, *Borderlands/La Frontera: The New Mestiza*, around Chicano/a experience including Mexican history, culture, language, myth and society, I find her most theoretical discussion one that reaches to universal identity issues while concurrently embedded in this community. Therefore I focus on the crucial chapter: "La Conciencia de la Mestiza: Towards a New Consciousness." It is here that she articulates ideas that I think help one to reconceptualize racial and ethnic identities (and not just Chicana/o ones). We can expand upon her discussion of the consciousness of la

Introduction

mestiza, "mestiza," meaning a woman of Mexican Indian and European ancestry, a woman who embodies the paradox of two things that should not be able to co-exist but do. I believe many ethnic and racial American women, and particularly lesbians, can be said to embody just such a meaningful paradox.

Anzaldúa begins her discussion by showing her indebtedness to Jose Vasconcelas's own theory of "una raza mestiza." She writes, describing both of their concepts of mestiza:

> Opposite to the theory of the pure Aryan, and to the policy of racial purity that white American practices, [it] is one of inclusivity. At the confluence of two or more genetic streams, with chromosomes constantly "crossing over," this mixture of races, rather than resulting in an inferior being, provides hybrid progeny, a mutable, more malleable species with a rich gene pool. From this racial, ideological, cultural and biological cross pollinization, an "alien" consciousness is presently in the making—a new *mestiza* consciousness, una *conciencia de mujer*. It is a consciousness of the Borderlands. (*Borderlands* 77)

This quote appears to emphasize a genetic concept of racial/ethnic consciousness; however, Anzaldúa is actually much more interested in exploring and describing a consciousness rather than in positing a biologically describable entity. She describes the inner nature of la mestiza thusly:

> Cradled in one culture, sandwiched between two cultures, straddling all three cultures and their value systems, *la mestiza* undergoes a struggle of flesh, a struggle of borders, an inner war. Like all people, we perceive the version of reality that our culture communicates. Like others having or living in more than one culture, we get multiple, often opposing messages. The coming together of two self-consistent but habitually incompatible frames of reference causes *un choque*, a cultural collision. (*Borderlands* 78)

This internal collision, this living with paradox, certainly goes against a traditional concept of race or ethnicity. How can something essential and natural, be a fluctuating collision? Anzaldúa gives us a hint of why she could conceive of identity in this way. She writes, referring to Chicana identity specifically:

> The new *mestiza* copes by developing a tolerance for contradictions, a tolerance for ambiguity. She learns to be an Indian in Mexican culture, to be Mexican from an Anglo point of view. She learns to juggle cultures. She has a plural personality, she operates in a pluralistic mode—nothing is thrust out, the good the bad and the ugly, nothing rejected, nothing abandoned. Not only does she sustain contradictions, she turns the ambivalence into something else. (*Borderlands* 79)

Anzaldúa here describes the subject taking an active role in identity formation depending on the circumstances. She does not discuss exactly how an agent accomplishes these roles but even the idea that one can perform different racial or ethnic identities could powerfully affect ethnic/racial subjects.

Anzaldúa, as a Chicana lesbian, is well aware of the inevitability of the existence of the ethnic lesbian and has a particularly interesting idea of the consciousness of the people within this community. She states:

> Being the supreme crossers of cultures, homosexuals have strong bonds with the queer white, Black, Asian, Native American, Latino.... We come from all colors, all classes, all races, all time periods. Our role is to link people with each other.... It is to transfer ideas and information from one culture to another. Colored homosexuals have more knowledge of other cultures...
>
> The mestizo and the queer exist at this time and point on the evolutionary continuum for a purpose. We are a blending that proves that all blood is intricately woven together, and that we are spawned out of similar souls. (*Borderlands* 84–5)

She even discusses a particular purpose for the person living in paradox: connecting and building bridges. If we give Anzaldúa's definitions validity, then all the comfortable categories break down. Accepting the paradoxical notion of identities in flux means questioning how lesbian and ethnic identities have been constructed in the past. It moves us from the task of categorizing to the more Foucaldian project of tracing genealogies of identity. Because she does not describe how the idea of la mestiza might apply to non Chicanas or how this concept of race might affect theory or literary criticism, her work leads into but does not anticipate all concepts of identity that pertain to the lesbian of color, by any means.

The fifth and concluding chapter focuses on an exploration of my theory of "performing la mestiza" as a theory of identity that can account for the specificities of external society, cultural traditions, and histories. I claim that lesbians of color routinely use performance as a tactic to travel within multiple communities and more importantly to affect cultural change by creatively revising portions of their own culture's traditions. This also has a major affect on the idea of authenticity within identity construction. I suggest that authenticity is impossible if identity categories are to be seen beyond the "biology is destiny" argument that has primarily lost its relevance. Indeed the successful lesbians of color that I discuss do not concern themselves with representing some "authentic" figure but rather with how this preconceived notion of authenticity must be undermined and reworked in order for her to have a place to stand within many communities.

Ultimately, I argue that the notion of revising concepts of identity as I have outlined is not just needed to "include minorities" into an already present identity theory which would continue their tokenization. Rather, focusing on these women shows the glaring limitations of performance that exist for any subject regardless of minority status. By conceiving of a theory with lesbians of color as its focus, I show the dramatic need to revise all constructions of identity that do not adequately account for the pressure of the external world(s) on any individual subject regardless of minority status. This assertion might cause confusion in regards to this project because I am speaking in generalities as well as specificities. I feel I must attend to both simultaneously because a focus on lesbians of color requires an attention to specificity but it also illuminates even wider disruptions for all identity-based studies. But by discussing "performing la mestiza" I don't wish to specify "the" theory that can be applied to all lesbians of color, rather I wish to illuminate the powers that entangle her, and discuss one possible strategy that opens up and affects a far-reaching dialogue within the academy and society. I don't intend for the theory of performing la mestiza to be taken only as a reaction to Judith Butler and thus easily restricted. I wish to emphasize the dynamism of identity and stay away from Yvonne Yarbro-Bejarano's warning that the task "is not a question of evolving a parallel theory of the performance of racial identity vis-à-vis a phantasmic racial ideal analogous to gender" ("Expanding" 129) but rather my goal is in agreement with Yarbro-

Bejarano's call to articulate a "reading of race, and political movement as well, into Butler's performative model" ("Expanding" 129) to affect both specified and general changes.

Performing La Mestiza

CHAPTER ONE
Rethinking Identity Construction: Placing the Lesbian of Color

Gender studies, Gay and Lesbian studies and Ethnic studies are all undeniably receiving more attention throughout the academy and increasingly tend to challenge traditional areas of study, canons, and modes of thought. However, in this chapter I'm particularly concerned with how these modes of thought have created paradigms that, for the most part, exclude lesbians of color. I believe it is particularly important to investigate how these theories construct subjectivity in order to discuss this exclusion. Therefore, by showing how these theories construct identities I show how lesbians of color problematize the political and theoretical assumptions upon which they are based.

One of the most important things that all three of these areas of study have in common is that they question constructions of identity that do not include a meaningful analysis of multiplicity. In my view the perfect way to explore this issue, within the literary field, is by focusing on the work of lesbians of color. It is within this subject position that all single representations of self break down. A meaningful consideration of this combination of selves, this combination of theories, is at the heart of this project and its intention is to illuminate and consider the consequences that strategic essentialism has created for lesbians of color.

Identity politics are considered important for all identity-based studies and they are crucial also within the strategic use of essentialism. Obviously, identity politics is emotionally charged and therefore, not surprisingly, gender studies, gay and lesbian studies, and racial/ethnic studies are emotionally charged as well. Therefore, the insistence upon definitions, categories, and labels is fraught with a very specific danger within these areas of study. Even though this is true, it seems that any identity-based field must account for the issue of definition either directly or indirectly. These definitions particularly affect lesbians of color because they disrupt essentially based identity formulations which means that identity politics is as dangerous to lesbians of color as they are to identity politics. Therefore, a consideration of identity politics is needed here to show why this is true.

Diana Fuss has an intriguing discussion of identity politics in her *Essentially Speaking: Feminism, Nature and Difference*. In the portion that is focused on identity politics, she centers her discussion specifically on gay and lesbian identity; but her words are still useful in a general sense as well. Fuss states that "In common usage, the term identity politics refers to the tendency to base one's politics on a sense of personal identity—as gay, as Jewish, as Black, as female" (97). Her discussion nicely illustrates the importance of identity-based politics in terms of strategic essentialism—empowering groups to speak and be validated. She does, though, rightly point to some problems inherent in these political coalitions and theories. She raises a number of questions:

> Is politics based on identity, or is identity based on politics? Is identity a natural, political, historical psychical, or linguistic construct? What implications does the deconstruction of "identity" have for those who espouse an identity politics? Can feminist, gay, or lesbian subjects afford to dispense with the notion of unified, stable identities or must we begin to base our politics on something other than identity? (*Essentially* 100)

Fuss also clearly understands the political reality for more disempowered subjects, who focus on an essential concept of identity because it is too threatening to their existence not to. In other words, she acknowledges the importance of strategic essentialism. She still, though, neglects to discuss a *combination* of disempowered identities, such as those present in the racial/ethnic lesbian, and how identity politics works in these situations. Do the politics work the same when one has what could be considered multiple distinguishable identities that are sometimes in conflict? Is the formation and recognition of these identities the same? A consideration of such a subject would complicate her already complex discussion but would also serve to further her ideas. Because lesbians of color are left out of this discussion there seems to be no strategy that has been devised for them.

How then might this woman accomplish her political goals through identity politics? or can she at all? It seems that her identity remains trapped in the plight Fuss describes: choosing a limited unified identity for political purposes or choosing a fiction that does not take into account real historical, cultural, and societal contexts. I will consider further the political aspect of this subject's identity later in this project.

One way to begin to construct a theory that considers multiple identities is to introduce the element of choice into its framework. For example, I *choose* to identify myself as a Latina as well as a queer critic.[13] Because I am of mixed race, I could choose other racial identities as well; in different places with different people I consider some parts of my identity to be foregrounded either intentionally or unintentionally. Also, different people interpret my identity in different ways at different times. What does this mean for identity? It means to me that identity is constantly in flux and being interpreted by others both with and without help from the subject. This has clear effects for the power of agency that Butler highlights as important to subversive performance. Because I feel I do have some element of choice, and therefore agency, I find performance theory to be an important avenue of exploration here. Performance theory would allow choice for some multiply identified subjects but I am particularly concerned with the limitations of choice/agency for the person of color.

To be defined as a person of color means, supposedly, that one has a skin color that is different than white (white not being read as a color). Obviously, there is some visual aspect connected to this identification. I don't intend to discuss in depth the whole area of "passing" but rather wish to focus on the point that much of ethnic/racial identity is a *visual* recognition of difference. Because I am light-skinned I can choose to be identified as a white non-Hispanic; but when I am tanned and clearly dark, do I have this same choice?[14] In a white supremacist society, the darker one's skin, the more readily one is interpreted *externally* and without choice rather than with choice. Clearly, the ability to choose is reflective of a position of privilege. However, I do not feel that this position is necessarily negative. I believe the possibility of choice shows the ability of movement within these categories and the person who might visually disrupt a category can be an effective reminder of its arbitrary nature.[15]

Feminism might be flagged as the defining moment in literary studies when "elite" theory was inextricably linked to "politics." Not only did feminist theory validate the search for women authors but feminist theorists also began to search for patterns of oppression and exclusion in previous constructions of literary history and theory. The early 1970s women's movement surely came on the heels of the Black civil rights movement as well as the Chicano and American Indian movements; in turn feminism opened the door for other "liberations": gay, lesbian, and those of other racial and ethnic groups. Feminism has constantly highlighted its attempts to embrace all other movements and peoples who seem to be in a similar state of oppression because of the legacy of white patriarchy but has never been able to meaningfully do so.

Because early constructions of the women's movement and feminism attempted to seek *unity*, many feminists of color denounced them for ignoring difference in the process. The apparent ease with which all women could connect and relate of course did not reflect other equally meaningful layers such as class, race, ethnicity, physical ability, and sexual orientation. There have been many people who have pointed out this white middle class blindness from early on. For example, in 1977 The Combahee River Collective stated that they:

> are actively committed to struggling against racial, sexual, heterosexual, and class oppression, and see as our particular task the development of integrated analyses and practice based upon the fact that the major systems of oppression are interlocking. The synthesis of these oppressions create the conditions of our lives. (272)

It was, arguably, Cherríe Moraga and Gloria Anzaldúa's volume entitled *This Bridge Called My Back: Writings by Radical Women of Color* (1983) that opened the floodgates of this debate. For the first time there was a collection of women of color who:

> want to express to all women—especially to white middle class women—the experiences which divide us as feminists, we want to examine incidents of intolerance, prejudice and denial of differences within the feminist movement. We intend to explore the causes and sources of, and solutions to these divisions. We want to create a definition that expands what "feminist" means to us (xxiii)

Of course there were, and continue to be, other texts wishing to speak about experiences that were subsumed in the "women's movement." For example, the volume *All the Women are White, All the Blacks are Men, But Some of Us are Brave* (1982) has been seen as another major voice as well as *Home Girls: A Black Feminist Anthology* (1983). Women of color have consistently voiced opposition to and proposed solutions for the limitations of a feminism that they consider to be dominated by white women.

Perhaps one of the clearest articulations of this problem has been made by bell hooks in her *Feminist Theory: From Margin to Center* (1984). She certainly describes the majority of work done by respected white feminist theorists when she writes that:

> Privileged feminists have largely been unable to speak to, with, and for diverse groups of women because they either do not understand fully the inter-relatedness of sex, race, and class oppression or refuse to take this inter-relatedness seriously. Feminist analyses of woman's lot tend to focus exclusively on gender and do not provide a solid foundation on which to construct feminist theory. They reflect the dominant tendency in Western patriarchal minds to mystify woman's reality by insisting that gender is the sole determinant of woman's fate. Certainly it has been easier for women who do not experience race or class oppression to focus on class and gender, they tend to dismiss race or they make a point of acknowledging that race is important and then proceed to offer an analysis in which race is not considered. (14)

Of primary importance here is the concept that white feminists consider race important but apparently not for their own ideas and work. hooks argues convincingly that the women's movement has been racist in its construction of the subject of feminism.

Indeed I suggest that this racism is responsible for the continued failure of mainstream feminism to meaningfully interrogate or integrate concepts of race as a subject for all feminists, and therefore feminists of color have still been forced to speak as the "Other" in comparison to "normal" feminists. Critics of color have seen this pattern in the work of many white feminist critics: Gilbert and Gubar, Elaine Showalter, Kate Millett, Catherine Stimpson, Jane Gallop among others.[16] The point here is not to criticize all that these and other feminist scholars have done or thought but rather to point out the need for feminism to confront the necessity of change. I think that the path that is most useful here is the one that Ann Russo suggests in her essay "'We Cannot Live Without Our Lives'": that it would be more useful to talk of "white supremacy" rather than "racism." She writes that:

> Central to developing feminist theory and organizing around specific issues, I feel [we] white women must analyze our relationship to race, ethnicity, class, and sexuality. Denying or ignoring our privilege as white and/or middle-class women will not build a strong women's movement, nor will minimizing the specifics of sexual oppression. . . . White supremacy correctly places the responsibility on white women and men, rather than focusing on people of color simply as victims of an amorphous racism. "White supremacy" as a concept forces us to look power directly in the face, and when we do that there is less room for denial, guilt, and paternalism in trying to change it, since it shifts the focus from people of color to white people. (Russo 299)

If feminist practice adopted this perspective, it would indeed turn people of color from a "problem" for feminism into active voices in the conversation of feminism. Another useful perspective to consider within this discussion of whiteness is Ruth Frankenberg. In her text *White Women, Race Matters: The Social Construction of Whiteness*, she explores how white women are indeed affected by issues of race through her interviews with selected white academic feminists.[17] Most useful here is her discussion of how these specific women characterize the meaning of white identity and the implications Frankenberg sees with the conceptions they describe. She states:

> The claim that whiteness lacks form and content says more about the definitions of culture being used than it does about the content of whiteness. . . . However, I would suggest that in describing themselves as cultureless these women are in fact identifying specific kinds of unwanted absences and presences in their own culture(s) as a generalized lack or non existence. (199)

Frankenberg posits that white identity is indeed constructed for specific purposes; primarily to maintain white supremacy. She feels that the fear of confronting this supremacy and privilege has limited white feminists.

She therefore calls for a specific study of whiteness that will change how white feminists conceive of feminism. For example:

> Attention to the construction of white "experience" is important, both to transforming the meaning of whiteness and to transforming the relations of race in general. This is crucial in a social context in which the racial order is normalized and rationalized rather than upheld by coercion alone. Analyzing the connections between white daily lives and discursive orders may help make visible the processes by which the stability of whiteness—as location of privilege, as culturally normative space, and as standpoint—is secured and reproduced. (242)

I further suggest that the absence of an articulated "white feminism" or "white feminist theory" also illustrates white supremacy. By considering the problems with a "white feminist" notion of whiteness, as reflected in feminist literary theory and criticism in particular, we can see that there is a need to articulate the absence of "white feminist theory." There have, of course, been statements of Black feminism and some of Latina feminism, etc., but it apparently seems unnecessary to specify a "white" feminism, suggesting that whiteness is still seen as universal and thus to be "of color" is to need a specific signifier in order to be validated. As Norma Alarcón states: "The fact that Anglo-American feminism has appropriated the generic term for itself leaves many a woman in this country having to call herself otherwise, i.e., 'woman of color'" (362). One wonders if the movement that so interestingly considered the generic term "man" to have power and privilege over "woman" has considered how its use of "woman" has power over the "woman of color."

bell hooks has claimed that the domination of feminism by white women is a continuing pattern. She sees Betty Friedan, author of *The Feminine Mystique*, as important because

> the one-dimensional perspective on women's reality presented in her book became a marked feature of the contemporary feminist movement. Like Friedan before them, white women who dominate feminist discourse today rarely question whether or not their perspective on women's reality is true to the lived experiences of women as a collective group. (hooks *Ain't I* 3)

This pattern of dominance by white women and the dominance of a consequent ideology has continued within lesbian literary criticism and theory. As Bonnie Zimmerman states: "Our process has paralleled the development of feminist literary criticism—and, indeed, pioneering feminist critics and lesbian critics are often one and the same" ("What Has" 117). This is certainly true in the best and worst ways: it assumes that lesbian literary criticism and theory is inextricably bound to feminist literary criticism and theory; it also means that the pattern that bell hooks exposes is replicated in the lesbian theory community.

Even though in Zimmerman's essay "What Has Never Been: An Overview of Lesbian Feminist Literary Criticism," she criticizes mainstream feminists for refusing to meaningfully incorporate lesbian perspectives into their critical work, she continues this pattern herself in her book *The Safe Sea of Women* by not meaningfully incorporating the perspectives of lesbians of color into her theory. She discusses the focus of her book when she claims that she "view[s] lesbian fiction as the expression of a collective 'myth of origins' with four primary divisions: the lesbian self, the lesbian couple, the lesbian community, and community and difference" (*Safe* xv). Zimmerman lists many texts written by lesbians of color in one chapter but disturbingly she keeps these lesbians separate in the section on "difference." This placement assumes that these women have nothing meaningful to contribute to her "myth of origins" but rather are contained under the heading of the "Other." These women do not enter the theoretical discussion and her main question regarding these authors appears to be: "How then is a white woman's novel not to be racist, either by omission or commission?" (*Safe* 178). This seems to be how Zimmerman sees these women's ideas as relevant: only in how they relate to white women's work. She does justice to summarizing their literary and theoretical works, giving these women a forum, but even after all the praise she gives them, she leaves them in "the House of Difference" (*Safe* 184).

In a similar but perhaps more problematic way, Sally Munt excuses the lack of diverse voices in her volume, *New Lesbian Criticism: Literary and Cultural Readings*, when she states "the fact that all five Black contributors commissioned to write articles for this collection did not deliver reflects the pressure on the few to represent the many" (xix). By publishing the book without their essays, however, she implies that these contributors are not considered important to understanding or articulating "new lesbian criticism." So while Munt recognizes the lack of diversity in her book, she doesn't view it as devastating to her concept of lesbian criticism.

Similar to more mainstream white feminists' intellectual need to recognize difference as a "problem" to deal with, not as something that requires change for them, white critics who identify specifically as lesbians have articulated the same notions that keep the generic term "lesbian" in relation to their own whiteness. Again it would seem necessary to introduce the concept of white supremacy into the consciousness of lesbian theory in order to recognize the limitations of "white lesbian theory." Therefore, I suggest that there needs to be an analysis of the ideology behind white lesbian theory; if lesbians of color write from the "house of difference" on what is this placement based? What would be inside the "house of sameness"? Clearly if you assume that the white perspective is *the* perspective then the more descriptors one has the further one is out on the margins and the less right one has to speak on any issue except those labeled with an equal number of descriptors.

As I touched on in the beginning of this chapter, all identity-based theories have been forced, from within and without, to define the representational figure whom it embodies. Therefore, in critiquing the present state of lesbian theory, or indeed to enter into the discussion at all, it seems necessary to attempt to define who a "lesbian" is. It is inescapable that one must determine who is the legitimate subject of any study involving lesbian theory. It seems that anyone who wishes to analyze from this perspective, not just the lesbian critic, must consider what or who is a worthy subject. As Zimmerman states "lesbian critics have ... to begin with a special question: 'When is a text a "lesbian text" or its writer a "lesbian writer"'? Lesbians are faced with this special problem of definition" ("What Has" 120). There have, of course, been a wide range of definitions offered from Catherine Stimpson's to Adrienne Rich's. Stimpson, in her essay "Zero Degree Deviancy: The Lesbian Novel in English," says:

> My definition of the lesbian ... will be conservative and severely literal. She is a woman who finds other women erotically attractive and gratifying. Of course a lesbian is more than her body, more than her flesh, but lesbianism partakes of the body, partakes of the flesh. That carnality distinguishes it from gestures of political sympathy with homosexuals and from affectionate friendships in which women

enjoy each other, support each other, and commingle a sense of identity and well-being. (Stimpson 301)

On the other hand there is Rich's definition in her essay "Compulsory Heterosexuality and Lesbian Existence" which is markedly more inclusive:

> I mean the term *lesbian continuum* to include a range—through each woman's life and throughout history—of woman-identified experience; not simply the fact that a woman has had or consciously desired genital experience with another woman. If we expand it to embrace many more forms of primary intensity between and among women, including the sharing of a rich inner life, the bonding against male tyranny, the giving and receiving of practical and political support... we begin to grasp the breadth of female history and psychology which have lain out of reach as a consequence of limited, mostly clinical, definitions of "lesbian". (Rich 648-9)

So clearly even in this microcosm of the debate there are major political consequences behind each position. If we accept Stimpson's literal definition, then we have reduced the woman to purely sexual terms; it is difficult to accept this concept as positive since it has been used by others to dehumanize her. If we accept Rich's liberal definition, then every woman could be a lesbian; there seems to be little difference between heterosexual feminists and lesbian feminists and so the identity of "lesbian" is problematic at best.

Any definition of who a lesbian is seems to be primarily motivated by the fact that historically others have defined her for their own ideological reasons. Even though Foucault notoriously omitted discussion of the history of lesbianism from his *History of Sexuality*, he discusses the effects of an ideology on an individual in ways relevant to the consideration of lesbian identity. Susan J. Wolfe and Julia Penelope rewrite Foucault to focus on lesbian identity in a way that is relevant to defining lesbianism by stating:

> Historically, men have controlled "talk about sex" and its meaning, both in public and in private. With isolated exceptions, such as Sappho and the Lesbians mentioned pejoratively by Martial, Lucian, and others, all women had been assumed to be heterosexual until the end of the nineteenth century, when it suited men's political purposes

to codify and stigmatize any and all intense female relationships explicitly, but especially those in which the physical passion of like to like might be acted upon.

Since then, Lesbians have lived under siege. Not surprisingly, the sexologists grounded their definitions of *Lesbian*, *invert*, and *homosexual* on the expression of genital sexuality, simultaneously locking several Lesbian generations into their discourse framework and erecting a physically intimidating barrier between those who act on their feelings and those who do not, between Lesbians and "heterosexual women." ("Sexual" 20)

Thus the definition of lesbianism is debated both from without and within the lesbian community. This difficulty has led to a wide range of lesbian criticisms, and to theories and philosophies about what the lesbian critic has to add to literary studies. For example, Wolfe and Penelope define lesbian theory as one that:

has had the task of positing a Lesbian subject, experienced through a collective history and culture we have had to construct before we can begin to *de*construct Lesbian identity. That is to say, we have had to deconstruct the notion that women can be seen only in relation to men, and defined only in terms of male discourse, in order to create a position from which to speak and be heard by non-Lesbian feminist critics. ("Sexual" 3)

The point here seems to be the possibility of speaking from a specific position of authority.

Joanne Glasgow and Karla Jay also describe lesbian criticism as a kind of tool for survival by "revisioning" ideas:

Sometimes the act of re-visioning becomes abstract and theoretical; sometimes it is personal and narrative.... But whatever the theoretical stance and whatever the methodology employed, lesbian criticism never loses sight of ... early activist assumption—unless we see with fresh eyes, unless we find our own language and inscribe our own experience, we will be again silenced or erased. We cannot survive without our words. It is a criticism about and for our lives. (2)

Interestingly they imply that lesbian theory and "the lesbian" are not static monoliths but rather that they inhabit a subject position or perspective with a political motivation, rather similar to the necessity of the sort of authoritative subject position that Wolfe and Penelope articulate. It should not be surprising that these lesbian theorists feel this need. Many other non-white heterosexual theorists desiring authority to speak attempt to define what this position is in order to set themselves up as legitimate speakers. If one cannot articulate a self, one cannot create a space from which to speak and therefore be recognized as a self.[18] Because we all inhabit subject positions it is not likely that this limitation will disappear; however, what I question is the inability of some theorists, typically white, to account for their own while at the same time stridently insisting that "others" do.

From the speaking of self, theorists have stepped to the analysis of that self (or selves) within existing society. In Diana Fuss's book *Inside/Out: Lesbian Theories, Gay Theories*, she discusses the metaphor that serves as the book's title stressing how it reflects the paradox of the political position of gays and lesbians. She notes that:

> Supporters of "Gay Studies," . . . must grapple with many of the same issues its predecessors confronted, including the vexed question of institutionalization and the relation of gay and lesbian communities to the academy, the issue is the old standoff between confrontation and assimilation: does one compromise oneself by working on the inside, or does one short-change oneself by holding tenaciously to the outside? (5)

She sees this metaphor of position as essential to considering "gay" identity. So her concept of queer theory then is reflective of political existence. I find this connection of theory with reality a beneficial one when considering lesbian identity. It definitely opens the door for not only political context to theories of identity but social, cultural, and historical contexts as well. Fuss states further that:

> To endorse a position of perpetual or even strategic outsiderhood (a position of powerlessness, speechlessness, homelessness . . .) hardly seems like a viable political program, especially when, for so many gay and lesbian subjects, it is less a question of political tactics than everyday lived experience. Perhaps what we need most urgently in gay and lesbian theory right now is a theory *of* marginality,

> subversion, dissidence, and othering. What we need is a theory of sexual borders that will help us come to terms with, and to organize around, the new cultural, sexual arrangements occasioned by the movement and transmutations of pleasure in the social field.(*Inside* 5)

This questioning of "outsiderhood" challenges the very nature of Gay studies (and other identity-based fields as I have articulated earlier) as legitimate *not only or because of* their outsider status. This interest in politics is developed further in a more recent text, *Fear of a Queer Planet: Queer Politics and Social Theory*. The editor, Michael Warner, begins the discussion by addressing the question of how to place queer theory in politics and social theory, as his subtitle implies. He succinctly remarks: "Following Marx's definition of critical theory as 'the self-clarification of the struggles and wishes of the age,' we might think of queer theory as the project to elaborating, in ways that cannot be predicted in advance, this question: What do queers want?" (vii).

From such political questions and concerns has come political positioning within literary criticism and theory. Similar to the other two perspectives described above, literary queer theory depends, to some extent, on a queer subject. One critic, Sally Munt, attempts both to show a specific lesbian subject as well as claiming a marginality for the subject. She describes Lesbian studies as an intersection of Gay Studies and Women's Studies and "the dinky crossover segment in the middle is of course Lesbian Studies, marginalized by and defined in relation to both" (xii). She continues by clarifying the space of lesbian theory:

> Critical Theory intersects with Women's Studies in the area of Feminist Theory, and with (Lesbian and) Gay Studies in the area of Sexuality (which has tended to privilege studies on heterosexuality or male homosexuality, heavily influenced by Foucaldian theory, and using gay male models of sexual transgression.) Nevertheless, this small triangle of Lesbian Studies tends to appear a bit beleaguered, framed on all sides by spheres of intellectual exploration more acceptable to the academy. (xii)

Of course the edition, framed in this way, has something to say about these intersections. Munt herself sees the lesbian as particularly empowered in theory *because* of these intersections. She claims that:

> Indeed, lesbians are particularly adept at deconstruction, patently reading between the lines, from the margins, inhabiting the text of dominant heterosexuality even as we undo it, undermine it, and construct our own destabilizing readings.(xii)

She continues:

> we are particularly adept at extracting our own meanings, at highlighting a text's latent content, at reading "dialectically", at filling the gaps, at interpreting the narrative according to our introjected fictional fantasies, and at foregrounding the intertextuality of our identities.(xxi)

Thus, Munt makes a claim for the existence of a lesbian subjectivity not only within history and politics, as the critics discussed previously have, but as situated within theory as well. Therefore, Munt has expanded upon the implied meaning of lesbian existence, specifically, that it is tied to a method of reading texts and realities. In this way Munt is opening a specific space for lesbian theory, but a space not devoid of problems.

Marilyn Farwell takes this subjectivity a step further and attempts to situate the lesbian as a metaphor for all women's creativity. To argue this point she says:

> Western metaphors for creativity present images—lover, androgyne, or mother—that exclude lesbian sexuality by privileging heterosexuality in assuming an analogy between creative production and reproduction. "Lesbian" is one of the few words in our language, if not the only one, that privileges female sexuality. For a cultural tradition that identifies sexual energy with creativity, then, lesbian as a metaphor is crucial to the redefinition of female autonomy and creativity ... [it is a] flexible image that both deconstructs the heterosexual pattern for creativity and creates a space for redefining the relationship of the woman writer to other women writers, to readers and to the text. (101)

Farwell here seems to intend only this metaphoric reading of the lesbian, but one must extend that metaphor to social and political reality when one explores the implications of her statement. Farwell asks us to reconsider the woman writer in relation to other writers, readers, and texts—in other words, social and political realities. How then are we to reconsider the lesbian beyond her function as a metaphor? Because clearly many "real" lesbians would object to this use of lesbian subjectivity as symbol and not as imbedded within social and political traditions. Here Farwell uses the troping of the lesbian to force the reader to reconsider who the "real" lesbian is. By critiquing Western culture's role in female sexuality, and by privileging the lesbian, she rewrites the marginality of lesbian identity.

Much of the most recent lesbian theory has excused itself from even attempting to define its speaking position but rather has focused on the many ways that the lesbian disrupts traditional theory and criticism. These critics have adopted the perspective that lesbian identity somehow relates to disruption: of power, of tradition, of binaries.[19] It seems that pluralism then is seen as a strength and not a liability; because there is no agreement on who a lesbian is, as I have illustrated within this section, the interest has turned towards what the lesbian disrupts and how she does it. For example, Laura Doan opens the preface of *The Lesbian Postmodern* not by speaking authoritatively about the text itself but by analyzing the possibility of doing so. Doan writes:

> The willingness to risk whatever might arise from the conflation of two such highly contested terms as *lesbian* and *postmodern* . . . is, in part, what this project is about One immediate result is this departure from a conventional introduction, that space where the editor does the trick with the round peg and square hole by proclaiming the magical cohesion of remarkably diverse approaches. . . . But it is unlikely that the articulation of any single unified formulation or construction of a lesbian postmodern will emerge. So how might we proceed, and more important, what expectations might we dangle before the reader? In entering this new and unpredictable terrain, we can at least express confidence that the configuration of something called the lesbian postmodern will enable us to pose and address questions, both provocative and critical, about the interventions of categories of sexual identity and difference into postmodern culture. (ix-x)

Arguably, Doan is able to dismiss the responsibility to define these subjects only because of the preexisting debate about lesbian identity. This decision not to define the parameters of one's theory is an interesting one; it results in a view that lesbian theory survives only by the virtue of the multiple voices within it that define and are defined by the theory simultaneously. This implies that lesbian identity is not so much defined by tradition and history but by the power of current theoretical trends. Although clearly this is problematic it also diffuses the obsession with definition.

As I have already argued earlier, any identity-based theory or criticism must address the problem of what qualities, actions, or characteristics make up the subject who can be characterized as having the particular identity. Also as I have touched on earlier, "identity" has many levels of meaning within literary criticism and theory: there is the material person (or subject), the subject's effect on the theory, the texts and/or authors to which this theory can be validly applied, and the identity of the critic who applies or even invents this theory. All of these concerns are present in different communities of theorists tied together by some notion of a "self" at stake, be it, for example, gay or lesbian, female, male, racial, national, or ethnic. I have already discussed feminist theory and lesbian theory in regards to this issue and have shown that, though wary of the traps of definition, early "identity-based critics" feel it necessary to use strategic essentialism in order to combat oppression. As identity-based theories and criticisms become more developed, making the necessity of essentialism less useful, the definition of the identity can withstand challenge and make the theories more meaningful and useful.[20] This trend is also relevant to a discussion of racial and ethnic theory.

These dialogues are particularly poignant in race or ethnicity based theory and criticism, as can be seen when one views the theory that has been produced. As with the previous two theoretical perspectives discussed, ethnic theory has also been dominated by specifically invested perspectives. Similar to those of other identity-based theories, the concerns of ethnic theory bring up the need to define the subject. So, we might ask the question: What person or what text has "race"? Also of concern here are the dynamics surrounding the many possible responses to this question. For example, how is race constructed in a text and what difference does that make?

Arguably the field of racial and ethnic theory has been dominated by African-Americans and the voices of these critics have undeniably influenced its vision. This could be related to the legacy of the enslavement of Africans in America or to the civil rights movement and its indelible consequences in the community. Because of the very clear racial violence perpetrated on this community its people and advocates were strongly motivated to speak.[21] For example, Barbara Christian connects the Black Arts Movement of the 1960s to the creation of not only Black Studies, but of both Women's Studies and the feminist literary movement as well. ("The Race" 338) I wish to discuss a few voices from within the complex field of African-American criticism, those who have generally be seen as the definers of the field, in order to illustrate the consequences of this assumption for the literary community.

In the field of literary criticism Henry Louis Gates Jr. and Houston A. Baker, Jr. are two of the most influential African-American theorists and both are primarily concerned with Black identity as it relates to orality. These theorists are well respected for good reason and I will discuss their work later in this section, but the wider white academic community has taken these scholars to be *the* spokespeople not only for the Black community but also for issues such as "multiculturalism," "race," and "ethnicity." Obviously, these issues are also important to other people of color as well as white people. It seems as if the white majority has generally found it easy to find one or two voices to define what "ethnicity" means and invest fully in them while disavowing the true complexity of non-white peoples; of course, such a move also assumes that white peoples are without race or ethnicity.

Toni Morrison provides some perspective on how the white literary community has historically viewed blackness as well as some of the consequences have been for Black subjects. In her book *Playing in the Dark*, she makes a strong argument for the recognition of the effect that the enslavement of Blacks had on the white American psyche. She claims that:

> Black slavery enriched the country's creative possibilities. For in that construction of blackness *and* enslavement could be found not only the not-free but also, with the dramatic polarity created by skin color, the projection of the not-me. The result was a playground for the imaginations. What rose up out of collective needs to allay internal fears and to rationalize external exploitation was an American Africanism—a fabricated brew of darkness, otherness, alarm, and desire that is uniquely American. (38)

This concept of the creation of a "fabricated brew of darkness" can be traced through the academy's treatment of "ethnic" literatures and theories by collapsing non-white peoples into the category of "blackness." It also parallels the academy's reductivist ideology that accounts for the behavior of choosing a "spokesperson" for theories and ideas not solely related to whiteness. In any case, whether positively or negatively, it is clear that African-American theory and texts have dominated the discussion.

In order to see how Black scholars have written about Black identity within and for the literary community, it is helpful to survey a limited overview of African-American criticism on the subject. 1970 could be pointed to as a landmark year for African-American theory. Many anthologies of African-American literature were published including Toni Cade Bambara's *The Black Woman*. Bambara seems very aware of the complexities of both essentialist and constructionist concepts of Black identity in this work. Even though the title of this volume would imply that there is such a person as "the black woman," Bambara instantly flips this assumption around as the opening page reads "Who is the Black woman? She is a college graduate. *A drop-out.* A student. *A wife.* A divorcée. *A mother.* A lover. *A child of the ghetto.* A product of the bourgeoisie. . . . *She is all these things—and more."* (n.p.) Perhaps it was this very early awareness of the competing pressures on the Black woman that forced this kind of articulation. Bambara also shows her sense of connection with other women of color when she describes the beginnings of the work of Black women as a movement. She describes American Black women desiring to form alliances on a "Third World Women plank." She concludes that "They are women who have not, it would seem, been duped by the prevailing notions of 'women,' but who have maintained a critical stance" (10). Interestingly, Bambara implies that a critical stance is inherent within the condition of the Black woman in America.

Both Alice Walker's "In Search of Our Mother's Gardens" (1974) and Barbara Smith's "Toward a Black Feminist Criticism" (1977) have been noted as important critical essays, but Smith's has probably had the greatest attention from academics. Smith argues that a Black feminist criticism is needed and then attempts to define what it might be. Primarily she feels that the existence of a Black female literary tradition needs to be recognized and the elements that are specific to the writing of Black women need to be considered. Smith argues that:

> thematically, stylistically, aesthetically, and conceptually Black women writers manifest common approaches to the act of creating

> literature as a direct result of the specific political, social and economic experience they have been obliged to share (Smith 164).

Smith further states that the critic employing Black feminism is indeed a Black woman with experiences and needs similar to those of any other:

> she would think and write out of her own identity and not try to graft the ideas or methodology of white/male literary thought upon the precious materials of Black women's art . . . The Black feminist critic would be constantly aware of the political implications of her work and would assert the connections between it and the political situation of all Black women. (164)

Here Smith implies an essential identity that is the basis of the criticism she envisions. Therefore, she illustrates a position of strategic essentialism not only pertaining to the subject of study but to the critic as well. She also implies that this identity's characteristics are obvious as she does not list them directly. Yet one is left to ask: would every Black woman have the same experiences as she asserts? Whatever the answer to this question, the criticism developed would certainly be affected making an essential identity difficult to maintain. I do not find it useful to judge Smith's use of essentialism but rather to make note of how it was important to the development of the dialogue on Black identity.

Surely essentialist versus constructionist ideas of race are at the heart of many discussions within African-American theory. Perhaps the most notorious discussion was within the *New Literary History* debate. Joyce Joyce argued against the Poststructuralist criticism of Gates and Baker and "the merger of Negro expression with Euro-American expression" (Joyce 339). She believes that "The Poststructuralist sensibility does not adequately apply to Black American literary works" (342). Ultimately it is the notion of race as a construction that Joyce refuses: "It is insidious for the Black literary critic to adopt any kind of strategy that diminishes or . . . negates his blackness" (341). These judgments, too, imply that there is an essential Black self that can be defined and understood and experienced and that certain avenues of inquiry are useless to penetrate it. Who does Joyce see as representative of this Black self? She seems to imply that Baker and Gates are not "real" Blacks because of their critical behavior. Could they be judged Black again in her view if they were to agree to an essential Black identity as she sees it? These questions illuminate the debate about how blackness gets defined, who defines it, and what qualities it might have. Clearly here these questions of definition are at issue both inside and outside the Black academic community.

Because, as I mentioned earlier, Gates and Baker have been treated as *the* spokespeople for African-American criticism and literature by the academy at large their work has been taken as *the* way to think about African-American literature. These critics have been both praised and criticized for their work and unfortunately their view of what equates to blackness, which I will discuss below, has been used to provide another method for limiting blackness. Obviously this consequence of their positive reception was imposed upon both scholars by the white academy. But it is when they seem to passively accept this role as spokespersons that each of these critics is at his weakest and most destructive for other people of color. Their work has also indirectly been used to limit the possibilities for lesbians of color because the academy has taken Baker's and Gates's definitions of blackness as the only ones, illustrating that the academy believes it needs no more.[22] It is important, then, to discuss how these two scholars envision Black identity.

Gates's main contribution to the field has been his concept of "signifying" as a critical theory. He has been seen as claiming a historical tradition for African-American theory through the culture of Africa; he has then attempted to rewrite present notions of race. He writes that:

> Race has become a trope of ultimate, irreducible difference between cultures, linguistic groups, or adherent of specific belief systems which—more often than not—also have fundamentally opposed economic interests. Race is the ultimate trope of difference because it is so very arbitrary in its applications. The biological criteria used to determine "difference" in sex simply do not hold when applied to "race." ("The Blackness" 5)

Even though Gates is advocating a constructionist view of race here, he still believes that there is something essential to Black identity and that is the ability to signify. He definitely focuses on a learned cultural tradition rather than on biology, yet the essential characteristic remains. He concurs with Smith, and argues that Blacks have an essential critical awareness and sense of linguistic play. How does this affect his concept of reconstructing race? Is it to be constructed only by his guidelines? Even though he has added much to the critical dialogue within African-American theory and hasn't claimed to be the only voice, the white academy has forced him to be.

Baker's most well known ideas revolve around the importance of the vernacular within African-American literature and criticism. Baker's theoretical perspective has been called "blues criticism." As a blues critic he discusses the blues as the "always already" of African-American culture and a useful way to discuss African-American poststructuralist theory. Baker envisions the critic as train-hopping hobo, and he claims that "The task of present day scholars is to situate themselves inventively and daringly at the crossing sign in order to materialize vernacular faces" (Baker 202). Again we have a theory that, while turning attention away from fixed signs like skin color, still essentializes by claiming the importance of the phantasm of the vernacular.

The reason that I point out these moments of essentialism is not to disparage these critics, or the use of essentialism, but rather to point out elements that have been used by other critics as definitive statements within their criticism. To take either of these ideas alone and consider no other theories within the African-American community is to hail these two but shut out everyone else. Clearly both of these critics have valid things to say and deserve attention, but for the academy to consider them as interchangeable, or as synonymous with ethnic literary theory, typifies the reductivist reception that greets critics and theories concerned with people of color and only serves the dominant white academy in limiting the effectiveness and importance of this material. Also this portion of the academy interprets the strategic essentialism and the moments of essentialism, even within work concerned primarily with construction, as moments of "truth" about racial subjects.

It should be obvious from even this very small sampling of some of the critical perspectives that African-American theory is extremely diverse and complex. The element that is startling to me, however, is that there is generally not much discussion about who is Black and yet there are clear omissions within African-American criticism that imply that there are members of the community who do not qualify.[23] An obvious omission relevant to this project is the lack of consideration of Black lesbian identity as part of Black identity.[24] Therefore, is there such a thing as "authentic" blackness? If so, how might it be defined? Why is it that blackness and/or African-American literature and criticism have many times represented all "ethnic" literature and all racial/ethnic theory? Is there some particular relationship that African-American literary criticism has with majority literary criticism that might answer these questions? Not surprisingly the answer here, I suggest, is yes. Paradoxically the primary reason for the status of African-American theory and literature is related to white supremacy. I argue that it is reflective of Morrison's description of a "brew of darkness" where whites see blackness as a total embodiment of otherness and therefore make it stand for everything that is not white thereby neglecting its complexity and that of other people of color. As Barbara Christian argues the binarism of "terms [like] 'minority and 'discourse' are located firmly in a Western dualistic ... frame which sees the rest of the world as minor and tries to convince the rest of the world that it *is* major" ("The Race" 337).

It seems that the non-Black-identified theorists of color who are concerned with ethnicity and race don't feel that somehow African-American theory has intentionally pushed them aside but rather they imply that the dominant "white" or "Western" theory has neglected complexity and therefore themselves, their writers, and their analyses. For example, as Eliana Ortega and Nancy Saporta Sternbach state in their text *Breaking Boundaries* they wish

> to explore the literary, social, political, and economic components that give rise and shape to a Latina literary discourse....Not surprisingly, there has been both resistance to and ignorance of this literary discourse from the various institutions of the dominant culture. Even in feminist criticism, where one expects broader paradigms than in the male establishment, little, if any attention is given to Latina literature.(3–4)

Even though these critics discuss the existence of "ethnic studies" and the discussion is broadening, they conclude that "In spite of the emergence of [Latina] literature and of the efforts by some critics to keep this work alive, there still prevails the resistance to acknowledge it ... In this stage of definition it appears to us that we are at the threshold of the unnamed" (9). This kind of "critical absence" is certainly evident in dominant criticism and theory.

Going back in time to one of the first books published related solely to Latinas, the editors of *Cuentos* (1983) discuss the motivations for creating the text. They link the silencing of their voices to both the history and culture of their own community and the history of their place within the dominant culture. And as in the other identity-based theories discussed, political oppression is seen as the primary motivation for speaking. Discussing their role within Latino culture they write "we are heirs of a culture of silence" (viii), and when discussing their place in dominant American culture, which again is specific to their place as women, they write:

> With the Third World liberation movements in the Sixties, a generation of people of color gained entrance (although limited) to the University. There our "cuentos" grew into literature. But even our "official" story-tellers—mostly male—did not tell our stories as women. The Latina fiction writer was the last to be fostered and recognized. And, the Latina as subject seldom extended beyond the role of virgin or puta (viii).

The placement of the Latina is without a doubt framed within cultural and historical parameters both white and Latino. Interestingly, in order to pave an opening for this text the editors discuss the Latina by *implying* an essential self but not stating any definition directly. They state:

> In *Cuentos* our intent is to mention the unmentionables, to capture some essential expression—without censors—that could be called "Latina" or "Latina identified." In short, we sought writings which put the concerns and struggles of the Latin woman first. And that in the naming, our cuentos could empower Latinas to believe we have the right to feel what we feel, in all its complexity (ix)

Clearly they imply that essential experience and/or qualities exist, but, unlike the lesbian critics previously mentioned, they do not explicitly list any such qualities thereby creating more room for inclusion. This is an important difference between lesbian and ethnic criticism because a more open racial definition might allow space for the inclusion of lesbians of color. From the beginning of this introduction the authors exhibit the complexity of the term "Latina." They distinguish U.S. Latinas from Latin American women because of the combination of cultures within the United States. They also distinguish the complexities of ethnicity and nationality among Latinas and in Latina identity. This discussion of identity differs from that in African-American theory;[25] this may be because of the domination of the white concept of "race" in the United States as a somehow more stable marker and one that belongs solely to Blacks whereas the more flexible marker of ethnicity belongs to other peoples of color.

This more flexible and therefore unstable notion of ethnicity has been a double edged blade. On one hand it allows the freedom of being something different than the permanent embodiment of a racial other, but on the other hand it also disavows the importance of the real life differences of these people of color. This is true both in "real" life and in criticism as many other peoples "of color" are not clearly marked by a "color" and therefore their "difference" can be easily ignored.[26] In this volume the editors have an interestingly empowering way of conceiving Latina identity that juggles the sword. They claim that:

> *Cuentos* goes against the grain of privilege we have been told is necessary for the development of "good"—meaning white—writing. Our aspirations are not to be more European. Instead, we *claim*, "la mezcla," la mestiza, regardless of each author's degree of indio, africano, or european blood. (x)

This inclusive move would also be a difficult one to define, and that appears to be what is at issue here, pointing out the real difficulty and futility of cataloging identity. Further, they establish that it is a white pursuit, this cataloging, one that internalized within the community of people of color can lead to fruitless divisiveness. This does not mean that all identity must be equal or all differences ignored, but rather they point out another way to conceive of such difference within cultural context.

It has primarily been within introductions to creative anthologies that many of these issues are addressed in specific relation to Latinas and although there have been other texts written about Latina literature I find these first resources of particular interest. Gloría Anzaldúa's text *Borderlands/La Frontera: The New Mestiza* has been an incredible step for theoretical notions of identity and much of my future discussion will focus on it. Here, however, I am concerned with primarily literary critical concepts of Latina identity and the major book length discussion focused on this aspect of Chicano literature is Ramon

Saldívar's *Chicano Narrative: The Dialectics of Difference* (1990). Therefore, even after all of the calls for the voices of Latinas to be heard, they are still primarily silent in the field of literary theory. There has not been a sustained call for a "Latina Feminist Criticism" for example.[27] So I'd like to explore the major literary statement on Latino/a identity-based literature and criticism that exists, which is Saldívar's.[28]

Saldívar's concept of Chicano literature is that it is "emphatically political" and he further aligns it with the narratives of other "radical writings" (4). Again the idea is expressed that the narratives' purpose is to allow the authors to speak their own representations. Saldívar believes that Chicano fiction illustrates that the concept of being the other is "potentially liberating when as the contrastive other Chicano culture has produced for Chicanos a consistent and highly articulated set of oppositions to the dominant cultural system surrounding it" (4). He does not attempt to generate a definition of what might be considered "Chicano," nor does he give the qualities that would define a text as a Chicano narrative, but he implies that a Chicano is necessarily concerned with politics and specifically with one's own oppression or "Otherness." Saldívar nicely articulates the fact that a consideration of Chicano literature must also cause a reconsideration of the "American canon." This is surely a worthwhile pursuit; however, there are many Chicano/a authors who don't make it into Saldívar's book because they could be seen as not "emphatically political."[29]

The editors of the first anthology of Asian-American writers, *Aiiieeeee!* (1974), also immediately claimed a rebellious stance to frame the selections; in this case against dominant definitions of the "Asian." The editors have their own definition of who an Asian-American is: "Asian-Americans are not one people but several—Chinese Americans, Japanese Americans, and Filipino Americans." (xi)[30] The editors describe, in similar terms to those in some of the Latina texts previously discussed, the immense differences within the community that must be considered to contain Asian-American identity. The authors also find it of major importance to foreground a critique of white constructions of Asians and their effects on Asian-Americans. They write that:

> Seven generations of suppression under legislative racism and euphemized white racist love have left today's Asian Americans in a state of self-contempt, self-rejection, and disintegration. We have

> been encouraged to believe that we have no cultural integrity as
> Chinese or Japanese Americans, that we are either Asian (Chinese or
> Japanese) or American (white), or are measurably both. This myth of
> being either/or and the equally goofy concept of the dual personality
> haunted our lobes while our rejection by both Asia and white
> American proved we were neither one nor the other. Nor were we
> half and half or more one than the other. Neither Asian culture nor
> American culture was equipped to define us except in the most
> superficial terms. However, American culture, equipped to deny us
> the legitimacy of our uniqueness as American minorities, did so, and
> in the process contributed to the effect of stunting self-contempt on
> the development and expression of our sensibility (xii).

This concept of the self-defined subject speaking for him/herself is consistent with other American minority perspectives, but it is strikingly different from the concept of claiming an identity in flux as the editors of *Cuentos* did. In contrast the editors of *Aiiieeeee!* see unstable identity as destructive to the Asian-American subject.[31]

The anthology *The Forbidden Stitch* (1989) was the first exclusively female Asian-American collection and one gets a sense of the editors' reactions to this "first" from its title. Interestingly, the concept of a definition of the Asian-American woman begins immediately. Shirley Geok-Lin Lim writes of identity much more broadly than did the editors of *Aiiieeeee!* when she claims that:

> I [know] there [is] no such thing as an "Asian American woman."
> Within this homogenizing labeling of an exotica, I [know] there [are]
> entire racial/national/cultural/sexual-preferenced groups, many of
> whom find each other as alien as mainstream America apparently
> finds us (10).

She continues by expanding the previously given definition of the Asian-American when she writes about difference:

> We do not share a common history, a common original culture or
> language, not even a common physique or color. We are descended
> from Hindus of Uttar Prodesh, Chinese from Hong Kong, Japanese
> from Honshu, Ilocanos from the Philippines, Vietnamese from Saigon
> (now Ho Chi Minh City), Koreans, Malaysians, Pakistanis (10).

So even in her inclusiveness and grouping, there again is no clearly articulated definition of who exactly an Asian-American is, although there is an implication that one does exist.[32] Interestingly she implies a multiplicitous Asian-American identity through her use of place, as she makes her reader consider all of the possibilities for Asian heritage and how they might change and/or combine.

As an overview of these issues, Jessica Hagedorn begins her anthology *Charlie Chan is Dead* (1993) with a kind of Asian-American literary history. She begins by describing the reaction to the publication of *Aiiieeeee!* as one typical of a groundbreaking text. She writes:

> it gave us visibility and credibility as creators of our own specific literature. We could not be ignored; suddenly, we were no longer silent. Like other writers of color in America, we were beginning to challenge the long-cherished concepts of a xenophobic literary canon dominated by white heterosexual males (xxvii)

Hagedorn does not *directly* attempt to define the Asian-American, but she implies her response to the question of identity, in a move reminiscent of Lim's, when she discusses the contributors to her book:

> Some were born in the Philippines, some in Seattle. A few in Hawaii. Others in Toronto or London. Some live in San Francisco. Oakland. Stockton. Los Angeles. New York City. Santa Fe. Family in Panama. Singapore. Tokyo. Manila. Pusan. Chicago. Hayward. Boston. Brooklyn. Beijing. Mindoro. Washington, D.C. Seoul. Greeley, Colorado. India. Penang. Moscow, Idaho.
> Asian American literature? Too confining a term, maybe. World literature? Absolutely. (xxx)

By listing the vast array of places where the contributors live, Hagedorn has an original way of critiquing stereotypes of Asian-Americans, as well as critiquing the desire to define the subject. I don't believe she is equating address with Asianness here, but rather she is asking her reader to confront their own idea of who an Asian-American is. Also she clearly critiques dominant white notions of race and ethnicity by critiquing the categories that are so easily created for "different" literatures and theories as well as the idea that a center and margins exist in the first place.

She continues with an analysis that could be considered a critique of the Asian-American community itself:

> We are asserting and continually exploring who we are as Asians, Asian Americans, and artists and citizens.... The choice is more than whether to hyphenate or not. The choice is more than gender, race, or class. First generation, second, third, fourth. Who is authentic or fake. Dead or undead. Mainstream or marginal. Uncle Tom or Charlie Chan. (xxx)

Perhaps the most compelling and most clearly theoretically oriented discussion concerning Asian-American literature is King-Kok Cheung's *Articulate Silences* (1993). She addresses many complex issues within any consideration of ethnicity: cultural specificity, white supremacy, authenticity, nationality, duality, categories, gender, experience, authority, canon formation, articulations of self, as well as theory. She does not directly address the need to define who an Asian-American is, but she does show the need to start the text off with some "terminology." She states that:

> I use the term "Asian American" to refer to North American writers of Asian descent.... the term "Asian American literature" generally describes works by writers of diverse national origins—Chinese, Japanese, Korean, Filipino, East Indian, Pakistani, Vietnamese, Thai, Cambodian, Laotian, and Pacific Islanders (n.p.).

Her choice to start her study this way implies that she sets this up as a necessary pragmatic move, and within her introduction itself she is much more critical of labeling and essential identity. In this way she can both be clear as to whom she is dealing as well as challenge those same parameters. She clearly states that she is not trying to make a claim that she can define *the* Asian-American theory. She reaffirms that "Asian American sensibilities vary in accordance with nationality, birthplace, age, social background, and individual endowment" (21).

In my opinion the most provocative statement Cheung makes is in describing how she positions herself within theoretical dynamics. This situating is also a pragmatic move parallel to her above use of terminology, however, at this moment her critique of academic dynamics is much clearer. She states that:

> Intellectually I situate myself somewhere between advocates of diverse feminisms, between those of feminism and nationalism, and between those of ethnicity and race. This position derives from my multiple allegiances and a deep ambivalence toward certain persuasions (22).

Intriguingly Cheung continues specifying that "Because I neither readily ally myself with nor reject out of hand any one school of thought, my own voice may come across as evasive or subdued" (22–3). She is astutely responding to criticism she knows will come after she has given her position as a critic and, in my view, Cheung here is correctly pointing out the limits of boxing certain theories and theorists in only one arena.

This discussion assumes, of course, that no theories overlap or can be employed simultaneously. Also, she critiques the idea that by "belonging" to one group necessarily means you cannot be part of another. Again this critic shows that the more "marginal" a theory or theorist is perceived to be the more categorized they become, and that because some labels are read as neutral, these theorists can pretend that their own theories cannot be contained in specific boxes. Cheung's pragmatic "admission" points to the real limits imposed by whites on all people of color.

One of the major limits placed on writers of color is that they are readily externally defined and boxed by the white academy (as well as publishing houses and other institutions). Barbara Christian nicely makes this point when she states that the definers:

> have the power (although they deny it) first of all to be published, and thereby to determine the ideas which are deemed valuable, some of our most daring and potentially radical critics (and by *our* I mean black, women, third world,) have been influenced, even co-opted, into speaking a language and defining their discussion in terms alien to and opposed to our needs and orientation. At least so far, the creative writers I study have resisted this language. ("The Race" 335–36)[33]

The main issue of importance to my discussion here is that Christian posits that "people of color have always theorized—but in forms quite different from the Western form of abstract logic" (336). It is most likely this fact that accounts for the minimizing of this "dynamic" theorizing by peoples of color by the white academy and for only a very select few to be recognized as contributing to theoretical debates.

I believe that Beth Brant has been one such writer who has been seen as important primarily as an editor of Native American women's texts and not also as a theorist. Beth Brant's important text *A Gathering of Spirit: A Collection by North American Indian Women* (1984), she does not make "academic" theoretical statements, but rather she uses a material perspective by discussing the process of compiling the anthology, including letters she received from contributors, and by including her own journal entries concerning her task. Even though this is not a typical theoretical discussion, and hasn't been seen as one, I suggest that Brant is indeed engaging in critical dialogue here. In her introduction she states

> I want to write about what it means to put together [a journal's special] issue by North American Indian women. I need to explain and share my feelings connected to that work. There is an urgency to relate to physical details, the spiritual labor, the ritual, the gathering, the making. Because in the unraveling, the threads become more apparent, each one with its distinct color and texture. And as I unravel, I also weave. I am the storyteller and the story. (8)

This discussion echoes the constructions of self that many other women of color articulate; also there are topics undeniably related to American Indian cultures and selves.

Perhaps the moment in Brant's introduction where she most clearly enters a dialogue with many other positions is when she writes:

> We are angry at Indian men for their refusals of us For their limited vision of what constitutes a strong Nation We are angry at a so-called "women's movement" that always seems to forget we exist. Except in romantic fantasies of earth mother or equally romantic and dangerous fantasies about Indian-woman-as victim. Women lament our *lack* of participation in feminist events, yet we are either referred to as *et ceteras* in the naming of women of color, or simply not referred to at all. *We are not victims.* We are organizers, we are freedom fighters, we are feminists, we are healers. This is not anything new. For centuries it has been so. (11)

This statement parallels the voices of other women of color, but also clearly represents a culturally specifically American Indian voice.

It could be argued that it is American Indian identity that is most hotly contended. It is within this racial category that we still count drops of blood as an indicator of authenticity.[34] Interestingly enough, though, it seems that within texts written by these authors the subject of identity is left more ambiguous than in any other group previously described. It is difficult to account for this tendency within the literary community, however, I suspect that it is based on how Native Americans have been traditionally categorized and labeled by white society and the American government. To my knowledge, it is the only minority group for which "realness" is defined by fractions of identity on government forms and the like. Perhaps it is because of this atmosphere that many Native American writers have so much difficulty in being defined both from within and without their communities.[35]

There is an interesting presentation of American Indian identity within Paula Gunn Allen's *The Sacred Hoop* (1986) when she discusses the characteristics that typify the essays included in the volume. The definition of an American Indian subject is not among the recurring elements included. Still, Gunn Allen implies that such a definable subject exists when she asserts that Native American literature exists. She claims that "There is such a thing as American Indian literature, and it can be divided into several interlocking categories" (4). A further discussion of these categories is not warranted here, but I mention this only to make the point that Gunn Allen, too, stays away from a direct definition of "Indianness" but implies that one could be stated.

It is within Gunn Allen's text *Spider Woman's Granddaughters: Traditional Tales and Contemporary Writing by Native American Women* (1989) that she discusses more elements of American Indian identity. She first points to the fact that has encouraged many other groups to turn to identity politics in the first place:

> When a people has no control over public perceptions of it, when its sense of self is denied at every turn in the books, films, and television and radio shows it is forced to imbibe, it cannot help but falter. But when its image is shaped by its own people, the hope of survival can be turned into a much greater hope; it can become a hope for life, for vitality, for affirmation. (18)

The need that Gunn Allen discusses here would certainly seem to call for some kind of definition(s) of the American Indian subject. She responds by stating "We are not so much 'women,' as American Indian women; our stories, like our lives, necessarily reflect that fundamental identity" (24). But again, what it means to be an American Indian woman or how one might define such a subject is not delineated, only implied.

Gerald Vizenor's text, *Narrative Chance: Postmodern Discourse on Native American Indian Literature* (1989) is a major book length literary critical study of American Indian fiction that posits a specific theoretical frame for its readings.[36] The authors in the volume do exactly what the title indicates, they give readings of texts through various Postmodern theories. By doing this with no apologies or explanations, the critics make it clear that American Indian literature is literature after all and should not *just* be studied by sociologists and anthropologists but literary theorists as well. On the back of the edition there is a portion of a review from *Great Plains Quarterly* that says "[Gerald Vizenor] is talking walking politics. . . . It's a politics opposed to academic constructions of 'Indianness.'" I would agree with this assessment but perhaps see it from a different perspective than is implied by this praise. There actually is very little discussion of "Indianness" at all. For what reason? To deny an externally imposed version of "Indianness"? Or to deny any validity to constructed identity? I find it particularly interesting that these questions are on the whole ignored which in this instance I perceive to be a consequence rather than a strategy.[37]

So, after exploring these various examples of how race and ethnicity are constructed within the literary realm it is particularly interesting that even though definition is deemed to be important, the subject at hand is never defined. Also because some subjects don't receive attention within ethnic/racial criticism they are, by implication, not part of its definition. Clearly, on the whole, lesbians of color, whose identities tend to disrupt essentialist constructions, are left out of this criticism because of its tendency to emphasize identity construction based on strategic essentialism. The lesbian "sexual identity politics", which I explored earlier in this chapter, are similar to those that occur within racial/ethnic criticism; though, the prior's definitions are generally less stringent than the latter. However, I pointed out earlier that lesbians of color are also left out of this criticism because of its

Rethinking Identity Construction

tendency to develop identity constructions out of white supremacist ideology. There are other factors that could explain the differences between how and why these two critical perspectives exclude the lesbian of color.[38] I believe numerous factors could be considered when discussing this issue; most important for this discussion though is the concept of a *visually* knowable identity. Typically, sexual identity is conceptualized in terms of *behavior* and not visual identification. On the other hand racial and ethnic identities are conceptualized not in terms of behavior but in terms of skin color or visual difference. Therefore, lesbian behavior does not seem to be taken as important to theorizing about constructions of race or ethnicity, and racial or ethnic visual difference does not seem to be considered important when theorizing about constructions of lesbian identity.

Because I have argued here that constructions of lesbian selves are slightly more free from the confines of definition than those of race and ethnicity I think it is useful to introduce an alternative approach to reading race and ethnicity.[39] A reconsideration of these theories will allow lesbians of color entrance into the dialogue, and more importantly, their experience can help transform many limiting concepts of racial and ethnic identity.

Werner Sollors's volume *The Invention of Ethnicity* (1989) is a useful place to begin considering racial and ethnic identities. Sollors describes the "traditional way" of looking at ethnicity and claims that most studies reflect that the existence of ethnicity is taken for granted:

> Ethnic groups are typically imagined as if they were natural, real, eternal, stable, and static units. They seem to be always already in existence. As a subject of study, each group yields an essential continuum of certain myths and traits, or of human capital The focus is on the group's preservation and survival, which appear threatened Conflicts generally seem to emerge from the world outside of the particular ethnic group investigated. Assimilation is the foe of ethnicity; hence there are numerous polemics against the blandness of melting pot, mainstream, and majority culture.... The studies that result from such premises typically lead to an isolationist, group-by-group approach that emphasizes "authenticity" and cultural heritage within the individual, somewhat idealized group—at the expense of more widely shared historical conditions and cultural features, of dynamic interaction and syncretism. (xiv)

Many of these traditions are still at the heart, in varying degrees, of the texts I have discussed within this chapter that summarize a particular racial or ethnic identity. Although clearly some of the critics I mentioned either refuse to define, or focus on the multiplicity of, identities. These are two useful approaches to escape a limiting definitive statement of identity. Sollors discusses that ethnic and racial identities can be seen as more flexible and less definitive in the postmodern context. He states that:

> The forces of modern life embodied by such terms as "ethnicity," "nationalism, "or "race" can indeed by [sic] meaningfully discussed as "inventions." Of course this usage is meant not to evoke a conspiratorial interpretation of a manipulative inventor who single-handedly makes ethnics out of unsuspecting subjects, but to suggest widely shared, though intensely debated, collective fictions that are continually reinvented. (xi)

If it is possible, then, to conceive of this identity as an invention and as ever-changing, how might this be beneficial to lesbians of color? Clearly there are undercurrents of the identity debate within the texts that I discussed earlier but the view of racial/ethnic identity as construction is not the primary one. Because lesbians of color straddle this debate, they simultaneously exist inside the community and challenge its stability, they are left to decide how to resolve this duplicity in order to actively exist as they choose.

Is a monolithic definition the most useful approach to take? If not, then is a complete abandonment of definition the best approach? Or is there a possibility of employing one or the other at different times? When considering people of color, then, I believe that individuals may *claim* the identity they feel defines their experiences and their position most accurately. This position is parallel to the one I described from *Cuentos* which I discussed earlier and is clearly volatile. The argument that identities can be determined by active negotiation within different communities and within different contexts, is one that acknowledges both limits and benefits to different historical constructions of identity. But it also leaves the subject open to assault by those, within and without the academic community, who wish to categorize and attempt to stabilize ethnic/racial markers.[40]

Self definition allows connections and difference to exist among different peoples of color.[41] I believe that the strength of ethnic identity is the ability to live with paradox. Even though some ethnic peoples see statements like this as reinforcing external limitations forced upon them by those whose identity has been constructed as definite and stable,[42] I still side with Gloria Anzaldúa's much more positive use of these paradoxical elements of ethnic American identity. I don't believe that this acknowledgment of the paradox of identity somehow "dilutes" a "real" identity but rather that it reveals its fictionality. In that case ethnic identity, when seen as something other than simply the opposite of "regular" identity, validates the "marginal," the borders, and not the existence of a center.

This rethinking of hierarchical structures of definition is of benefit to lesbians of color because their identities are disruptive and yet are always threatened by erasure. These very real threats are incredibly important to understand and acknowledge because they are fundamental to the lesbian of color's construction of identity. Thus, in order to account for lesbians of color within critical discourse one must explore the social and cultural contexts in which she attempts to exist.

CHAPTER TWO
Naming the Enemies: Multiple Threats to the Existence of the Lesbian of Color

The primary voices within lesbian studies that attempt to make a place for their work, and sometimes for themselves, see compulsory heterosexuality and its resulting oppression as their major threats. As I have already discussed in the previous chapter many of these scholars feel that the lesbian has been erased from history and literature, as well as from consciousness and therefore part of their work is "rediscovering" a history and a tradition that serves to validate her existence. This is, of course, similar to the feminism of the 1970s, when bringing back "forgotten" women's texts was a major goal, which had some positive results for lesbians, and indeed all women, in the academy as well as in society. However, what has been for the most part ignored is the specific difficulty that the lesbian of color faces. This difficulty, these oppressions, are not important just because they are different from white lesbians' experiences but because an understanding of these oppressions, as well as the strategies the lesbian of color employs to survive them, profoundly questions the content of lesbian studies and identity theory in general.

Makeda Silvera, the editor of *Piece of My Heart: A Lesbian of Colour Anthology*, summarizes the difficulty that the lesbian of color has in merely speaking her existence. She describes this fear thusly:

> Fear of the loss of family, fear of obliteration from a whole community, a whole culture. For often times it is not just the loss of

blood family we fear but that entire cultural community, where we go for comfort, for music, for food; where we go to when our daughters and sons get jerked around by a system that is plain racist. A system that tells us we are nothing but a bunch of criminals—that we have no voice. A culture that tells us that gay/lesbian, women who love women of any colour are to be scorned and ridiculed. Our community, our family, are no exception, they are often embarrassed, scandalized, ashamed and fearful of us—lesbians—oddities. This is frequently what silences us, because without that home, without family, we often have only that hostile white world.

But we can remain silent for only so long, because with each silent day, with every denial of who we are, we die a little.

It is a serious and brave act each time one of us comes out, because for some of us the danger is real There is always that threat of physical violence depending on the community that we live in, and depending on our socio-economic condition. Always, we must be on guard because violence against us is lurking. We are women, we are lesbians, we have no race privilege. (xv)

Just considering these differences is not enough. Because this woman is in such jeopardy, as Silvera aptly makes clear here, just recognizing her existence does nothing to change it.

If white lesbian and white feminist theories are going to be relevant and remain relevant, to both literary studies and liberation movements generally, they must include considerations of these lesbians' experience of identity. Lesbian and feminist theorists must acknowledge what role they have within "that hostile white world" in order to make these theories more complex in their constructions of identity. This is clear from looking at the difficulty that Anglo feminist theorists have had in understanding the fact that a consideration of women of color should necessitate a different feminist theory (instead of just "adding" them to classes, texts, conferences, and so on.).

This problem has continued within lesbian theory as well. Ann Ferguson has pointed out, within *Lesbian Philosophies and Cultures*, that these differences should illustrate the need for a re-consideration of the general term "lesbian," or more specifically "lesbian culture." She states that it is:

> plausible to argue that there are historically different gender and sexual formations in place in different societies—different family structures, economies, forms of the state, which embed different forms of patriarchy and sexual hierarchy.... Many of these can be associated with lesbian sexual practices that will involve different senses of self identification, not only between one country or region of the world and another, but within cultures, between different economic classes, racial and ethnic groups. Our lesbian history thus should conceive of a number of lesbian subcultures rather than one universal lesbian culture. (81)

That Ferguson implies lesbian studies should take this direction is encouraging, although I think that we should go beyond a consideration of lesbian history/culture and into an investigation of lesbian (and indeed all) identity formation as well. By looking at texts where the authors or characters articulate the communities that they are excluded from because of their multiple identities, one can see the complications that the lesbian of color brings to conceptions of identity.

In order to do justice to the differences among women of color I feel it is necessary to discuss the specific cultural contexts that differentiate racial and ethnic groups from one another. There are specific historical, cultural, religious and mythic institutions/aspects of heritage that these women exist in relation to; it is necessary then to give a brief contextual discussion before placing the primary texts within their own framework. I do not attempt, however, to give definitive cultural histories in this chapter, as a comprehensive study of all of these communities is beyond the scope of this project. It is through these contexts that the specific experiences of the lesbian of color finds its resonance. In this chapter I will focus on the hostilities the lesbian of color faces within her community and try to show that they exert influence on their ability to construct her identity amidst community opposition. While this is an important element within these texts, it is not the only element. Thus, many of the primary texts discussed here will recur in following chapters where I will focus on different elements that reflect how lesbians of color construct their identities.

As I have already discussed in the previous chapter, African-American women have probably been the most focused on of all women of color. Therefore, there is a plethora of writings concerned with their place in history and literature as well as literary theory and criticism. Many scholars see the slavery of Africans in America, and the consequential "birth" of the African-American, as the major force within African-American consciousness and history that affects not only the literature they produce but the lives they lead. Within African-American literature the connection between history and literature has been strong, although some might argue that until relatively recently it has been almost invisible because there is not a long tradition of studying the spiritual autobiographies, slave narratives, as well as musical traditions as worthwhile "literature." During slavery achieving literacy was a dangerous and powerful act and one that was deeply connected to freedom. There are many examples in early literature that connect reading and writing both to danger and freedom.[43] Being denied the opportunity of being literate, slaves developed a wide array of oral storytelling forms such as: folktales, sermons, work songs, and spirituals.[44] The experience of slavery had devastating effects on both men and women, and they both wrote about their experiences and developed what we can today call the African-American literary tradition. Women, though, had specific difficulties and experiences within the bonds of slavery that differentiate them from men and complicate their status as women.

Hazel Carby has explored the experiences of Black women slaves and the consequences of these experiences on Black women today in her text *Reconstructing Womanhood: The Emergence of the Afro-American Woman Novelist*. She also discusses the effect that the enslavement of Black women had on Black men. Specifically Carby focuses on the sexual abuse that women suffered which, she argues, had the effect of defining black men as helpless. She writes that,

> The victim appeared not just in her own right as a figure of oppression but was linked to a threat to, or denial of, the manhood of the male slave. Black manhood, in other words, could not be achieved or maintained because of the inability of the slave to protect the black woman in the same manner that convention dictated the inviolability of the white woman. The slave woman, as victim, became defined in terms of a physical exploitation resulting from the lack of the assets of white womanhood: no masculine protector or home and family, the locus of the flowering of white womanhood. (35)

The Black slave woman became the symbol of Black male bondage and her children were a constant reminder of the continuation of slavery and/or of the power of the white master. Carby continues by showing that the male slave has historically been seen as the symbol of the oppressed Black whereas the female slave has been seen as somehow complicit with white men and the system of slavery. She states that:

> the institutionalized rape of black women has never been as powerful a symbol of black oppression as the spectacle of lynching. Rape has always involved patriarchal notions of women being, at best, not entirely unwilling accomplices, if not outwardly inviting sexual attack. The links between black women and illicit sexuality consolidated during the antebellum years had powerful ideological consequences for the next hundred and fifty years. (39)

Perhaps the most stunning consequences for the Black woman have been the stereotypes of her that survive within both literature and society. Some of the typical "types" are: the matriarch, the Sapphire and the Queen Bee (or "B"). The matriarch, of course, is the individual woman who is the head of the Black family. bell hooks claims that

> The argument that black women were matriarchs was readily accepted by black people even though it was in image created by white males. Of all the negative stereotypes and myths that have been used to characterize black womanhood, the matriarchy label has had the greatest impact on the consciousness of many black people. The independent role black women were obliged to play both in the labor force and in the family was automatically perceived as unladylike....The matriarchy theory gave the black male a framework on which to base his condemnation of working black women. (*Ain't I* 78-9)

hooks defines the Sapphire as a black woman who "w[as] depicted as evil, treacherous, bitchy, stubborn, and hateful....The Sapphire image had as its base one of the oldest negative stereotypes of woman—the image of the female as inherently evil" (85).

Jean Carey Bond and Patricia Perry also offer a definition of this "type" in their essay "Is the Black Male Castrated?" They write that the Sapphire image of the Black woman is that "she is depicted as iron-willed, effectual, treacherous toward and contemptuous of Black men, the latter being portrayed as simpering, ineffectual whipping boys" (116). SDiane A. Bogus defines the Queen B image as "a euphemism for Queen Bulldagger or Bulldyke" (275) used in a pejorative way to refer to "the black woman who assumes the male sexual prerogative" (276); in other words she is in control of her own sexuality. Gayl Jones's novel *Eva's Man* illustrates some examples of this figure and she is always connected directly with death. One woman talks about this figure: "They call her the queen bee . . .cause every man she had end up dying. I don't mean natural dying, I mean something happen to them. Other mens know it too, but they still come" (17).[45] They all have in common the concept that a powerful Black woman is a destructive woman, an emasculating woman, a threat to the identity of the Black man as well as to the survival of the community in general.

Ann Allen Shockley's contribution to *Home Girls*, "The Black Lesbian in American Literature: An Overview," contains a discussion of the apparently necessary placement of Black women characters within a male context. She argues that many women writers feel the necessity to stick with heterosexual perspectives because of the fear they will be labeled lesbians and so rejected whether they are or not. Shockley writes that the

> threat of being identified as gay, queer, funny, or a bulldagger in Black linguistics is embedded deeply within the overall homophobic attitude of the Black community, a phenomenon stemming from social, religious, and "biological" convictions. The enmity toward homosexuality has long been rampant in Black life. (84)

She gives examples such as: the power of religion (both Muslim and Christian) in the community and the dominance of its male-centered attitudes/practices and the Civil Rights movement of the sixties with its promotion of Black male identity in order to debunk the myth of Black matriarchy. Shockley concludes that

> In view of this [need to enhance Black manhood], naturally, the independent woman-identified-woman—the Black Lesbian—was a threat. Not only was she a threat to the projection of Black male macho, but a *sexual* threat too—the utmost danger to the Black male's designated role as 'king of the lovers' (85).

Even though she does not connect the legacy of slavery with this male dominant definition of womanhood a connection is definitely there. If, as Carby argues, the woman was seen as a threat because of the fact she was a slave, her very existence was troubling to Black manhood. The Black lesbian then, as seemingly contradictory to heterosexual institutions, is viewed as the ultimate destroyer of community and enemy to Black males ascension to manhood as it is defined by dominant culture. Because she can never be a "symbol" of Black male manhood, she is apparently at odds with the possibility of power within the Black community.

Cheryl Clarke exposes some of this blatant homophobia within the Black community especially as it relates to the concept of the community's survival. She focuses first on the Black Liberation Movement's view of community. She quotes directly from a flyer from the conference that she attended:

> Revolutionary nationalists and genuine communists cannot uphold homosexuality in the leadership of the Black Liberation Movement nor uphold it as a correct practice. Homosexuality is a genocidal practice.... Homosexuality does not produce children.... Homosexuality does not birth new warriors for liberation... homosexuality cannot be upheld as correct revolutionary practice.... The practice of homosexuality is an accelerating threat to our survival as a people and as a nation (198).

Clarke clearly shows that the Black Power movement, though desiring to change class boundaries, still mantained the centrality of male superiority. The rhetoric here seems to guarantee that women are always already heterosexual and exist to support the heterosexual male's ability to be a "warrior." In other words, reproduction legitimates male political power and the use of females as breeders. After discussing various sites of homophobia within her community she states that:

> it is exceedingly painful for us to face public denunciation from black folk—the very group who should be championing our liberation. Because of the level of homophobia in the culture in general, many black gay men and lesbians remain in the closet, passing as heterosexuals. Thus, when public denunciations of our lifestyles are made by other black people, we remain silent in the face of their

hostility and ignorance. The toll taken on us because we repress our rage and hurt makes us distrustful of all people whom we cannot identify as lesbian or gay. Also, for those of us who are isolated from the gay or lesbian community, the toll is greater self-hate, self-blame, and belief in the illness theory of homosexuality. (207)

The pain that Clarke so aptly describes here is represented in numerous works of fiction by and about Black lesbians. And although I do not agree with the position that Anita Cornwell posits, in her *Black Lesbian in White America*, that all males are inherently evil, I do agree that lesbians are at the mercy of the society males have constructed (17–22). It is worthwhile then to explore how creative writers have constructed Black lesbian characters within the parameters of these cultural traditions and ideologies.

One of the most notorious characterizations of Black lesbians is within Gloria Naylor's novel *The Women of Brewster Place*. She most poignantly portrays how patriarchal dominance within the Black community can be devastating for Black lesbians. In this text she dramatizes many of the dangers that threaten the Black lesbian's survival specifically in the chapter entitled "The Two." This chapter incorporates the rest of the women she has discussed in the previous pages, but it is the lesbian couple Lorraine and Theresa that are the focus here. Naylor has been describing the women as they fit into the community of Brewster Place; she proceeds telling her story as if putting together a puzzle with one woman's story connecting to the next and building Brewster Place into a character in its own right. It is during a tenants' meeting organized by Kiswana, the resident activist, that the disparate people try to unify. Instead of discussing the topic at hand they debate what they should do with the "bad element" that has moved into their building—in other words the lesbians. Some of the women discuss how lesbianism affects them: one woman disapproves on religious grounds, but the most interesting discussion occurs between Mattie and Etta who attempt to find out what is wrong with the idea of women loving each other.

"But I've loved some women deeper than I ever loved any man," Mattie was pondering. "And there have been some women who loved me more and did more for me than any man ever did."

"Yeah." Etta thought for a moment. "I can second that, but it's still different, Mattie. I can't exactly put my finger on it, but . . . "

"Maybe it's not so different," Mattie said, almost to herself. "Maybe that's why some women get so riled up about it, 'cause they know deep down it's not so different after all" (141).

It is after this moment of realization and acceptance that the meeting disintegrates into a shouting match over the issue of lesbianism, making it difficult for these people to form a truly powerful community. As Maxine L. Montgomery summarizes "The implication is, of course, that they can never find complete, unconditional acceptance in a context where heterosexual relationships are considered to be the norm" (11).

An even clearer articulation of a threat of danger towards these two women occurs after Kiswana apologizes to Lorraine for the other tenants' behavior at the meeting. As the two women stand outside Brewster Place and talk they are approached by a group of young men who belligerently verbally attack Lorraine for being a lesbian and Kiswana for being seen with her. Naylor describes one young man, C.C. Baker, and his reasons for hating Lorraine:

> C. C. Baker was greatly disturbed by the thought of a Lorraine. He knew of only one way to deal with women other than his mother. Before he had learned exactly how women gave birth, he knew how to please or punish or extract favors from them by the execution of what lay curled behind his fly. It was his lifeline to that part of his being that sheltered his self-respect. And the thought of any woman who lay beyond the length of its power was a threat. (162)

This is a perfect example of the very real danger that the lesbian faces from within her own community. Naylor's own powerful image representing this danger is Lorraine's brutal rape at the hands of C.C. Baker and his group of friends:

> So Lorraine found herself, on her knees, surrounded by the most dangerous species in existence—human males with an erection to validate in a world that was only six feet wide.
>
> "I'm gonna show you somethin' I bet you never seen before." C.C. took the back of her head, pressed it into the crotch of his jeans, and jerkily rubbed it back and forth while his friends laughed. "Yeah,

now don't that feel good? See, that's what you need. Bet after we get through with you, you ain't never gonna wanna kiss no more pussy."
(170)

The torment that these men perpetrate causes Lorraine to lose her mind and brutally murder her only friend in the community.

The violence of this devastating rape has a chain reaction in the community of Brewster Place. This includes the death of Ben, the "patriarch" of the building, at the hands of his friend Lorraine. Interestingly, it was the "specter" of lesbianism that threatened to destroy a budding unity within Brewster Place, and it is Lorraine's plunge into insanity, Ben's death, and the subsequent departure of Theresa that seem to destroy the symbol of unity, the block party. It is only Ben's death, though, that they openly mourn and that they wish to understand. Naylor describes in deep detail the connection between Ben's death and the well-being of Brewster Place and its residents:

Rain. It began the afternoon of Ben's death and came down day and night for an entire week, so Brewster Place wasn't able to congregate around the wall and keep up a requiem of the whys and hows of his dying. They were forced to exchange opinions among only two or three of themselves at a time, and the closest they could get to the wall [where Ben was murdered] was in the front-room windows of the apartments that faced the street. They were confined to their homes and their own thoughts as it became increasingly difficult to tell a night sky from a day sky behind the smoky black clouds. The rains became the heaviest after dusk; water snaked down the gray bricks and flowed into the clogged gutters under sulfurous street lights like a thick dark liquid. . . .The corner bar did a record business that week, and electric bills rose sharply as portable heaters, televisions, and lamps stayed on night and day as Brewster Place tried desperately to bring any kind of warmth and light into their world. By midweek, hopes for the block party started to disappear, the weeks of planning washed through the rusted drains with the gutters' debris.
(175)

It is particularly poignant that the exterior gloom appears to be a requiem for Ben but Naylor's description of the "unspeakable" nature of the community's response to Lorraine's rape is much more reminiscent of a haunting of Brewster Place.

Naylor also connects the memory of the attack on Lorraine and her subsequent insanity specifically to the women and girls:

> Although only a few admitted it, every woman on Brewster Place had dreamed that rainy week of [Lorraine] the tall yellow woman in the bloody green and black dress. She had come to them in the midst of the cold sweat of a nightmare, or had hung around the edges of fitful sleep. Little girls woke up screaming, unable to be comforted by bewildered mothers who knew, and yet didn't know, the reason for their daughters' stolen sleep. The women began to grow jumpy and morose, and the more superstitious began to look upon the rains as some sort of sign, but they feared asking how or why and put open Bibles near their bed at night to keep the answers from creeping upon them in the dark. (176)

Clearly, Lorraine is a problematic figure for these women: is it because of their guilt? or of the fear of the men who raped her and drove her insane? or of the community's hate? Naylor does not leave an easy answer but it is obvious that Lorraine's fate is the lasting image of the novel—the one that connects all of the women of Brewster Place. Perhaps the difficulty in reading what happens to Lorraine shows the text's resistance to treating the Black woman as merely symbol. Indeed, I will discuss further elements of this novel later.

Audre Lorde's biomythography *Zami: A New Spelling of My Name* is sometimes taken as the epic of literature by lesbians of color. It is the text that most frequently appears in predominantly white lesbian critical and theoretical collections and it is with an awareness of this background that I explore it here.[46]

Lorde describes the complexity of the Black lesbian within her text and she also has quite an elaborate concept of the place that performance has within her life. The element of performance is not always one of hostility, however, I discuss it here as it is reflective of the many limitations that Lorde experiences as a Black lesbian within her own community. She discusses how costume fits into her life at different moments of her maturity—from playing dress up with a friend to an awareness of dress from both within the gay community and from without. Always, though, Lorde describes the act of performing as integral to her identity as a lesbian. For example, she describes her relationship with her friend Gennie before she identified herself as a lesbian and before she realized that she was in love with her. Lorde describes their outings:

> We took hours and hours attiring each other, sometimes changing entire outfits at the last minute to become two different people, complimenting each other always. We blossomed forth, finally after hours of tacking and pinning and last-minute ironing-board decisions.
>
> Bandits, Gypsies, Foreigners of all degree, Witches, Whores, and Mexican Princesses—there were appropriate costumes for every role, and appropriate places in the city to go to play them all out. There were always things to do to match whomever we decided to be. (88)

After she enters the lesbian community she realizes that there are rules about one's clothes and consequences for ignoring them. Lorde describes her hangout a bar called the Bagatelle:

> If you asked the wrong woman to dance, you could get your nose broken in the alley down the street by her butch, who had followed you out of the Bag for exactly that purpose. It was safer to keep to yourself. And you were never supposed to ask who was who, which is why there was such heavy emphasis upon correct garb. The well-dressed gay-girl was supposed to give you enough cues for you to know. (221)

Lorde describes her discomfort with these roles, and although she respects the rules, she tends to see her clothes very differently. She describes herself wearing "straight clothes" for going outside the community and wearing clothes she liked within it.

More important to Lorde than clothes is her idea of how her blackness is a kind of costume to other people. Even though sometimes Lorde is silenced, and sometimes liberated, by others' interpretations of her she always stresses her control of her own signification through dress. While at the same time she notes that race inflects her signification in ways that she is unable to control. She describes what the combination of her blackness and gayness means to others' interpretation of her; it is more far reaching than being butch or femme. White lesbians attempt to connect to Lorde through their oppression as lesbians. Lorde writes that:

Naming the Enemies

> I was gay and Black. The latter fact was irrevocable: armor, mantle and wall. Often, when I had the bad taste to bring that fact up in a conversation with other gay-girls who were not Black, I would get the feeling that I had in some way breached some sacred bond of gayness, a bond which I always knew was not sufficient for me. (181)

Even more difficult for her is her white lover's belief that race didn't enter into their relationship:

> Even Muriel seemed to believe that as lesbians, we were all outsiders and all equal in our outsiderhood. "We're all niggers," she used to say, and I hated to hear her say it. It was wishful thinking based on little fact; the ways in which it was true languished in the shadow of those may ways in which it would always be false. (203)

Clearly here Lorde hurts because of the lack of recognition that white lesbians' have of their own privilege. She summarizes her anger when she says that "we would all rather die than have to discuss the fact that it was because I was Black, since, of course, gay people weren't racists. After all, didn't they know what it was like to be oppressed?" (180)

Lorde not only describes the hostility that comes at her from the white community she deals with but the animosity she feels from within the Black community as well. Similar to the lack of understanding Lorde receives from white lesbians is the lack of understanding from Black heterosexual women. Lorde describes the attitudes of her straight friends:

> My straight Black girlfriends . . . either ignored my love for women, considered it interestingly avant-garde, or tolerated it as just another example of my craziness. It was allowable as long as it wasn't too obvious and didn't reflect upon them in any way. At least my being gay kept me from being a competitor for whatever men happened to be upon their horizons. It also made me much more reliable as a confidante. I never asked for anything more. (180)

Black men appear as more threatening in their hostility to Lorde's identity as a Black lesbian and her description is reminiscent of Naylor's description of Lorraine enduring the brutal rape. Lorde puts an ironic play on the term "brother" when she describes the scene: "when your Black brother calls you a ball-buster and tricks you up into his apartment and tries to do it to you against the kitchen cabinets just, as he says, to take you down a peg or two.... I finally got out of being raped although not mauled by leaving behind a ring and a batch of lies" (181–2).

These kinds of descriptions poignantly show the initial failure of performance for Lorde. In certain situations she feels power in costume, and sometimes limitations, but more than anything she feels hostility. She summarizes her identity in relation to the attempt to empower herself as a Black woman through a variety of vehicles:

> As I say, when the sisters think you're crazy and embarrassing; and the brothers want to break you open to see what makes you work inside; and the white girls look at you like some exotic morsel that has just crawled out of the walls onto their plate (but don't they love to rub their straight skirts up against the edge of your desk in the college literary magazine office after class); and the white boys all talk either money or revolution but can never quite get it up—then it doesn't really matter too much if you have an Afro long before the word even existed. (182)

Even though Lorde clearly feels alienated from these various communities for various reasons, because the Black lesbian community in general is also forced to deal with all of these hostilities Lorde cannot count on them either. Each Black lesbian's decision on how to survive has drastic consequences for them and for Lorde as well. She describes this situation thusly:

> Most Black lesbians were closeted, correctly recognizing the Black community's lack of interest in our position, as well as the many more immediate threats to our survival as Black people in a racist society. It was hard enough to be Black, to be Black and female, to be Black, female, and gay. To be Black, female, gay, and out of the closet in a white environment, even to the extent of dancing in the Bagatelle, was considered by many Black lesbians to be suicidal. And if you were fool enough to do it, you'd better come on so tough that nobody messed with you. (224)

Some of the other choices that these women made besides being tough were being deeply invested into roles and distancing themselves from one another and accepting a white male concept of beauty. Lorde describes these choices as ones of survival coming from a need to put self-preservation before community:

> The Black gay-girls in the Village gay bars of the fifties knew each other's names, but we seldom looked into each other's Black eyes, lest we see our own aloneness and our own blunted power mirrored in the pursuit of darkness. Some of us died inside the gaps between the mirrors and those turned-away eyes (226).

Also, within this description is Lorde's own view of external interpretation of performance. Here she describes the connection between Black lesbians as solely visual and totally empty. Surely, the Black lesbians she describes above cannot convincingly perform an identity for each other because they are all defined by common experiences of themselves. Lorde poignantly describes this when she shows that they could not even make eye contact with one another because of their painful self-recognition. It is a powerful description of a microcosm where the lesbian of color exists.

Lorde has felt the need for a definition of self that includes her concept of herself and it solidifies when she contemplates the varying hostilities that she lives within: "*Being women together was not enough. We were different. Being gay-girls together was not enough. We were different. Being Black together was not enough. We were different. Being Black women together was not enough. We were different. Being Black dykes together was not enough. We were different.*" (226)

Many critics see Lorde's work as the most important representative of lesbian literature that exists, and as I have already stated it is widely seen as "the" canonical text by a lesbian of color. On the other hand, Gayl Jones's work is widely seen as homophobic.[47] Her writing is definitely not centered on lesbian identity, but she does have some lesbian characters in her texts who, although they have small roles, also make indelible impressions on the main character of each novel as well as on the reader. They strongly illustrate the symbolic role that the Black lesbian has in the community: as threat to the roles formed by heterosexuality.

In her novel *Corregidora*, Jeffy is one such character. Jones aptly describes the main charatcer Ursa's disgust at a young Jeffy's advances toward her. Probably most dramatic is the contrast between the possibility of a lesbian identity and that of the outwardly very heterosexual Ursa, whose main task was intended to be "making generations" in order to continue to bear witness to her female relatives' suffering through slavery. I would not say that the heterosexual relationships are depicted as particularly positive, but none is so negatively imagined as the encounter that Ursa has with Jeffy. Jones writes about Ursa waking up and feeling Jeffy's hands on her body:

> I was drowsy, but I felt her hands on my breasts. She was feeling all on me up around my breasts. I shot awake and knocked her out on the floor. It wasn't even daylight yet. It couldn't have been more than three o'clock. There was a smell of vomit in the room, like when you suck your thumb. (39)

Before this encounter Jeffy is badgering Ursa about her inability to have children because of a hysterectomy resulting from an injury caused by her husband in an interesting twist of the guilt of reproduction that Clarke discussed. This dramatic contrast is disturbing and certainly unclear.

Much later Ursa runs into Jeffy again in a rather uncomfortable moment. Jeffy is talking to Ursa about Cat, an older lesbian who has helped Ursa in the past, implying that Ursa once had questions about her own sexuality because of her strong relationship with Cat. The dialogue between Jeffy and Ursa begins with Jeffy:

> "I knew there was nothing between y'all," she said "I knew even if you didn't."
>
> I played like I didn't know what she meant. And then, I was thinking, maybe I didn't. "I don't have to listen to you," I said quietly.
>
> "Who do you listen to?"
>
> I said nothing.
>
> "Do you have anybody?"
>
> I wouldn't answer.
>
> "You know I got something for you when you ready for it."
>
> "I don't want no shit from you, Jeffy."
>
> "Woman like you got to get something, ain't she?"
>
> I turned and walked away from her. She said it softly, but I still heard. "You *know* it felt good that time." (178)

Naming the Enemies 55

The tension in this scene and Ursa's apparent confusion within this dialogue suggests that a lesbian identity could be possible for her. Indeed critic Janice Harris claims that Ursa has an "unadmitted desire for her black sisters, Cat and Jeffy" (1) and further she claims that Ursa "wants the lesbian relationships Cat and Jeffy hold out to her, and yet walks a wide path around them" (4). Jones makes nothing clear but only implies these possibilities—leaving us to ask, why does Ursa have these confusing feelings?

At first she associates a lesbian affair with the smell of vomit and infantile thumb sucking and later she is unable to accept or deny a lesbian identity and/or pleasure in lesbian experience. What is clear, though, is that the world of *Corregidora* is a highly heterosexually charged one; where most of the Black women identify themselves solely in terms of men. Indeed, because in the novel, non-slave identity is signified by breeding generations to bear witness to the forced nature of oppression then heterosexuality must be maintained at all costs. Clearly this is an inhospitable environment for lesbian existence because of her threat to the existence of generations.

On the other hand, Ann Allen Shockley has been a pioneer of lesbian fiction although not one free from criticism.[48] She wrote the first novel that included a Black lesbian as a main character so one imagines her women might have more options within the textual society. Within her novel *Say Jesus and Come to Me* Shockley focuses on the world of the Black church and how the church can be hostile toward Black lesbian identity. The main character Reverend Myrtle Black is a lesbian who must define herself within the limitations of the church. There are many moments within the story where she must be wary of how she comes across because of her lesbianism; there are other times when she appears to use her ministry just to seduce beautiful women. In either case Shockley explores this complex woman through her life as a reverend and a Black woman. One moment where Shockley illustrates the tension Myrtle feels is when she is talking to a Black professional woman, Iffe Degman, about trying to organize Black feminists to attend a rally. Iffe describes what she thinks about the meaning of feminism in the black community much to Myrtle's chagrin:

> We met a few times, then they voted to change the name from Black Feminists to the Black Women's Improvement Club. You see, the word feminist was anathema. It antagonized their black men, and men

> *are* important to black southern women, you can believe it! To top that, they equate the word feminist with man-haters, white women, and lesbians. And, like wow! Lesbians are something that can't be dealt with in the black community—queers and funny people. (133)

These comments anger Myrtle but she realizes that she cannot say anything in response that would give away her own lesbian identity because of her tenuous position inside the Black church. Shockley writes:

> A hot flush went through Myrtle at Iffe's remarks about lesbians. It was such times as these, by her locked-in secrecy, she felt a traitor to herself. This silence she justified by weighing the burden of the consequences. She had her career as a minister who headed her church. Together with that, her sight was set on expanding her secular leadership role, an aspiration that was beginning to materialize. For her to come out now, declare her lesbianism, could be disastrous for both herself and her church. The core of her existence was rooted in black life Black people had not yet come fully to grips with homosexuality. For these reasons, she had to conceal her sexuality. Religion and race mattered first to her. (133)

Myrtle further articulates the problem for Black lesbian identity when she responds to Iffe's comment that Black southern women don't like to be in the forefront of the women's rights struggle. Myrtle responds that the reason is the "Fear of perpetuating the myth of castrating matriarch" (134). Clearly here Myrtle is articulating some of the stereotypes that limit the Black woman in her own community; images that are particularly devastating for the Black lesbian. Most destructive in this novel is the lack of support that the all important church has for the lesbian. The church can only offer solace for the lesbian if she denies her identity or confesses her sin.

Many of the limitations that create formidable barriers to the Black lesbian's survival also limit the Latina lesbian; although there are cultural variances that differentiate these limitations within the constructed category of Latina identity. In both cultures religion is an important source of coherence and identity, but whereas the Black woman holds the hope of becoming the symbol of her man's power if he can protect her, the Latina may be read culturally as partaking of

The Virgin Mary's/Guadalupe's purity and maternity; but not if she is a lesbian. Even within this frame of religion the individual components of the category Latina have many subtleties. Categorizing the Latina has been an incredibly difficult, but much attempted, pursuit.[49] Not only does this grouping account for people from multiple continents and numerous countries, but also different races. Many of the terms that we use to categorize people from Mexico, Central, and South America have colonialist connections. For example, the term "Hispanic" focuses on one's Spanish ancestry, the ancestry of the colonizers, and even the term "Latino" connects one to a territory so named because of the colonizing Europeans' imposition of laws and customs from ancient Rome. Many Mexican Americans feel the term "Chicano" to be more accurate than any other because its use is a response to the imperialist's power to name.

Interestingly, Chicano writers have been dominant within the academic study of Hispanic authors. I suspect this is so for two reasons: the Chicano movement of the sixties that brought Chicano life and issues into the forefront, and Mexico's proximity to the United States that makes Mexican immigrants much more numerous than those from the Carribean, Central or South America. Also likely is the desire to categorize Hispanic peoples into one knowable and definable group. In any case multiplicity is integral to the study of these women; oneness is impossible, detrimental and generally externally imposed.

Indeed, Debra Castillo argues that it is essential for those studying Latin America to question how they themselves fit into various institutions and/or traditions, most importantly their relationship between developed and developing countries. She writes:

> In relation to the particularities of Latin American women's lives Latin Americanists need to explore concrete questions of their opposition to or complicity in the established orders and their relationships to specific social, historical, political, and legal structures in their respective countries, how the problem of a continuing colonialism in some realms intersects with postcolonial structures in others. Moreover, the particular relationship between women and development in develop-*ing* countries demands closer examination. (10)

Even though there are enormous differences between Latinas, there are some similarities within their cultures/societies as well. These similarities are worth exploring further here so that I can give a sense of the general limitations that Latina lesbians face. One main legacy that Latinas share is that of their national conquest and colonization by such countries as Spain, Portugal and France and the differentiation between the indigenous peoples and the conquerors. The native peoples (whether Aztec, Maya, Toltec, Inca, etc.) who were enslaved, both physically and through cultural and religious imperialism, tended to combine their own traditions with the imported customs of the Europeans. Therefore the indigenous traditions exist side by side with the imported Christian ones. Perhaps the people could be best described as constructing, and constructed by, an entirely new tradition. This act of combining is reminiscent of the blending of races, or the beginning of the "mestizo" culture. In contemporary Latin America that which is indigenous is generally maligned and that which is European is celebrated; to be Indian is not something that gives pride but rather something to be denigrated. Indeed, in most situations it is an insult. Therefore, skin color and European versus Indian features are of great significance. These prejudices play out differently in the United States (but clearly the European is generally celebrated here as well) however the tradition of prejudice toward people of color is not reserved for the United States.

For example in Latin American countries typically the representation of everything negative is embodied by the Indian woman; she is the ultimate shame for those of her own culture, just as she is the ultimate romantic image for American culture.[50] As Debra Castillo states within her book *Talking Back: Toward a Latin American Feminist Literary Criticism*:

> the lower-class woman—mulatta, mestiza, or Indian—is generally misconceived/misrecognized by the institutionalized culture under the image of an ignorant (uneducated, unused to metropolitan customs, clinging to quaint and inapplicable rural practices or superstitions) or stupid (uneducable) childbearer (generally as producer of many children), associated with food preparation and consumption (the overweight woman in braids perpetually patting out tortillas), primarily concerned with housework or, if in the workplace, relegated to those jobs traditionally associated with domestic work (as servants, cleaning women, works in clothing factories). (21-2)

In many ways, women are incredibly important in Latin American cultures. There are many myths where women are of central importance and arguably La Virgen de Guadalupe (the brown-skinned Virgin Mary) is cherished more than any other figure within Christian religious iconography. The central image of the ideal Latina is represented by two core mythological figures: La Virgen and La Llorona. Both of the figures' origins are Spanish and Indian. La Virgen is said to be the descendant of Tonantzin, an Indian Earth Mother and Aztec goddess of fertility and feminine energy. She was seen as the true essence of womanhood: as mother, protector and nurturer. These two figures were fused under colonization. La Llorona, "the weeping woman," is a mythical native woman who was betrayed by her husband, committed infanticide and was condemned to an eternity of sorrow. She supposedly can be found wandering by rivers (where her children died) and can be heard wailing for them. Both of these women are praised for their motherhood: La Virgen as the essence of motherhood and La Llorona as the victim, an oppressed mother whose only choice is to turn against her own people. The paradoxical nature of La Llorona is typical to the Latin American sensibility: the consequences of cultural syncretism are powerful, sometimes confusing and sometimes restorative.

Clearly these powerfully maternal figures, as representative of the ideal for women, leave little room for real Latinas, both straight and lesbian, to exist. D. Soyini Madison claims that "These representations symbolize the extremes of purity, guilt, and betrayal that both Latin and European traditions have ascribed to womanhood" (12). The legacy of sexual repression is a burden that Latinas endure as it is deeply ingrained in their religion, culture, mythology and law.

Cherríe Moraga summarizes the history behind this repression that is specific to Chicanas though representative of many Latinas:

> The sexual legacy passed down to the Mexicana/Chicana is the legacy of betrayal, pivoting around the historical/mythical female figure of Malintzin Tenepal. As translator and strategic advisor and mistress to the Spanish conqueror of México, Hernán Cortéz, Malintzin is considered the mother of the mestizo people. But unlike La Virgen de Guadalupe, she is not revered as the Virgin Mother, but rather slandered as La Chingada, meaning the "fucked one," or La Vendida, sell-out to the white race.

> Upon her shoulders rests the full blame for the "bastardization" of the indigenous people of México. To put it in its most base terms: Malintzin, also called Malinche [and Marina], fucked the white man who conquered the Indian peoples of México and destroyed their culture. Ever since, brown men have been accusing her of betraying her race, and over centuries continue to blame her entire sex for this "transgression." (99–100)

This history has led to the view that Latinas can only be either virgin/long suffering mother (La Virgen de Guadalupe) or whore (Malintzin); therefore the male remains at the center of women's sexual identity and culture in general.

For a Latina not to put a man at the center of her existence is to be a traitor to her race and her culture. To be a Latina lesbian then seems a contradiction in terms. Moraga states that "The Chicana lesbian bears the brunt of this betrayal, for it is she, the most visible manifestation of a woman taking control of her own sexual identity and destiny, who so severely challenges the anti feminist Chicano/a" (112). She is then, as was the Black lesbian, the ultimate destroyer of family and community. Juanita Ramos writes that:

> As Latinas, we are supposed to grow up submissive, virtuous, respectful of elders and helpful to our mothers, long suffering, deferring to men, industrious and devoted. We also know that any deviation from these expectations constitutes an act of rebellion, and there is great pressure to conform. Independence is discouraged, and we learn early that women who think for themselves are branded "putas" or "marimachas."
>
> Being a lesbian is by definition an act of treason against our cultural values. Though our culture may vary somewhat from country to country, on the whole, to be a lesbian we have to leave the fold of our family (xxvi).

Similarly Carla Trujillo wonders what place the Chicana lesbian has within Chicano culture. She too believes that because Chicanos are of primary importance to Chicano culture all women have a limited and tenuous position within it. She writes:

> How does the Chicana lesbian fit into this picture? Realistically, she doesn't. As a lesbian she does many things simultaneously: she rejects "compulsory heterosexuality"; she refuses to partake in the "game" of competition for men; she confronts her own sexuality; and she challenges the norms placed upon her by culture and society, whose desire is to subvert her into proper roles and places. This is done, whether consciously or unconsciously, by the very aspect of her existence.... [Chicana lesbians] must be selling out to Anglo culture.... this equivocation of sexual practice and cultural alliance is a retrograde ideology, quite possibly originating from the point of view that the only way to uplift the species is to propagate it. Thus, homosexuality is seen as "counter-revolutionary." ("Chicana" 189)

These limits for the Latina have continued both within the various liberation movements as well as within the literary world. Generally Latinos are outspoken both for liberation and for various aesthetic principles judged as important for their community's literature. Thus, all Latinas, but especially lesbians, are seen as appendages at their best and traitors at their worst. Political activism in any form is sometimes taken as a rebellion against one's own people. This is especially true if it is for causes important to women. Debra Castillo describes the specific context:

> Streetwalking as a political activity ... is officially ignored as unintelligible madness, a displacement made possible by the tradition of seeing all deviance from the model of self-restricted, enclosed femininity as insane. *Una loca* represents the most common appellation for any woman who crosses the threshold of the home and who steps outside the traditional bounds of a proper, womanly *pudor* (decorum, but also modesty, humility, and purity) and *recato* (prudence, caution, shyness, also coyness). (16)

Latinos have always been at the forefront, claiming certain aesthetics and history for their tradition. This is similar to the Harlem Renaissance when men dominated and many women were ignored or disparaged because they did not follow the prescribed "rules that would further black unity and 'progress'." Likewise, the contributions of many Latinas have been ignored and/or disparaged because their work does not fit into the mold or because it does not show Latin American culture/people in a wholly positive light. For example, Latin American literature has sometimes been seen as of interest only for historical or sociology study, a problem that afflicts most ethnic literatures, and therefore the issues that would be of interest to these disciplines have taken precedence. These characteristics are more easily applied to Latino writing than to Latina writing and therefore much of women's writing has been ignored as of only marginal importance.

Yvonne Yarbro-Bejarano writes about the burdens of the Chicana feminist specifically (but her words can also be applied to all Latinas). She states that "While recognizing her Chicana cultural identity and affirming her solidarity with all Chicanos and other Third-World men and women to combat racial and economic oppression, the Chicana feminist also spearheads a critique targets heterosexist as well as patriarchal prejudice" (733). Again, in order to speak her own liberation she must accept being seen as a traitor to "the cause" and to her family and culture because she undermines the man's pride in himself as the center of both.

Bernice Zamora illuminates the differences between Latinas and Latinos well in her poem "Notes From A Chicana 'Coed.'" Within this poem she nicely illustrates the frustrations that limitations from her own community create for her. She writes:

> To make the day easier
> I write poems about
> *pájaros, mariposas,*
> and the fragrance of perfume I
> smell on your collar;
> you're quick to point out
> that I must write
> about social reality,
> about "the gringo who
> oppresses you, Babe."
>
> To give meaning to my life
> you make love to me in alleys,
> in back seats of borrowed Vegas,
> in six-dollar motel rooms
> after which you talk about
> your five children and your wife
> who writes poems at home

> about *pájaros, mariposas,*
> and the fragrance of perfume
> *she* smells on your collar.
> Then you tell me how you
> bear the brunt of the
> gringo's oppression for me,
> and how you would go
> to prison for me, because
> "The gringo is oppressing you, Babe!"
>
> you're quick to shout,
> "Don't give me that
> Women's Lib trip, *mujer,*
> that only divides us,
> and we have to work
> together for the *movimiento;*
> the *gabacho* is oppressing us!'" (131–2)

Even though Zamora is not a lesbian, this piece clearly illustrates some of the limitations that all Latinas face. She shows this strongly by identifying the similarities between her situation and that of her lover's wife: they both write poetry about their lives as Latinas who are controlled by Latinos. There are severe double standards for women as well as limitations (aesthetic and moral) from men in the community and/or the liberation movement. It should be clear that the Latina lesbian is seen as even more of a threat than Zamora's speaker who is an independently sexual woman. Zamora shows that protecting the woman from the gringo's oppression has become the definitive moment for Latino manhood, and because the lesbian is not dependent on the Latino's rescue it is clear that she threatens his very existence.

Cherríe Moraga, a Chicana, sees the predominant image of a Chicana lesbian existing within multiple societies as "loving in the war years." Within a poem of this name Moraga writes about what it is like to exist as a lesbian within her community—it is to exist within a state of war. She writes:

> Loving in the war years
> calls for this kind of risking
> without a home to call our own
> I've got to take you as you come

> to me, each time like a stranger
> all over again. NOT knowing
> what death you saw today
> I've got to take you
> as you come, battle bruised
> refusing our enemy, fear.
> We're all we've got. You and I
> maintaining
> this war time morality
> where being queer
> and female is as bad
> as we can get (30)

Moraga here creates a compelling vision of what it is like to exist as a lesbian. She lives within constant hostility where the description of a potential encounter between women is made parallel to an encounter between prisoners of war. This risk taking that defines the lesbian's existence is also shown as mutual which contrasts greatly with Zamora's vision of Latino existence as dependent on Latina submission.

Perhaps the tensions that exist between Latinos and Latinas are best illustrated by Ana Castillo, a Chicana writer who has been disparaged by her own literary community for the lack of "Chicanoness" in her writing. In an interview she discusses the differences that she sees between Chicano and Chicana writing:

> I think that Chicano and Chicana literature reflect something very important about ourselves. Chicano men took issue with society as brown men, Catholic men, and poor working class men. They entered into a confrontation with society from the privileged view of a dialogue amongst men. "We are the men who have been treated badly by those men who are privileged." But the Chicana doesn't have any place at all to enter into a dialogue. So that's the first thing, having to make that assertion, that she can say anything at all, that she can critique society. But then she also does something that's very particular to Chicanas: to be openly self-critical and abnegating at the same time.... We don't really find that in male Chicano literature. They're not willing to look at themselves and say, "I am a horrible cabrón who isn't worth the time of day anyone has given me." They romanticize themselves, or they glorify themselves, or they objectify

themselves, and their courage and their history, but none of them is
ever willing to look into each other as an individual. (Navarro 116)

Clearly Castillo is pointing to an element that is embedded in Latin culture that can be connected to male dominance and the prominence of male interests that I have already illustrated.

Castillo is probably the best known Chicana novelist and clearly the most widely accepted by the larger literary community. She writes poignantly about the lives of Chicanas and Chicanos and their relationships and community. In her first novel, *The Mixquiahuala Letters*, she writes about two women, Teresa and Alicia, and their experiences with one another as well as with the societies they move within. Teresa describes various cultural limitations that she grew up with or constantly faces as a Chicana. She describes in a letter to Alicia her most important experience with the Catholic church in which she was immediately cast as the pandora's box of sexual temptation and desire:

> The last time I went to CHURCH, genuflecting my way to the confessional, I was eighteen years old.
> I was a virgin, technically speaking, a decent girl, having been conditioned to put my self-respect before curiosity. This did not satisfy the priest, or should I say, stimulate his stagnant duty in that dark closet of anonymity and appointed judgment.
> He began to probe. When that got him no titillating results he suggested, or more precisely, led an interrogation founded on gestapo technique. When I didn't waver under that torment although feeling my knees raw, air spare, he accused outright:
> *Are you going to tell me you haven't wanted to be with a man? You must have let one do more than . . . than what?* (30)

Teresa and Alicia both are traveling through a string of male lovers looking for fulfillment and using the other primarily for comfort and empathy when the need arises. Teresa describes an interesting female community that she and Alicia inhabit—one that exists only out of necessity, one that exists for women who still keep men at the center of their lives at the cost of everything else. She describes their behavior towards each other after their failed affairs as "resenting each other because of our desperate acts. Each time we've parted it has been abruptly. We picked, picked, picked at each other's cerebrum and when we didn't elicit the desired behavior, the confirmation of allegiance, we reproached the other with threatening vengeance" (29).

Each woman has been taught to relate to other women in this way by her family. Teresa describes her own female role models who influenced her own view of Chicana womanhood:

> My mother had only been close to female companions during her adolescence. My older sisters never maintained close relationships with women after marriage. When a woman entered the threshold of intimacy with a man, she left the companions of her sex without looking back. Her needs had to be sustained by him. If not, she was to keep her emptiness to herself (35).

Castillo here writes provocatively of the loss that Latinas suffer if they are to put men at the centers of their worlds as they are supposed to. Teresa writes again of one of her affairs with a Mexican man: Alvaro Pérez Pérez. She describes his attitude toward her as a Chicana:

> He wanted to spend the night with me. It was that plain. To a drunkard, it was plain. To me, it was ridiculous and i said so That's when he declared himself in that honorable fashion of men of my culture. He wanted me to stay so that we could be together always. His father would find employment for me, if that was what i wanted. He loved me. He had a right to spend one night with me. (57–8)

Teresa later describes a night at a friend's house in Mexico when a man approaches her and asks if she is "liberated." She understands and explains his real concern:

> In that country, the term "liberated woman" meant something other than what we had strived for back in the United States. In this case it simply meant a woman who would sleep nondiscriminately with any man who came along.
>
> "What you perceived as 'liberal' is my independence to choose what i do, with whom, and when. Moreover, it also means that i may choose *not* to do it, with anyone, ever."
>
> The dark man winced. The crow's feet of his black eyes gathered momentarily. He hadn't expected that move by a long shot He cleared his throat. Like an expert chess player, gave up a soldier graciously, "Really?" His voice cracked. "Well, you gave me that

> impression, you know . . . of being 'liberal' and frankly, you appeal to me What do you say?"
> Liberal: trash, whore, bitch. (79)

Teresa and Alicia run into numerous examples such as these. And yet they still cling to the notion that they need a man to appear complete in the eyes of their families and cultures. Teresa and Alicia seem desirous to escape these many limitations but ultimately Teresa concludes that "We weren't free of society's tenets to be convinced we could exist indefinitely without the demands and complications one aggregated with the supreme commitment to a man" (45). And this keeps them trapped in a competitive relationship with one another and sexually repressed by men.

Ana Castillo has written, in many different forms, about Chicana/o sexuality and her second novel, *Sapogonia*, explores this issue even more deeply than her first.[51] This novel centers around Máximo Madrigal who is a Latino playboy who seems to need to have sex with every woman he can in order to feel that he exists. He becomes obsessed with one, Pastora Velásquez Aké, whom he sees as so different that she threatens his sense of self. When he first sees Pastora she is performing with her friend Perla at a concert. Máximo, taken by their beauty asks his friend about them. Their discussion follows:

> I leaned over to Jacobo and whispered, "What do you know of those two women?"
> "They're both conceited as the devil. You can't get anywhere with them, believe me, my friend. I've known plenty of men who've tried. I think they're lesbians," Jacobo replied generously. It seemed to me, however, that there were women who were puzzles to Jacobo and this complexity was too much for my poor friend, who thought life was as two-dimensional as a script.
> It was incredible to me that I could not persuade one or both with my unfailing charisma (25)

Obviously, neither of these men can fathom the possibility of a lesbian relationship they cannot conceive of themselves not being at the center of any woman's world.

When Máximo attempts to meet Pastora he transforms her rejection of him into a symbolic castration. He describes the scene as he catches her eye and he wonders "Was it possible to castrate a man with a glance? She had looked up at me and at once chewed my existence and spit me out" (25). Afterward he goes home with a woman he doesn't even know whom he feels somehow indebted to because she "inadvertently saved me from the jaws of a bloodthirsty female vampire" (26). Later Pastora is described again in relation to her sexuality, after she and Máximo have become lovers. Castillo writes that "Máximo was under the impression that Pastora was his sexual counterpart in every sense, that she was as much a manizer, a Jezebel of a thousand lovers, as he was the Cortés of every vagina he crossed" (124). It is this fact that makes Máximo need to control her in every sense.

Pastora herself, who is rumored by men to be a witch, has her own take on herself as a sexual being. The novel centers on this, on the signification of Pastora's body and life. How will they be represented and who will represent them? Castillo describes Pastora thusly:

> She said Latino men always thought that a woman who allowed herself to be thought of sexually and denied any reason to feel shameful of it and had none of the inhibitions or insecurities with relation to commitments as it was considered women should—had to be a witch. Likewise, she said, men had similar distorted and archaic perceptions of their own sexuality. (125)

Máximo, the stereotypical Latino male, is obsessed with Pastora but is also afraid of what she represents for his identity. Madrigal thinks to himself:

> Admit it, Máximo Madrigal, Pastora Velásquez Aké has you by the balls, los puros huevos, those two nitrate-filled nuts you lug around like a pair of trophies. the world's greatest lover, el gran chingón. Face it, Max, she's got you whipped.
>
> Pastora was a witch, an unequivocal bruja who'd undoubtedly used her wicked powers to hex him; a drop of spitballed wax on the back of his neck one night, his hairs left on her pillow, pulled from his chest the moment he'd drifted into a heavy sleep after coming. Somehow, she had managed to take something so vital and potent from his being, like the umbilical cord his grandmother had severed with her teeth the dawn he was born, the remains, shriveled ten days later, wrapped and hidden away to protect his soul. (172)

This novel is dominated by the male perspective and only Máximo is allowed to speak in the first person. He desires to define every person in the story in relation to him; if they are male they are either gay or competitors, if they are female then they are sexual conquests. Obviously, Castillo has created an environment where Latinas are inherently limited by the various pressures of the community, primarily pressures exerted by the heterosexual male who seemingly controls the community and the meanings it generates.

The Argentinean poet, Judit, writes of a more abstract oppression for herself as a Latina lesbian—that is categorization. She writes

> I live in constant negotiations
> trying to resolve
> the border conflicts raging inside of me
> at the place where I stop being Argentinean
> and start being Jewish
> at the line that separates
> the ghetto and tenements of my parents' childhoods
> from the suburban house where I grew up
> at the wall where my assimilated North-American part
> yearning for the Supremes and Elvis Presley
> crashes into a voice that says
> anything North American is trash
> but only national products
> listen only to samba and tango
> Some borders I can quietly walk through
> while others are impenetrable barriers
> one day I can be on the Argentinean side
> and the next on the Jewish side
> with the only condition
> that I never leave my cultural baggage behind (218)

Clearly Judit explores her cultural baggage here which extends beyond male domination. She nicely illustrates the very physical borders, as well as psychic ones, that appear in her ever changing sense of community. Judit writes of a very amorphous barrier that is much more difficult to recognize and resist than stereotypical machismo.

Cherríe Moraga writes in a similar way about being a multiply identified woman. She writes as a mestiza:

> I am the daughter of a Chicana and anglo. I think most days I am an embarrassment to both groups. I sometimes hate the white in me so viciously that I long to forget the commitment my skin has imposed upon my life. To speak two tongues. I must. But I will not double-talk and I refuse to let anybody's movement determine for me what is safe and fair to say (vi).

She describes here what restrictions are present for her. She must be limited by all the different "movements" that she might seek liberation through because of the risks she poses towards their singular goal. For Moraga these movements include the women's movement, the Gay and Lesbian movement, and the Chicano movement. If the lesbian of color is to align herself with anyone, Moraga concludes, she must somehow choose: "To whose camp, then, should the lesbian of color retreat? Her very presence violates the ranking and abstraction of oppression. Do we merely live hand to mouth? Do we merely struggle with the 'ism' that's sitting on top of our heads?" (53) Should Latina lesbians choose an "ism," any "ism," to exist and be recognized?

In a similar move Natashia López, in her aptly titled poem "Trying to be Dyke and Chicana," writes about the difficulty of combining two apparently incompatible elements of self. She also points out the attitude that a lesbian somehow taints the community she comes from and is a potentially destructive force. Also important is the issue of categorization and its limitations and frustrations. López writes:

> Dyk-ana
> Dyk-icana
> what do i call myself
> people want a name
> a label a product
> what's the first ingredient
> the dominant ingredient
> can you taste Chicana
> or smell Dyke
>   call me Dyke
> race destroyer
> i darken the color of my people's skin
> polluting the bad recipe
> call me Dyke
> feeling pressure to choose

>   between
>   brown   white/women/loving
>   call me Chicana
>   call me Dyke
>   Chyk-ana (84)

It should be clear here that the Latina lesbian sees herself as, at best, ignored by her own community, and at worst as a degradation of her race and a destroyer of her family and culture. These literary selections represent the lesbian as an aberrant sign not given much room to attempt to rewrite herself as acceptable to her community. The more freedom she is given by the community the more of a risk she becomes to it. So, ultimately any demand for existence becomes an entirely selfish attack.

Arguably no other group of women of color is more diverse or complex than Asian-Americans. The people who are categorized thusly have vast differences including: race, religion, ethnicity as well as culture. It is therefore incredibly difficult to generalize about this group; however, I must take the risk of oversimplifying in order to discuss some of the similarities that exist for the authors I am concerned with. I am, though, very aware of the historical tendency of critics to make sweeping definitions of this group in order to safely retain dichotomous thinking; this is not my intention here.

One important factor in Asian-American experience is that of immigration. The first Asians to immigrate to the United States in the 19th century were primarily Chinese, but there were also Japanese, Indian, and Korean men, who primarily came to work on the Central Pacific Railroad, and also in mines, on plantations or in fields on the Hawaiian Islands or West Coast. Hence immigration policies had a strong affect on Asian-Americans. The government's policies toward immigrants from Asia responded to the changing needs of American industry.[52] Even during times when Asian laborers were welcomed their wives were generally not allowed entry. Other women were disuaded because of the lack of opportunities and support for women in frontier culture. Whatever the case the Asian family suffered fragmentation and confusion with immigration. Thus the separation of family members is powerfully connected to Asian American experience. Women were affected in very particular ways dependening on their cultures, family circumstances and environment.

Japanese women immigrated in great numbers in the early 20th century primarily as "picture brides." As a result these first generation immigrants, or Issei, formed families and had some stability. They still faced many limitations within their new culture and economic position as well. Instead of the prosperity they hoped for they primarily encountered hard work and poverty as well as discriminatory legislation. One law, The Alien Land Law of 1923, prohibited Asians who were ineligible for citizenship from buying any land in the states where there were already numerous Asian American farmers. Of course the most infamous legislative restriction was the internment of all Japanese Americans after the bombing of Pearl Harbor. Japanese people were considered the enemy and other Asians were left to attempt to distinguish themselves as "good" and worthy of trust in order to survive in America.

This confusion over the inability to prove their "worth" as Americans and also as Asians was to be a long lasting legacy for Japanese Americans. Jeanne Wakatsuki Houston describes her experience in Manzanar Camp as growing up in a separate, third country:

> It was if the war were forgotten, our reason for being there forgotten.... In such a narrowed world, in order to survive, you learn to contain your rage and your despair.... The fact that America had accused us, or excluded us, or imprisoned us, or whatever if might be called, did not change the kind of world we wanted. Most of us were born in this country; we had no other models. (qtd. in Madison 15)

She reflects the ability of marginalized Americans to reinvent community, although clearly this community existed because of external forces.

Asian immigration, then, was guided by America's need for cheap labor followed by a slowdown in the economy and the consequential restrictions. These particularly racist policies were many and long lasting; from the Gentlemen's Agreement of 1907 focused on limiting Japanese and Korean immigrants, to the Tydings-McDuffie Act of 1934 that restricted Filipino immigration. Rights of citizenship were also limited. Indeed, it was impossible for an Asian to be a citizen until 1943 when, over the next few years, the policies were changed one country at a time. Even though there are individual differences for these peoples because of their varied destinations, the different immigration policies, and the status derived from leaving colonies of the United States or independent nations, immigration was (and is) of great importance in shaping Asian-American families and therefore the psyche of Asian-American individuals.[53]

The traditions of the country of origin are also influential, in varying degrees, for Asian-Americans. Differences in age and generation are typically important to Asian-Americans (as they are for most racially "other" immigrant cultures) in that the cultures of Asia vary so greatly from the culture of the United States, and the Asian-American born in America has a distinct conception of her ethnic/racial identity. Also important, though, and in some ways connected to generational difference, is the cultural limitations that women in particular face. Most of the Asian women who came as immigrants came as commodities; they came as picture brides or they came as prostitutes (or became prostitutes). For many Asian women, their home cultures greatly influenced their existence in America. For example, Madison claims that for Chinese women:

> nineteenth-century Confucian ideology governed Chinese culture, and one of the principles of Confucianism emphasizes feudal loyalty and filial piety. Women were expected by duty and custom to remain at home while men ventured out to seek adventure and riches. Some of the first women to arrive in the United States did not emigrate of their own accord. (Madison 15)

This heritage makes the Asian-American woman's role as signifier within her community different than other women of color. The Asian woman's historical subordination can be seen as a symbol of the attempted preservation of traditional Asian cultures which, in contrast to African cultures and mestizo cultures, can be kept "pure" in the minds of patriarchs.

This subordination many times determined women's opportunities upon their arrival. Though some women saw their travel to America as a release from traditional limitations their hopes were usually not fulfilled in the realities they found in America. Because of the disproportionate number of Asian women in America, and because of the negligible opportunities for women to support themselves financially, prostitution blossomed. The general sentiment was that these "Oriental" women were immoral and depraved and soon the stereotype of the sexually servile and agile Asian woman was born. The racial difference made it possible to blame Asians for this "immorality" rather than the numerous other frontier prostitutes and/or communities served by prostitutes. Most women's experiences paralleled those of the Chinese women described here by Judy Yung:

> Captives of an organized trade, most of these women were kidnapped, lured or purchased by procurers ... brought to America by importers, and sold to brothel owners who paid [professional killers], policemen, and immigration officials to protect the business. Most prostitutes did not have the individual or collective means to resist their fate. ... For some, suicide, madness, or violent death proved to be the only way out of misery.(qtd. in Madison 18)

This oppression created a lasting legacy for Chinese women with the birth of stereotypes of all Asians as depraved and of the women as oversexualized.

Sucheta Mazumdar writes about the effects of racism and oppression on Asian-American women thusly:

> the sexuality of "Oriental" women, depicted as somehow immoral and different, underlined the "heathen" values of the Chinese and became yet another reason for advocating the exclusion of Asians. The myth of the "erotic Oriental" and her objectification as a sexual mannequin, born of the 1870s racist environment, continues to haunt portrayals of Asian women (3).

This commodification of Asian women as willing sexual toys for men also, of course, reestablishes the dominance of compulsory heterosexuality.

The importance of marriage within one's own community is generally seen as integral to the building and survival of Asian-American communities in the United States. The traditional notion that a woman's worth is only as wife and mother is also a lasting legacy that is not peculiar to Asian-Americans but perhaps can be described as more important to them than to other groups because of the perception that the existence of the Asian-American community is tenuous. For instance, the disruption of the family and therefore the community was quite common with the introduction of new immigration laws so when women were allowed into the country they tended to be seen in terms of their sexual value. Indeed, Mazumdar posits that the stream of

Japanese and Korean picture brides into America was necessary as "a lifeline to survival" for these communities. (7)

This attitude towards women also varies in relation to generation. As Muzumdar writes "While the idea that female children are of less value than male children permeates all Asian cultures to greater or lesser degrees, the effect of this value system on an American-born woman is quite different than on an immigrant one" (15). The consequences of these generational differences have many times been conflict and rebellion. Mazumdar elaborates:

> Though some of this conflict is intergenerational and common to all societies, the disparate cultural values of East and West are a source of particular anguish. On the one hand, the preservation of ethnic identity within an environment often hostile to people of color has meant a closer allegiance to Asian cultural norms; on the other, these same cultural norms and values have been a source of oppression and discrimination, especially for women. Marrying outside the community has served as one way of expressing dissatisfaction with the traditional role. (16)

Clearly the limitations and roles that Mazumdar elucidates for heterosexual women are even stronger for homosexuals, but they don't enter her discussion at all, perhaps for this reason. Rakesh Ratti writes of the difficulties faced by South Asian homosexuals in particular because of traditional pressures and limitations. He writes that

> In the South Asian cultures, sex is an issue that is rarely discussed, and this tends to make the discussion of homosexuality quite taboo. Consequently, gays and lesbians go largely unacknowledged. This avoidance, coupled with the traditional pressures to marry and raise a family, can cause tremendous strain for the individual trying to live his or her life in a healthy, honest way Millions of gays and lesbians in South Asia find themselves pressure into entering heterosexual marriages, ultimately, these marital bonds become chains that enslave both partners and deny them the full existence they deserve. (13-4)

Therefore, instead of outright hostility, as within Black and Latino cultures, the Asian homosexual is ignored and silenced. This strategy is not peculiar to the issue of homosexuality and indeed, is another way that many see Asian Americans as the "model minority."

Pamela H. voices the limitations that the Asian-American lesbian faces from many different communities. She describes some of the issues that the lesbian might face from her family and community:

> Homosexuality is seen as Western concept, a product of losing touch with one's Asian heritage, of becoming too assimilated. One Asian American woman, when she revealed to her parents that she was a lesbian, was met with shocked stares. Her parents said, "But how can that be? Being gay is a white disease. We're Korean; Korean people aren't gay." The perception that homosexuality does not "afflict" Asians is pervasive. Asian parents are incredulous when they learn *their* daughter is a lesbian; indeed, most Asian languages do not even have a word meaning "lesbian." In essence, Asian lesbians do not exist for many Asian cultures. (284–5)

Pamela H. continues by stating that even beyond the incomprehension of this identity comes the family's strong rejection of its possibility for women. Indeed she feels that the tendency for Asian-American families to be a source of strength for most is actually limiting for the lesbian. She writes:

> In Asian culture where marriage and family are stressed for every woman, the Asian American lesbian often succumbs to the familial pressure Parents' expectations are that she fill the "dutiful daughter" role and become a loyal, obedient wife, an asset to her husband's career. Being a lesbian would smear the perfect Asian image and reflect negatively on the woman's family.
>
> Concern that family honor will be tarnished motivates many women to hide their lesbianism. This family shame factor reflects the tightness of many Asian communities and how one's community itself may inhibit a woman from coming out. . . . Therefore, it is not uncommon for Asian American lesbians to move outside the Asian community so as not to be found out. (287)

One of the biggest differences between generations of Asian-Americans has been the perceptions that others have of them. With the lifting or lessening of immigration restrictions for professionals in particular there came many more opportunities for later generations of professionals and their families. Mazumdar voices concern that the stereotype of the "yellow peril" has been replaced by the stereotype of the "super successful model minority" which doesn't account for much of the community (13). Asian-Americans have never been seen as actively involved in civil rights issues or other "movements" as have other peoples of color, and it has been wrongly assumed that because the people from this group apparently have nothing to "complain" about they must not be limited by white society.[54]

Finding work by Asian lesbians is extremely difficult perhaps for the reasons that Pamela H. discussed above. In any case, the small amount of published works by Asian lesbians accounts for the brevity of this section. However brief this discussion might be these women speak loudly for themselves and their communities.

Willyce Kim, in an untitled poem, describes a lesbian speaker's response to her first generation immigrant mother's attitude towards her. She illustrates that in these communities mother/daughter, rather than male/female conflict hostility conflict, tends to be the site of lesbian resistance. Her poem further illuminates some of the limitations that have already been discussed. She discusses both the issue of the "super success" and the roles of Asian-American women. She writes:

> Mother, I want to sit down
> and swing my words across
> the table at you.
> Rap like an honest woman
> at a soul sister's gathering.
> But mother, you have suspended yourself
> above your children,
> and hang in anticipation of our marriage
> with a professional world
> that is borne across your forehead
> like a trading stamp.
> Your daughters seek liberation from the
> very role that has had you captive;
> there is fire brimming out of their
> passive oriental eyes.
> You have asked us to be pillars, mother.
> We choose to be of the earth, instead. (n p.)

Kim aptly describes the roles that seek to confine her. The speaker wishes to do battle with her mother's traditions and desires to choose a different path as an Asian-American woman. Clearly this choice would complicate her position not only in her family but in the larger community.

Barbara Noda, in her poem "Mother and Daughter" describes the alienation she feels from her family, specifically her mother, because of her lesbianism. Noda also shows the feelings of separation from her community that Pamela H. discussed as a cause for many Asian-American lesbians remaining closeted.

This discussion also resonates with some of the generational differences that Asians, especially women, must face. For example:

> the living room was deserted
> except for you and I and the color t.v. . . .
> we sat there staring at each other
> I tried to say, mother, I am a lesbian
> you must have heard my thoughts
> your eyes were wrinkled and tired
> and I could still smell the bleach, on your
> hands that had been scrubbing
> there is a difference there is a difference
> it has taken years for the shine to come through
> now we both know that mornings for you
> are different for me (n.p.)

Noda interestingly connects work and consumer culture with the differences between the women. The fact that the daughter and mother seem to communicate through silence reflects the power of the statement "I am a lesbian." The silent response and almost physical emptying of the mother with these words shows their devastating impact.

Kitty Tsui writes of this alienation between family members and with one's appropriate family role. much more directly in her poem "A Chinese Banquet" that she dedicates to her lover who was not invited to the family gathering. She writes:

> it was not a very formal affair but
> all the women over twelve
> wore long gowns and a corsage,
> except for me.
> aunts and uncles and cousins,

> the grandson who is a dentist,
> the one who drives a mercedes benz,
> sitting down for shark's fin soup.
> my mother, her voice beaded with sarcasm:
> you're twenty six and not getting younger,.
> it's about time you got a decent job.
> she no longer asks when i'm getting married.
> one day, wanting desperately to
> bridge the boundaries that separate us,
> wanting desperately to touch her,
> tell her: mother, i'm gay,
> mother i'm gay and so happy with her.
> but she will not listen,
> she shakes her head.
> mother, i say,
> you love a man.
> i love a woman.
> it is not what she wants to hear. (12-3)

Again Tsui writes of generational difference, consumer culture and silence. Tsui's speaker clearly could devastate this banquet by challenging the silences. However, she does seem hesitant to sever these traditional connections.

Kitty Tsui also writes provocatively about the complications of being an Asian-American lesbian in her essay "Breaking Silence, Making Waves and Loving Ourselves: The Politics of Coming Out and Coming Home." She describes the cultural limitations that she inherited as equal to, but different from, the oppressions her Chinese grandmother suffered. She states:

> In the China of my grandmother's time, girl children born into poor families were drowned or sold. Girl children born into prosperity had their feet bound, their marriages arranged. My grandmother escaped the horror of having her feet bound because she was born poor. I and all my contemporaries escaped because we were born to a new generation. But we were not born free. We cannot walk on the streets without being accosted by a whistle, a catcall or a car horn. Taunts ranging from "Ching chong Chinaman" to "Suzy Wong" to "china doll" are never far away. Social stereotyping is still running rampant in this modern age. (54)

Obviously she is describing her identity as a Chinese American as oppressive, and as a lesbian it is even more so. After she came out as a lesbian she writes that "It was one of the hardest periods of my life. I was rejected by my family, rejected by my peers, rejected by my community, rejected by my friends" (55). It is interesting how she specifically connects the heritage of Chinese women's suffering to the silences that these "freedoms" in America bring to Chinese American lesbians. She also makes the connection between China's institutionalized limitations of women and those directed toward lesbians by these same women.

C. Allyson Lee summarizes what the paradox of being a Chinese American lesbian means for her. She describes the pressures her Chinese father put on her by telling her she needed to "act" Chinese in order to be a good daughter.[55] His definition of a "nice Chinese girl" meant "that I should be a ladylike, submissive, obedient, morally impeccable puppet who would spend the rest of her life deferring to and selflessly appeasing her husband" (116). Lee describes her inability to accept this role but also her difficulty in knowing how to define herself. She writes: "Becoming a lesbian challenged everything in my upbringing and confirmed the fact that I was not a nice, ladylike pamperer of men" (16). She feels alienated by her own community and family but at the same time not at home among whites—straight or gay.

Kaushalya Bannerji, an Indian lesbian, writes similarly of her experiences coming out within her various communities. She describes her first awareness of herself as a lesbian thusly:

> My first encounters and relationships with women were not the results of choice, but rather of being overwhelmed by what appeared to be a startling awakening of sexual feelings. At that time these feelings appeared right to me, but they were not always acceptable to the world I lived in. Being comfortable with homosexuality in societies that view your life as being not only abnormal, but in fundamental opposition to patriarchal notions of the family, love, and heterosexual norms of desire is never an easy process (59).

Especially interesting here is Bannerji's particular problem with role playing in the North American lesbian community and her own culturally determined ideas about womanhood and her identity as an Indian.

She describes her own difficulty sorting out the limitations she feels both from within her own community and from the white lesbian community as well. She writes:

> In those early days of sexual discovery, not many faces like mine were out in the lesbian scene. I was almost seduced into believing that I could not be an Indian and a lesbian without betraying either the culture of my birth and family, or the culture I had chosen as a lesbian and a feminist. Just as men had silenced me in the solidarity committees and meetings of the left, so too I found white lesbians talking for me and about me as though I was not present (60)

White lesbians not only alienated her by their white supremacy and racism but also by interpreting the way she looked (her clothes and hair, etc.) through white definitions of beauty and womanhood. She discusses the integral relationship of her gender identity to her racial identity; a relationship that white women do not understand and so do not acknowledge. For example:

> As a lesbian of Indian origin with an active relationship to India and to my family, I was struck by the conformity to androgyny that appeared to be the norm of white lesbian beauty. Having grown up with a body and an aesthetic value system that was utterly different than this white androgyny, I struggled to accept my Indian woman's body against all white heterosexist odds. My breasts, hips, and long hair were not seen by everyone as symbols integral to my identity as an Indian woman; they were reinterpreted by white lesbians as manifestations of my being "femme." It was difficult to fight against the white feminist canon of androgyny, particularly as my coming out was a recognition of the fact that I loved flesh-and-blood women, not symbols. (60)

Here, Bannerji gives a perfect example of a misreading of a culturally significant tradition or symbol by those who are attempting their own symbolic transformation within a different cultural system.

Again it should be clear with these examples that Asian American lesbians find only small and problematic spaces within their communities. Their American female identity is inherently tied to sexual submission as duty and therefore their primary experience is one of silence.

Paula Gunn Allen has stated that Native American women have similarly been misread and misunderstood by American society, and their culture has been misused most disturbingly by white feminists. American Indian history is profoundly different from that of the other groups I have discussed in that they were a native people who were conquered and subjected to oppression by an invading people.[56] The history of relations between Indians and Americans is one riddled with broken treaties and selective genocide. The interests of the European settlers constantly came first and their concerns guided much of the oppressive legislation that afflicted Native Americans.

One example is that of the Indian Removal Act of 1830 which forced all eastern tribes to move west of the Mississippi and out of European settlements. This area was then officially called "Indian Territory" and meant to be a place for natives to exist peacefully. This all ended, though, in 1849 when gold was discovered in California which brought a mass influx of settlers and further development. Legislation soon followed which divided this territory further and led to the removal of more Indians and the retraction of the promise of a permanent homeland.

Paula Gunn Allen describes some of the consequences of these white settlements:

> With loss of population on the Native side and enormous increase on the Western side, our land holdings, rights to self-governance, water, hunting, fishing, and religious rights were abrogated, and our most precious mainstay, the community of being with all our relatives, was severely curtailed. Not only were Native peoples held prisoner in forts, camps, and on reservations, not only were they forbidden to practice their religions or prevented from doing so by having their mobility restricted (most groups practice many religious ceremonies in places outside of the village or camp, sometimes great distances away), but the life forms and the land itself were altered beyond recognition, and in the course of white settlement from 1850 to 1950 all but destroyed. (16)

In spite of this tragic history most Native American authors wish to highlight the fact that they are a community who has resisted and survived. And most importantly, that contrary to popular belief and American mythology Native Americans are not extinct.

As Beth Brant ardently argues, victimhood is not the essential descriptor for American Indianness and indeed it has been one way that stereotypes have limited them, their work, and their communities.[57] Gunn Allen has her own "facts of life" for Native people that relate to their stories and their lives:

> First, for Native Americans, humans exist in community with all living things (all of whom are known to be intelligent, aware, and self-aware), and honoring propriety in those relationships forms one of our basic aesthetic positions. Second, in the eyes of America, we (like other wildlife) are extinct or soon will be. Native women must contend with yet a third fact, one more difficult to notice or tell about: if in the public and private mind of America Indians as a group are invisible in America, then Indian women are nonexistent. Finally, we are ever aware that we are occupied peoples who have no military power on earth ready to liberate us (as the Allies liberated France, say, or Greece or Lebanon earlier this century). . . . These four truths are always present in our consciousness and none takes precedence over the others. They are all givens, like the mountains or the sky, part of what is. (9)

She nicely summarizes traditions of culture, gender and Anglo American perceptions that have both limited and defines Native peoples.

In Gunn Allen's essay "*Hwame, Koshkalaka,* and the Rest: Lesbians in American Indian Cultures" she specifically discusses the traditional and modern concepts of the American Indian lesbian. She finds fault for their invisibility both within the work of non-Native ethnographers and anthropologists and in portions of the modern Native American community itself. She states:

> The lesbian is to the American Indian what the Indian is to the American—invisible. According to ethnographers' accounts, among the tribes there were women warriors, women leaders, women shamans, women husbands, but whether any of these were lesbians is seldom mentioned. On the few occasions lesbianism is referred to, it is with regard to a specific individual who is noted because she is a lesbian. This fosters the impression of uniform heterosexuality among Indian women except for a very few who deviate from that norm. It is an impression that is false. (*The Sacred Hoop* 245)

Gunn Allen explores the lesbian within the framework of: the tribal community, women's roles within the family and different types of women's power. She is generally not seen as a symbol of some aspect of man's identity, rather she is ignored altogether. She ultimately concludes that, while unusual, the "American Indian foresister ... could find safety and security in her bond with another woman because it was perceived to be destined and nurtured by nonhuman entities, as were all Indian pursuits, and was therefore acceptable and respectable (albeit occasionally terrifying) to others in her tribe" (255).

She therefore discusses the reasons she thinks that the perception of this kind of relationship has changed in the modern American Indian community. She states that the invisibility of the lesbian can be attributed to:

> the historical events connected with the conquest of Native America; the influence of Christianity and the attendant brutal suppression of medicine people and medicine practices; the patriarchal suppression of all references to power held by women; Christian notions of proper sexual behavior, and, recently, an attempt on the part of a number of American Indian men to suppress knowledge among their own people (and among Europeans and Americans) of the traditional place of woman as powerful medicine people and leaders in their own right, accompanied by a dismissal of women as central to tribal ritual life. (259)

Most important to the modern American Indian lesbian then is the intent by her own community to erase her and her rightful place in society. Gunn Allen therefore states:

> Under the reign of the patriarchy, the medicine-dyke has become anathema, her presence has been hidden under the power-destroying blanket of complete silence. We must not allow this silence to prevent us from discovering and reclaiming who we have been and who we are. We must not forget the true Source of our being, nor her powerfulness, and we must not allow ourselves to be deluded by patriarchal perceptions of power that rob us of our true power, regardless of how many feathers those perceptions are cloaked in. As Indian women, as lesbians, we must make the effort to understand clearly what is at stake, and this means that we must reject all beliefs

that work against ourselves, however much we have come to cherish
them as we have lived among the patriarchs. (259)

Gunn Allen very interestingly then both uncovers a part of a richer lesbian history and also how that history is found in Native American tradition and history.

Beth Brant uses poetry and short fiction in her book *Mohawk Trail* to convey a vision of what it means to her to be a Native American lesbian. In her poem entitled "Her Name is Helen" she describes one Native American lesbian whose existence might not be described as that of a prisoner of war, in the words of Cherríe Moraga, but even worse as someone existing in solitary confinement from herself and others. Helen's life as a lesbian of color is much more hopeless than that which Moraga's describes because she cannot even articulate a sense of injustice, cannot describe the war that she is forced to inhabit. Rather Helen has incorporated the various hostilities directed at her and determined that "'I'm a gay Indian girl./A dumb Indian./A fat, ugly squaw'" (64). Brant shows Helen's alienation from other people as well as from herself as the non-Indians in the poem are constantly identifying her as Indian, in stereotypical ways, and Helen shows neither real acceptance nor real refusal of the identity they create. She is constantly passive to all external concepts of her identity as a lesbian of color. Brant writes:

> When she was laid off from the factory
> she got a job in a bar, serving up shots and beer.
> Instead of tips, she gets presents from her customers.
> Little wooden statues of Indians in headdress.
> Naked pictures of squaws with braided hair.
> Feather roach clips in fuschia and Chartreuse.
> Everybody loves Helen.
> She's such a good guy. An honest-to-god Indian. (62)

In this poem Brant has a fascinating way of illustrating her ideas about how American Indian women are treated. She shows that it is the "acceptance" of Helen that is destroying her. Her customers erase her individuality and transform her into a stereotyped object; and most destructive is that they expect her to be appreciative of, and instructed by, this treatment.

In her text *A Gathering of Spirit* Brant describes the situation she perceives: "We are angry at the so-called 'women's movement' that always seems to forget we exist. Except in romantic fantasies of earth mother, or equally romantic and dangerous fantasies about Indian-woman-as-victim" (11). Brant illustrates this pain, in this case without visible anger, by using Helen's relationships with white women as indicative of the problem she described above. She continues:

> She's had lots of girlfriends.
> White women who wanted to take care of her.
> who liked Indians,
> who think she's a tragedy.
> Her girlfriends took care of her.
> Told her what to wear
> what to say
> how to act more like an Indian.
> "You should be proud of your Indian heritage.
> Wear more jewelry.
> Go to the Indian Center."
> Her breasts that white women have sucked
> and molded to fit their mouths. (62–4)

Certainly the representative white woman is treating Helen both as an exotic earth mother and as a victim, which has caused destruction, as Brant describes. The white speaker really functions here as an extension of the American institutions that control and dominate Native lives.

Another poignant example of hostility is within a story called "The Fifth Floor, 1967," where Brant describes an unnamed woman who is placed, by her husband, into a psychiatric ward. It is implied that because the woman might be uninterested in her heterosexual life, that she is "losing herself" and therefore in need of medical treatment. Brant writes in the voice of the woman "Why I am here has something to do with losing myself. I used to be there—a young wife and mother in my house—washing dishes, bleaching diapers, reading a book, watching TV. Then I lost me. My husband tells me I am not myself" (69). This description of incarceration is frighteningly similar to the original imprisoning of Native Americans onto reservations. Interestingly Brant uses this metaphor as a way to show the hostility toward the Native American lesbian as medically incompetent as something inherently incompatible with Native American survival. Nonetheless, this unnamed woman is as alienated as Helen is, if not more so, from herself and her identity.

In Paula Gunn Allen's novel *The Woman Who Owned the Shadows* she traces the mental breakdown and quest for spiritual balance of a half breed woman named Ephanie Atencio. She has a breakdown when her husband leaves her and explores various means in order to regain her sense of wholeness in herself. Interestingly, Gunn Allen places a narrative of Ephanie's childhood relationship with another girl, Elena, at the beginning of the novel when Ephanie is drifting in and out of confusing dreams; it is not until later that the reader understands its importance. However, it is clear that the girls' relationship is of major importance to Ephanie's identity and psychic balance. Gunn Allen describes their relationship thusly:

> The events that measured their shared lives were counted in the places that they roamed, and Ephanie always remembered her childhood that way. The river, the waterfall, the graveyard, the valley, the mesas, the peaks. Each crevice they leaped over. Each danger they challenged, each stone, each blade of grass. A particularity that would shape her life.
>
> All those years, in spite of distance, in spite of difference, in spite of change, they understood the exact measure of their relationship, the twining, the twinning. There were photographs of them from that time. Because Elena's gold-tinged hair looked dark in the photograph's light, no one could say which was Elena, which Ephanie. With each other they were each one doubled. They were thus complete. (22)

There is no distinction here between the natural setting and the girls' relationship which definitely implies a connection with lesbian identity and psychic balance. This closeness is soon brought to a halt when Elena explains that they must not be friends anymore. She says to Ephanie:

> "You know," she said, her voice low. "The way we've been lately. Hugging and giggling. You know." She looked down at her hands, twisting against themselves in her lap. "I asked the sister about that, after school. She said it was the devil. That I mustn't do

> anything like that. That it was a sin. And she told my mother. She says I can't come over any more."
>
> Ephanie sat. Stunned. Mind empty. Stomach a cold cold stone. The hot sun blazed on her head. She felt sick. She felt herself shrinking within. Understood, wordlessly, exactly what Elena was saying. How she could understand what Ephanie had not understood. That they were becoming lovers. That they were in love. That their loving had to stop. To end. That she was falling. Had fallen. Would not recover from the fall, smashing the rocks. That they were in her, not on the ground. (30)

It is this devastating moment—a moment when Ephanie identifies herself as a lesbian—that she suffers her first loss. This first loss is echoed throughout the rest of the text and in the rest of Ephanie's story which I will explore at a later time.

Even though there are numerous differences in the cultures and traditions of these women of color, they all clearly suffer limitations from within their own communities. This is because their communities demand that they be read in relation to the identities of other, more powerful members of those communities, be they machos or mothers. If their own communities will not accept them as lesbians, but the larger community either doesn't understand them as women of color and also refuses them as lesbians, then where are they to turn? How can they define themselves as lesbians of color if their "color" won't co-exist with their lesbianness? This is the problem of multiplicity that the lesbian of color must confront. How can these two elements of herself, which various societies believe should not exist at all or cannot exist simultaneously, live peacefully inside herself? If the vision of the lesbian of color is to live within a constant state of war, how can she survive?

In Judith Butler's complex text *Gender Trouble* she confronts the notion that feminism, and arguably any theoretically/politically allied group, needs a defined "subject" in order to exist. She then challenges the notion that identity politics, in order to be effective, must have "a doer behind the deed." She states that

> The foundationalist reasoning of identity politics tends to assume that an identity must first be in place in order for political interests to be

> elaborated and, subsequently, political action to be taken. My argument is that there need not be a "doer behind the deed," but that the "doer" is variably constructed in and through the deed. (142)

By conceiving of identity in this fashion, she opens up a space for individuals to challenge "normal" constructions of gender and to find a place for themselves as they choose.

In order to open up this space, she assumes that the subject can be an active agent within the environment of signification where it is defined. She argues that:

> The subject is not *determined* by the rules through which it is generated because signification is *not a founding act, but rather a regulated process of repetition* that both conceals itself and enforces its rules precisely through the production of substantializing effects. In a sense, all signification takes place within the orbit of the compulsion to repeat; "agency," then, is to be located within the possibility of a variation on that repetition. If the rules governing signification not only restrict, but enable the assertion of alternative domains of cultural intelligibility, i.e., new possibilities for gender that contest the rigid codes of hierarchical binarisms, then it is only *within* the practices of repetitive signifying that a subversion of identity becomes possible. (145)

If this view of identity—as something that can be challenged and circumvented—is accepted, then the ability to deploy a universal subject for political or theoretical purposes is impossible. Butler states that the "critical task is, rather, to locate strategies of subversive repetition enabled by those constructions, to affirm the local possibilities of intervention through participating in precisely those practices of repetition that constitute identity and, therefore, present the immanent possibility of contesting them" (147).

This theory of identity is a seductive one for the person facing as much hostility from different societies as the lesbian of color does. However, is Butler's performance theory useful to such a person? Butler's theory of subverting limiting constructions of gender identities assumes that gender identity is *the* central or only identity that feminism need focus on. As I have already argued, this position assumes that femaleness can be separated from racial or ethnic identity and considered separately.[58] For the lesbian of color though there are not just the limitations of heterosexism, or the limitations of racism, but as I have outlined here, the very specific limitations of her own culture. She cannot, therefore, easily separate her gender identity out and subversively perform a different one that allows her to exist as a lesbian. Just as Butler has argued that the naturalness of gender identity (and consequentially its external signifiers) is an illusion, I suggest that the separability of identities is also. Likewise, when both the exterior culture and her own culture insist upon reading woman as a sign, in ways determined by race, subversion of her signification within their systems may present near insurmountable problems for the lesbian of color who attempts to perform identity subversively.

I have already articulated the limitations for lesbians of color with Butler's theory of identity construction. However, it is useful to understand these limitations if we consider the kinds of threats that exist from all of the hostile forces that I have discussed in this chapter. At times, then, lesbians of color who attempt to enact gender trouble in order to escape these hostile limitations end up in "gender danger" instead.

CHAPTER THREE
Strategies of Survival: The Limits and The Consequences

If the hostilities that bombard lesbians of color account for the inherent presence of contradictory and destructive elements for the lesbian of color, how then can she survive? How can one exist within both identities, lesbian and racial/ethnic identity, without just temporarily passing in either community? As I have previously stated, Butler's performance theory fails to meaningfully incorporate cultural, social, and historical contexts which makes it of limited use for lesbians of color. However, Butler's consideration of racial identity and performance within her text *Bodies That Matter* is a useful place to begin. I find the most pertinent section here is her study of the film *Paris is Burning* wherein she theorizes about the performances of individual Black and Latino drag queens (*Bodies* 124–40).

Within "Gender is Burning: Questions of Appropriation and Subversion" Butler considers differences between performances of gender that subvert heterosexual norms and performances that reinscribe those same norms. She also considers how one can have subversive power within various categories of oppression and specifically here she explores sexism, racism, and heterosexism. She argues that using sexist, racist, or heterosexist language does not always reinscribe its power but rather this language can be subversive if it can:

> be repeated in directions that reverse and displace their originating aims. One does not stand at an instrumental distance from the terms by which one experiences violation. Occupied by such terms and yet occupying them oneself risks a complicity, a repetition, a relapse into

> injury, but it is also the occasion to work the mobilizing power of injury, of an interpellation one never chose. Where one might understand violation as a trauma which can only induce a destructive repetition compulsion (and surely this is a powerful consequence of violation), it seems equally possible to acknowledge the force of repetition as the very condition of an affir-mative [sic] response to violation. (123–4)

This theory of mobilizing language to subvert the power of racism, sexism, and heterosexism has some power. There have been numerous examples of this negative language being turned upside down and used as a spark that ignites a liberation movement; this is true of "Chicano," "Queer," and "Dyke." However, I don't believe that a construction of identity for the lesbian of color can be solely based on choosing a name or even turning a negative name into a positive one. Because, after considering the kind of destructive consequences that lesbians of color face by just conceiving of themselves as such, the notion of this kind of affirmative response to violation seems to be spoken from a place of privilege because it doesn't meaningfully incorporate the reality of destruction. If we were considering *only* verbal violation then this strategy would be quite useful; but after the word games, one still has to venture into one's streets, community, and home. Simply appropriating racist or sexist language in order to demolish its intended effect seems a tiny gesture in the face of a far more devastating pain.

I believe most poignantly representative of this privilege is Butler's disturbing use of the life and death of Venus Xtravaganza, from the film *Paris is Burning*, to illustrate her ideas. Venus is a Black drag queen who apparently attempts to pass as a light-skinned woman in order to climb out of poverty and prostitution and into middle class safety. Butler sees this performance as a way to enter into the norm not subvert it. As a result of her inability, as a preoperative transsexual, to believably perform white femaleness "her life is taken presumably by a client who, upon the discovery of what she calls 'her little secret,' mutilates her for having seduced him" (130).

Apparently Butler sees this as a failure on Venus's part to conceive of her performance as subversive. In other words, because she hopes to benefit from embodying "realness" but is not able to do so convincingly Venus is murdered. In Butler's terms:

Strategies of Survival

> In the pursuit of realness this subject is produced, a phantasmatic pursuit that mobilizes identifications, underscoring the phantasmatic promise that constitutes any identificatory move—a promise which, taken too seriously, can culminate only in disappointment and disidentification. (131)

Butler should add here: and death. Butler may see this example as supportive of her theoretical exercise but it is difficult for me not to see it as symptomatic of her inability to deal fully with the social contexts and the dangerous consequences of this use of performance theory as a panacea for all identity. She does not seem to be aware that in some cases, it doesn't matter if the individual's *intention* was to affirm a different identity, or to disguise one's own identity, because even agents are externally interpreted sometimes with dangerous consequences.

Further, even though Butler reads the film's use of race within performance as subversive, she does not adequately discuss the context of whiteness that these performances are embedded within and defined through. For example, bell hooks is not impressed with the account of race that the film gives. Indeed, she feels that the film *worships* whiteness. She states that:

> The whiteness celebrated in *Paris is Burning* is not just any old brand of whiteness but rather that brutal imperial ruling-class capitalist patriarchal whiteness that presents itself—its way of life—as the only meaningful life there is. What could be more reassuring to a white public fearful that marginalized disenfranchised black folks might rise any day now and make revolutionary black liberation struggle a reality than a documentary affirming that colonized, victimized, exploited, black folks are all too willing to be complicit in perpetuating the fantasy that ruling-class white culture is the quintessential site of unrestricted joy, freedom, power, and pleasure. (149)

Butler does not see the drag in this film as upholding white supremacy but rather she feels that it "both appropriates and subverts racist, misogynist, and homophobic norms of oppression" (*Bodies* 128). The limitation for Butler's concept of performance then is that she cannot see, or she chooses to ignore, the importance of historical and societal contexts. These elements are exceedingly crucial to the lesbian of color because of the central role they play within her ability to articulate her identity.

hooks is most critical of Venus's disappearance from the film without explanation; in other words, she is angered that it's only the performance that counts in the film not the external reality that intrudes upon the "trouble makers." hooks writes:

> That tragedy is made explicit when we are told that the fair-skinned Venus has been murdered, and yet there is no mourning of him/her in the film, no intense focus on the sadness of this murder. Having served the purpose of "spectacle" the film abandons him/her. The audience does not see Venus after the murder. There are no scenes of grief. To put it crassly, her dying is upstaged by spectacle. Death is not entertaining.(154–55)

Butler critiques hooks's argument when she states that in hooks's view:

> the spectacle of the pageantry arrives to quell the portraits of suffering that these men relate about their lives outside the ball. And in her rendition, the pageantry represents a life of pleasurable fantasy, and the lives outside the drag ball are the painful "reality" that the pageantry seeks to phantasmatically overcome. (136)

Butler, on the other hand, sees this as a way that the drag queens rewrite concepts of kinship and family that make any external family irrelevant. While this is a valid comment and critique Butler still manages to skirt hooks's main complaint that once Venus is murdered, because a client discovers his "little secret," and mutilates her for having performed a role, Livingston offers no connection from the acceptable performances of the pageant to the life threatening performances outside of it. Clearly Butler does not offer any discussion of this context either. She does not discuss the fact that Venus must make a living as a prostitute nor does she discuss the possible consequences of Venus's various abilities to pass. hooks also discusses the apparent desire of the black men to "play" white as well as female; she also finds important the cultural and historical background of this previous desire. hooks states that

> in many ways the film was a graphic documentary portrait of the way in which colonized black people (in this case black gay brothers,

some of whom were drag queens) worship at the throne of whiteness, even when such worship demands that we live in perpetual self-hate, steal, lie, go hungry, and even die in its pursuit. (149)

Butler apparently sees no need to explore these issues within her analysis but rather seems to conclude that because the men are involved in performance the subversive element of this performance dominates other elements. Certainly there are subversive elements at play within this film, but I find it disturbing that all things external seem unimportant or omitted entirely. Clearly, no agent lives in an entirely self constructed vacuum and only in a vacuum would external realities not affect an individual's performance or the many interpretations of that performance. When we consider the real risks to agents who enact "gender trouble" without, or even with, all of the assets that society values (whiteness, maleness, straightness, upper class status etc.) then there is a definite need to consider the material implications of making and living in "trouble."

It is hard to deny that because much of Poststructuralist theory tends to validate the exposure of an incoherent self, a disruption of the self, and because the lesbian of color is the site of disruption within multiple communities, she could be swept up within a theoretical context solely as a romanticized object. This possibility might be useful in order to engage in current critical dialogues. However, as with Butler, this view neglects a consideration of the very real dangers and terrible consequences that lesbians of color face. To claim that they have the opportunity to make trouble, that they have the arena to perform subversively is to gloss over a minefield. It is to neglect a fundamental part of the lesbian of color's very existence: her identity is not a luxury but a victory both within and without the theoretical exercise that wishes to contain her.

Some critics have even speculated that the current interest in Poststructuralist theory exists in reaction to people of color beginning to focus on constructing their own identities. Indeed, Lourdes Torres illustrates this when she writes of the difference between theories from locations of privilege and those from sites of invisibility:

it is important to note that as people of color have begun to define and construct their subjectivity, [and so their right to speak and to exist] the construction of a "subject" suddenly has become antitheoretical and problematic according to the dictates of current critical theory (273).

Barbara Christian also makes a very similar statement when she discusses the timing of the white literary academy's focus on Western philosophy. She states that:

> I feel that the new emphasis on literary critical theory is as hegemonic as the world which it attacks. I see the language it creates as one which mystifies rather than clarifies our condition, making it possible for a few people who know that particular language to control the critical scene—that language surfaced, interestingly enough, just when the literature of peoples of color, of black women, of Latin Americans, of Africans, began to move to "the center." ("The Race" 338)

Yvonne Yarbro-Bejarano sums up the situation that people of color exist within when she states that "this multiple subject recalls that of postmodern theory, Guillermo Gómez Peña of the Border Art Workshop noted its historical specificity when he said 'we've always had postmodern, only ours was involuntary'"("The Multiple" 66).

Because this is the case, many people of color attempt to come to terms with this state within a dominant culture that values hegemony. Therefore, an exploration of a multiplicitous identity is not a solely theoretical pursuit but a real life one as well. This is clearly reflected by Karin Aguilar-San Juan's statement about Kitty Tsui's writing: "Tsui's writing reflected her discovery that as a *matter of survival*, she must assert her multiple identities as a Chinese American Lesbian" ("Exploding" 937, my emphasis). This question of survival is central to all lesbians of color and these identifications are multifaceted attempts at survival. They include: the psychological, emotional, financial, political, physical and more. Aguilar-San Juan reflects that it is:

> clear to me how critical the assertion of identity still is to our . . . lesbian community. Twenty-three years have passed since Stonewall, but we are still arguing merely for the right to exist. We confront not only homophobia but also racism in our struggle for visibility. Much of our activism, and therefore our writing, continues to be focused on claiming multiple identities and making ourselves whole. ("Exploding" 937-8)

Because many of these writers desire the opportunity to articulate and experience wholeness, they have been seen as untheoretical in the current atmosphere. This search to experience wholeness does not exclude the lesbian of color's experience of multiplicity; it does mean though that she has agency in regards to her identity construction and subjectivity. One must be willing to see beyond typical "Western" modes of theoretical discourse in order to appreciate the theories these writers construct. Even though their writing is connected to realities, physical and political, this does not mean that it is necessarily devoid of theoretical concepts. Thus, my point here is that as lesbians of color articulate their identities they must negotiate two important elements: the theoretical, to participate in and transform the critical dialogue, and the real, how they can survive in society.

Obviously the varying hostilities that I discussed in Chapter Two are crucial to a consideration of the methods of survival these women employ, as well as with the limits and the consequences of their strategies. These authors, then, use different strategies in order to show the effect that the battleground they inhabit has on their selves.

In this chapter I will discuss these strategies as well as their consequences. There seem to be two choices for these women then: either to articulate their identities as a lesbians outside of their own racial/ethnic communities or not to articulate it at all; in other words, not to conceive of themselves as lesbians. These are clearly choices that she can make for herself that could be described as subversive in Butlerian terms, but they are both choices not without consequences for her. They are choices that aren't just opportunities for subversive change, as Butler describes them, but challenges to the lesbian of color's existence.

As I have already discussed in Chapter Two many of the "home" communities (that is, those defined by their race or ethnicity) are male dominated so that within them all women are defined in relation to men. This is especially true for lesbians who, rather than being viewed as objects to dominate, are seen as threats to masculinity. Because racial/ethnic communities are so invested in a strong masculine identity, they tend to the value the heterosexually structured family. In other words, they see that the existence of "strong" males and "nurturing" females protects and preserves the family so that it can peacefully exist.

Many lesbians of color write about the numerous boundaries that these labels create for them within their creative works. As with the last chapter, in the forthcoming sections I will discuss only the relevant parts of each text; some of these texts will be discussed later to illustrate a different focus. Thus, these moments should be read as a further stop on the lesbian of color's journey to self-identification.

One of the major consequences that results from the hostilities that bombard lesbians of color, that I discussed in the last chapter, is the repressive atmosphere. In some cases this atmosphere makes it impossible for women of color to even conceive of themselves as lesbians. In other cases speaking this potentiality is impossible. Therefore in this section, I will consider creative texts that further illuminate this problem, as well as selected analyses of its foundations.

Audre Lorde's *Zami: A New Spelling of My Name* is useful to illuminate the problems that specific societal roles and expectations have on Black lesbians. This text is generally seen as focusing on the author's reflections on her experience as a Black lesbian. However strongly Lorde understood and accepted her identity later, much of the text describes her at a young age coming to terms with her various differences. Some of the most intriguing moments in this text are the moments when Lorde herself articulates her burgeoning awareness of her identity as a lesbian of color.

She describes a moment when she had a relationship with a man, Peter, and her feelings about it. It is an amazing description of the power of compulsory heterosexuality in her early life. Lorde describes the relationship as parallel to her rebellion against her mother as she moves out of her mother's home and in with Peter. Lorde writes that:

> I spent the summer feeling free and in love, I thought. I was also hurting. No one had even tried to find me. I had forgotten at whose knee I learned my pride. Peter and I saw each other a lot, and slept together, since it was expected.
>
> Sex seemed pretty dismal and frightening and a little demeaning, but Peter said I'd get used to it, and Iris said I'd get used to it, and Jean said I'd get used to it, and I used to wonder why it wasn't possible to just love each other and be warm and close and let the grunting go. (104–5)

So although Lorde didn't think of herself as a lesbian at first, she definitely was aware of something lacking in her conception of her sexuality. The expectation that she put a male at the center of her life, and therefore her conception of herself, seemingly caused her to play the role she thought was necessary for her as a "good" Black woman.

Anna Wilson describes this need as a consequence of African-American tradition of transmitting its culture through the metaphor of generations. She sees African-American lesbian authors as feeling the need to reappropriate the traditional family because "African-American literature [is] a literature that has emerged from the experience of a people whose heritage and familial structures have been distorted and suppressed by slavery and white cultural imperialism" (76). She believes that Lorde then is placed within a problematic position because "by virtue of her self-identification as a Black lesbian, [she] is always only with difficulty to be accommodated within a communal or literary structure that is conceived as based in the family" (76–7).

Soon after the summer with Peter, Lorde started a job where she worked with many other women. It is with one of these women, Ginger, that she has her first lesbian experience and consequently her first thoughts of herself as a lesbian. Lorde first describes other people assuming that she was a lesbian and her own processing of what these people might mean. As Ginger flirts with her, Lorde describes her own confusion as to Ginger's intentions: because Lorde doesn't conceive of herself as a lesbian she initially does not know how to interpret Ginger's desire for her. Lorde writes:

> For some time, I had known that Ginger was flirting with me, but had ignored it because I was at a loss as to how to handle the situation. As far as I knew, she was sweet and attractive and warm and lovable, and straight as a die

Ginger is also actively interpreting Audre seemingly by methods other than verbal communication. Instead of seeing the uncertainty that Lorde highlights, Ginger sees her quite differently:

> Ginger, on the other hand, was convinced that I had everything taped. She saw me as a citified little baby butch—bright, knowledgeable, and secure enough to be a good listener *and* make the first move. She was sure that I was an old and accomplished hand at the seduction of a young divorcée. (133)

This indirect communication and these varying attempts at interpretation, are originally scary for Lorde because it makes her confront herself and her own construction of herself. Because she does not have any experience as an "out" lesbian she does not know what to do. However, when Ginger asks her outright if she is gay the consequences come into their full focus for her. Lorde describes her feelings thusly:

> "Look, it's no big thing." She took a deep breath. "Are you gay or aren't you?" She took another deep breath.
> I smiled up at her and said nothing. I certainly couldn't say *I don't know*. Actually, I was at a loss as to what to say. I could not bring myself to deny what I had just this past summer decided to embrace; besides, to say no would be to admit being one of the squares. Yet, to say yes might commit me to proving it, like with the vodka. And Ginger was a woman of the world, not one of my high school friends with whom kissing and cuddling and fantasizing sufficed. And I had never made love to a woman before. Ginger, of course, had made up her mind that *I* was a woman of the world and knew "everything," having made love to all the women about whom I talked with such intensity. (135)

Even though Lorde eventually answers in the positive, she still remains fearful of what it means. She feels that it is right for her, but she only has the idea of what this difference means for her and her relationship to the world she has previously known. Interestingly, Lorde shows a consequence of her seemingly unintended performance as a "citified little baby butch" in that she is expected to *prove* that she is in essence what Ginger suspects. Lorde fears, as well as desires, anticipates, and delights in, the performance that Ginger desires because it would somehow solidify an identity that she is not sure she wants to, or is able to, claim. I believe this is reflective both of her "performance anxiety" as well as her uncertainty over what the performance would mean for her identity. She must confront the context that Ginger understands is inherent to lesbian identity if she is going to acknowledge her identity to this "woman of the world."

Ann Allen Shockley's novel *Say Jesus and Come to Me* focuses on a different element of the repressive atmosphere that exists for lesbians within the Black community. She nicely illustrates the homophobia within the Black community and its affect on the women who are at its center. Travis Lee is a popular rhythm and blues singer who surprisingly sees herself as a powerful woman who is also constantly under the control of men. It's only after her boyfriend Rudy beats her up that she begins to question her dependence on men. She says "'And men! I always had to have one around. I felt that I needed them. Now, I wonder why. Just for sex, I guess, for that was all they were good for'" (89).

Earlier though she has answered her own question when she discusses her views of homosexuality in the Black community with her manager. She states that:

> "I almost got into it once when I was a kid. Experimenting with mama and papa games—playing with each other," she giggled. "But the boys just swept it all away." She made a face. "Dykes turn me off, trying to imitate men when they know they don't have what men have down there. Wonder why some women go that route?" (72)

At this part of the novel Travis can conceive of the Black lesbian only in stereotypical terms; an existence that, in her mind, is in direct competition with the possibility of strong Black men. This assumption reflects the cultural tradition of male dominance that I discussed in the previous chapter. It is because Travis is totally invested in her role as objectified heterosexual female that she allows herself to be so dominated. She feels her power is in the display of her overt sexuality and attractiveness (presented through her singing), and she cannot yet conceive of that sexuality other than in this frame. Travis eventually has a lesbian relationship with Reverend Myrtle Black but even after that she still cannot conceive a connection between her identity and the "dykes" she describes here.

Interestingly Jewelle Gomez finds Shockley's premise and characters unbelievable and rather lightly treated, so much so that she feels that Shockley "trivializ[es] Black Lesbians and their sexuality" (114). Whereas I agree that Shockley's novel is not an in-depth treatment of character (indeed many of the characters' actions are rather confusing and alienating to the reader), nor does it have a particularly poignant issue at its center, it does, I think, brilliantly portray the investment that the larger Black community has in compulsory heterosexuality.

Particularly striking here is her portrayal of various Black men and their reactions towards the women. Rudy, Travis's abusive lover, can only see her as a successful woman if she is under his thumb. He sees Myrtle as direct competition for Travis and responds to her with anger, by trying to slander her character and destroy her life. Reverend Cross sees Myrtle as a threat to his leadership in the church because she is a strong female. He simply fears her. Bobby, a gay Black man, loves and supports Travis and finds her abuse of him painful. Shockley aptly describes the chain of consequences that compulsory heterosexuality has on both straight and gay men and women.

Audre Lorde, in *A Burst of Light*, also discusses the issue of the connection between Black lesbians and the larger Black community in her essay "I Am Your Sister: Black Women Organizing Across Sexualities." Lorde also finds the dominance of men to be deadly to the relationship of lesbians and straight women. She also focuses on the stereotypes that Ann Allen Shockley brings to life in her novel. She writes poignantly: "I have heard it said—usually behind my back—that Black Lesbians are not normal. But what is normal in this deranged society by which we are all trapped? I remember, and so do many of you, when Black was considered not normal" (21). Lorde progresses through all of the stereotypes of Black Lesbians: that they hate men, threaten the Black family, their concerns are not "political" and that their lesbianism is actually a consequence of their "whiteness" because lesbianism is a "white" disease. She refutes all of these labels by using herself and her life as an example. However, Lorde is well aware of the fact that Black lesbians still have a tenuous place in the community as she feels that Black men's voices dominate even the strongest Black women. She writes: "let anyone, particularly a Black man, accuse a straight Black woman of being a Black *Lesbian*, and right away that sister becomes immobilized, as if that is the most horrible thing she could be, and must at all costs be proven false" (22). Within this atmosphere it would not be surprising that a Black woman would deny her lesbianism to others and to herself.

A comparable atmosphere prevails in Ana Castillo's first novel, *The Mixquiahuala Letters*. Castillo is concerned with the sex lives of her two female protagonists Teresa and Alicia. As I described in the previous chapter, both of these women are obsessed with their connection with men. They both construct their identities according to a heterosexual male perspective of themselves and, even though they attempt to separate themselves from men again and again, they ultimately cannot see their lives as successful without approval from men. If men don't find them attractive, or if their relationships with

Strategies of Survival

men aren't deemed to be leading towards marriage, then they feel worthless. For example, Teresa becomes the lover of Sergio Samora and feels good about herself as having indigenous heritage because: "Hadn't he toasted to the incomparable bronze skin of the tropical woman? All of his friends reached high up with filled glasses and smiled in open admiration at my indigenous heritage" (66). Soon he asks her to marry him and, even though she reveals she doesn't love him, she agrees to be his wife. She informs her family who have been angry at her over her behavior: "i sent a letter to my mother and her reply (which came with unusual rapidity) told me she was ecstatic. Finally, I was redeemed" (67).

Even though this novel focuses on the relationship between these two women, they can only allow themselves to view each other through these heterosexual male blinders. Teresa constantly describes Alicia in super sensual terms, and yet whenever they describe their relationship they can ultimately see the other only in terms of heterosexuality. Alicia, because she thinks Teresa is the heterosexual male's ideal, sees Teresa as competition and as a reminder that she herself does not embody that ideal. Teresa describes this situation: "Men's glances on the street, their apparent pleasure when eyeing me told you that skinny was fine for high fashion but did no good when you wanted to appeal to men's passions" (62).

Teresa sees Alicia quite differently than as a failure to reach an ideal when she writes of Alicia thusly:

> You were the ocean, immense and horizontal, your hair the tide that came in to meet the shore. You watched as i walked alongside you, head erect, dressed in torn muslin, a small bundle tightly pressed against my bosom, unaware of the trail of faceless male figures in slow pursuit.
>
> Now i think i know how you saw me that first summer, although at times i was ethereal to you, i was part of the culture that wouldn't allow me to separate. You, on the other hand, saw yourself isolated, even unwanted by men and their world, observed me from that reality. (27–8)

Teresa continues to describe Alicia with sensual language when she attempts to give Alicia the picture that she herself sees. Teresa writes:

> You keep your virgin hair long, long, a snake hung by its tail down the narrow ripples of your vertebrae. Putting antiquated values regarding feminine beauty aside, it *is* lovely. You know that. That's why you keep it, brushing fastidiously nightly like a weaver of precious silk.
>
> But that isn't your most admirable asset, while you've confided in me that you don't believe it so, your legs, the angular lines of your body at once reminiscent of a child transforming into a woman, in this day and age society bestows an approving eye.
>
> Why don't you see that?
>
> Why do you shun the plum breasts, the raisin nipples that stand perpendicular to your torso—as if nature deprived you of a harvest?
>
> You, the artist, must've observed in the mirror, the graceful curve of the slender neck, as you tilted your head just so when embarking on a new sketch
>
> The pianist's elegant fingers with the simple silver band of abalone on the middle finger of which hand i forget.
>
> That's the secret of your beauty, subliminal, momentary, a sunrise, a sunset, a cyclic experience for the one who bothers with infinite details, awaits suspended at the onset of the symphony for the first moments when all the musicians tuck violins under chins with stirring patience watch for the conductor's baton to begin.(51–2)

However, Teresa also sees her inability to support and encourage Alicia, who has such low self esteem, as connected to the fact that they are both dependent on the words of men. Perhaps it is because Teresa sees the power that this framework has in their lives that she comments: "i, the poet, never praised you lyrically, instead scolded to put an end to your timid inhibitions; i've imagined it's done no good. They were only the words of another woman" (52). Yarbro-Bejarano finds that "Much of their bonding, both positive and negative, is established through their relationships with men and their internalization of various discourses on femininity and sexuality" ("The Multiple," 66). The discourses that Yarbro-Bejarano refers to include those about motherhood and womanhood both tied to a Chicano culture that states that women should be submissive in order to preserve the family and the centrality of men.

Castillo herself sees an inability to articulate a lesbian desire or a lesbian self as directly tied to Latino culture; specifically the placement of men as central to the culture. In an interview she claims that:

> In *The Mixquiahuala Letters* ...the relationships between Alicia and Teresa, ...are frustrated by what Adrienne Rich has called compulsory heterosexuality: I'm gonna find a man to love even if it kills me.... So that inability to love comes from the fact that they don't have the option to explore an alternative. As brown women, as poor women, as Catholic women repressed by their religion, as artists ...they're all marginalized ten times over, and this is an impossible place for them to be. They don't ever get a break, or the only break they may get is through some association with a man to give them visibility. Teresa and Alicia are not considered escorts for each other. One *x's* out the other.
>
> What's important for us, as Mexicanas and Chicanas, is to reflect our actual reality, which is not always a pretty picture, which does not always have a happy ending, which is not always opting for the woman lover ...[*The Mixquiahuala Letters* can be defined as a story] of two women who find it impossible to love each other in a world of men. (120–1)

Castillo explores the effect that this male dominance has on women's subjectivity more directly in her novel *Sapogonia* because she gives the first person perspective to a man: Máximo Madrigal. Yarbro-Bejarano describes him as a man whose "subjectivity is constructed in opposition to Woman as inaccessible enigma and *vagina dentata*. His masculinity is defined contradictorily in relation to his desire for primordial unity ... and his terror of the absorption of his identity in that unity" ("The Multiple," 68). He imagines Pastora as the representative of this unity that he describes as fused with Coatlicue, a pre-Columbian goddess who is a union of opposites.[59] He says that

> And like a thing, an abstract idea, he prayed to her. He worshipped her as he soldered metal and bent it into any likeness but hers. Her image, this one before him, consumed his brain until it burst like a circus balloon, pained him into nothingness, and he went back to find her, again and again, in other women (7).

Yarbro-Bejarano sees him as dependent on this view of Pastora: "Máximo needs to see Pastora in this way to maintain a fixed sense of identity; paradoxically, she is threatening to him if she does represent wholeness and threatening to him if she does not" ("The Multiple," 69). The critic sees this view as potentially violent towards women and even more disturbing is Pastora's own complicity with this violence. She does have a few options available to construct her identity around, yet she always chooses to be objectified by Máximo and she is "hooked on her own objectification as enigma and object of desire" (Yarbro-Bejarano, "The Multiple," 69). Indeed, it is clear throughout the novel that in order for this construction of masculinity to continue to exist Pastora must continue to behave this way. Castillo illustrates the deadly consequences of her behavior by showing how Máximo continually narrates the discourse of "strong" maleness to the detriment of independent female subjectivity.[60]

One of the possibilities that exists for Pastora is to have a relationship with Perla beyond that of friendship. The opportunity and the feelings are both present, but presumably because Pastora is not able to "escape" the boundaries that Máximo builds, and she accepts, nothing else is possible.

Castillo has some interesting things to say about this novel and its two main female characters in relation to their inability to articulate lesbian selves. She states:

> There's a place early on, the first time that Pastora and Perla meet, that Perla wants to sleep with Pastora, but she wants to do it like in a ménage-a-quatre to make it okay, but she won't let herself admit that that's what she really wants to do. So those feelings may come, but you're constantly telling yourself, "I'll lose my mind if this is really what's going on." You won't let yourself act upon it.
>
> Lesbianism is not just about sexual attraction, or whether it exists. It's about the status for each of them. . . . Lesbianism has to be when you make some kind of very clear declaration that that's what it is going to be. It's not about having once had an affair, or experimented, or anything like this, and that's what it would've been because neither . .Pastora or Perla was willing to give up that hope for identity through the male. (Navarro 120)

Even though Pastora has one transcendent moment with another woman, she cannot conceive of herself in lesbian terms. Castillo describes the result that this has for both Pastora and Perla when she states that "Perla and Pastora, who are very much in love with each other, know that neither one gives the other validation. So Perla has to go and marry a white man for that validation, and Pastora gets married and presumably gives up her music for motherhood" (Navarro 121).

Strategies of Survival

Clearly these examples illustrate the dangers that patriarchal dominance has for both straight and lesbian female subjectivity. This danger exists within every community and nowhere are they more strongly felt than within communities of color. Shirley Geok-lin Lim reiterates this situation by analyzing some Asian-American women's texts that contain articulations of the difficulties of creating a successful female self within established male-centered parameters. She states that "the Asian American female, in order to pursue her interest in a race-conscious society, has to modify her rejection of patriarchal ethnic identity" (588). In other words, many women's texts posit that she cannot critique her male-centered culture and survive as a female self. Lim describes Mitsuye Yamada's position on subjecthood of women thusly:

> Her position assumes an overlapping of categories that will enable the conventional and stereotypical hostility between ethnic cultures, traditionally organized for patriarchal ends, and emerging women's identities, expressed in socially transforming concerns for the rights of women, to be defused, synthesized, or merged into a new sensibility. (588)

Within this text though this rewriting seems only to apply to straight women as Lim only considers straight women's texts and characters in her piece; apparently in her view Asian-American lesbians have not even begun to articulate their identities much less be rejected for them.

Many lesbian writers do indeed articulate their identities and attempt to create a space for themselves within this paradigm by describing lesbian relationships in a way that the heterosexual family mandates—primarily that of marriage—in order to naturalize it as valid within the dynamic. It is one strategy that has a variety of consequences. In an interview, Paula Gunn Allen describes her writing's constant connection with family as a natural occurrence. She implies that only the homophobic community would distinguish lesbian and gay ideas and descriptions of family as somehow different or inappropriate. She states that

> I think that Indian writers, Chicano writers and black and Asian American writers do a lot of family stuff, because we don't distinguish ourselves from the family base. We exist within the

matrix of the people who are our relatives or family friends, or our tribe. (*This is About Vision* 98)

Because of the importance of family acceptance for people of color, the investment in family creation is important. So reorganizing or reinterpreting family is a logical choice for lesbians.

Beth Brant also discusses this impulse, specifically for Native lesbians, in her short essay "Giveaway: Native Lesbian Writers." She discusses these women's desire to connect their identities to land and Nation because

> When one is a Native lesbian, the desire to connect all becomes an urgent longing. Faced with homophobia from our own communities, faced with racism and homophobia from the outsiders who hold semblances of power over us, we feel that desire to connect in a primal way. (944-5)

Ultimately she sees this need to articulate a family as a brave act within the hostile environment they inhabit. She simply states that "I think the courage of naming ourselves as lesbian is a significant act of love and community" (945).

This use of accepted family metaphors also occurs in *The Mixquihuala Letters* as Teresa occasionally conceives of her relationship with Alicia as stronger than a friendship; indeed, she describes them as an "old wedded couple" (53). She sees them as deeply connected though not sexually. Teresa writes:

> When we
> were twenty-seven, we saw each
> other twice, both occasions indirectly associated with a member of the opposite sex. We were experts at exchanging empathy for heart-rending confusion known only to lovers, but you and I had never been lovers.
>
>   It is true we slept together curled up on the double seat of a rickety Mexican bus that wound its way through the nocturnal roads from one strange place to another; a soft shoulder served as a pillow for the other's head. A sleeping bag on foreign ground made us into siamese tamales. Like delicate creatures of an alien world we balled up immersed in networks of dreams, a foot spasm kicked the other awake for a half-conscious moment. It is true we bathed together in

Strategies of Survival

>the most casual sense, scrubbed each other's back, combed out one another's wet hair, braided it with more care than grandmothers who invariably catch it on broken tooth combs We pierced each other's ears.
>
>For the first half of the decade we were an objective one, a single entity, nondiscriminate of the other's being. (127-8)

Clearly here Teresa is trying to articulate the extent of their relationship but without the ability to articulate an "out" lesbian one because of the pervasive compulsory heterosexuality.[61] She summarizes and at the same time evades the sexual dimension, when she states that:

>When i say ours was a love affair, it is an expression of nostalgia and melancholy for the depth of our empathy.
>
>We weren't free of society's tenets to be convinced we could exist indefinitely without the demands and complications one aggregated with the supreme commitment to a man.
>
>Even greater than these factors was that of an ever present need, emotional, psychological, physical . . . it provoked us nonetheless to seek approval from man through sexual meetings. (45)

Teresa continuously needs to use heterosexual metaphors to describe her relationship with Alicia (marriage, star-crossed lovers, etc.) and seemingly does not connect these feelings with anything but empathy over the pain of heartbreak.

In an interview, Castillo has an intriguing description of this relationship and its connection with lesbianism. She states about Teresa and Alicia that:

>In this case, with these two women, it's up to the reader to decide whether or not they were in love with each other. But they're so much in a state of denial that it doesn't reach lesbianism, I think it doesn't reach that. I think that probably, for lesbians, that would be a tragedy, because of Alicia and Teresa's unwillingness to see that they are constantly betraying each other . . . they are always disloyal to each other, they're always picking on each other, because they're so much part of each other. However, that also happens in lesbian relationships with regard to internal homophobia. . . . Unfortunately, they have the most loyal friendships with women, and they spend most of their time complaining about their commitments to their husbands or their long

term lovers, and miss the true love and devotion that they're getting
and giving to each other. (119-20)

I find Castillo's description to be an appropriate one and I believe that
the reason these women behave as they do is because they have both
swallowed the cultural limitations that force themselves into their lives.

In *Sapogonia* Pastora and Perla are the two close friends. The first
time that we are introduced to them they are at a small party and feel an
instant connection. Perla clearly is interested in a sexual encounter with
Pastora and is disappointed when it doesn't happen. Castillo describes
the scene thusly:

> As she talked with Pastora, Perla's voice grew shrill. Her
> adrenaline had begun to flow and nothing could explain it but the
> excitement of having met the transfixing Pastora.
>
> All this she confided in the serene woman, whose eyes engulfed
> her with compassion. Pastora hardly said a word, and yet Perla knew
> that Pastora was with her, understanding the tragedy of her young
> life.
>
> They forgot about the men they had been dancing with, tangoing
> across the massive, dusty floors. Eventually, with the excitement and
> the alcohol, Perla had to dash to the bathroom. When she returned
> Pastora and Diego were out of sight. "Where did they go?" She tried
> to sound casual. In effect, she felt let down by their sudden
> disappearance. (19)

After this disappointing beginning the two women move in together as
roommates.

Castillo describes Pastora and Perla's life together in a way similar
to Teresa's description of her relationship with Alicia: that of a
heterosexual married couple. For example:

> During their first months together they were not too unlike a pair
> of newlyweds, blissful within the tight cocoon they had woven for
> themselves.
>
> Each morning, before Pastora went off to work, Perla prepared
> for her friend a cup of café con leche, dashed with cinnamon. She
> poured it into an earthenware cup that was painted with gladiolas. She
> knew this pleased Pastora very much

> Perla found dozens of small ways to please her friend, whom she now loved. She might prepare dinner, though out of a can, or save Pastora the trouble of warming up her car in the morning by starting out first to confront the cold. It made Perla uneasy, however, if she allowed herself to think of it, that she behaved this way with a woman, while having no patience whatsoever with the wishes of men.
>
> She felt uneasy, too, when she sensed that Pastora, who at times had the reserve of a queen, appeared to take her kindness in stride. Yet, she was happy. They were happy. Perla had moved in with Pastora. As there was only one bedroom, they shared the same bed, the only closet, each other's clothes, make-up, toothbrush. In their new relationship, they celebrated all the possible advantages of sharing life with another woman, while counting the disadvantages one had when sharing it with the opposite sex. Lovers were allowed to come by only when it was found necessary (69)

Castillo is describing a very close relationship but one that is devoid of the sex that would consummate a marriage. Interesting here is that the relationship provides the women everything they need except sexual satisfaction. I believe that Castillo shows the relationship in this light to show what *could* be for these two women if they can escape from the constraints of their culture's ideology.

It seems, though, that it is primarily Pastora who does not attempt to consider the possibility of a different kind of relationship with Perla. She does not seem astounded by Perla's kindness, or perhaps she doesn't consider the reason for her kindness. Perla, on the other hand, is definitely aware of what she feels for Pastora and that's why it scares her. Ultimately, confronted with Pastora's lack of reciprocity Perla feels she must find a man. Castillo writes that:

> What did bother Perla, what had disturbed her from the first, when she and Pastora began to share their lives, was how devoted she herself was to Pastora. Perla cried when alone at times (for no one was like her in having such a dread of being alone) for fear that one day Pastora would reject *her*, might think her too trivial, abandon her. Perla decided she would find a man who would love her as Pastora was loved. (125-6)

Perla eventually does distance herself from Pastora and eventually marries a white man. Interestingly, her separation from Pastora is seen as negative not just for its own sake but because she chooses an Anglo partner. I believe Castillo shows this result to show how far outside her own culture Perla must travel to receive what she thinks she wants. This is how the text frames her marriage in any case, that Perla adopts the privileges of whiteness and it is the loss of the possibility of closeness with Pastora that is mourned.

Pastora soon realizes what she has lost. Indeed, Castillo states that "Pastora resigned herself to Life Without Perla" (203). After talking to Perla and hoping that she could somehow "save" her friend from her fate she gives up. For example:

> Pastora turned away. In the end, it was Perla's fear of losing her man. She would risk a great many consequences, but not that one. Pastora wished she had money, enough to wave in Bob's face, to show him and his segregated world that they could not run a Latina woman so easily and she would buy her Perla back. (206)

Here Pastora wishes that she had all of the external attributes that apparently account for Perla's marriage. She realizes though that she cannot compete on this plane. It is not clear here if Pastora is acknowledging that she wants a lesbian identity and relationship with Perla. Castillo only makes it clear that Pastora regrets that Perla is taken away from her. Perhaps it is because Pastora cannot conceive of anything but the heterosexual paradigm that dominates the novel that she can only see "male" attributes that attracted Perla and sees herself only as Perla's protector in the face of the Anglo threat.

Another way that these authors point to and illuminate the limits to the articulation of self is to describe what is needed for these women to come to a recognition of their desire and to start the healing process. This space is not primarily seen as a place of liberation or individual exploration but rather one of incarceration: prison and the psychiatric ward. However, both Castillo and Beth Brant use these spaces as positively woman centered *because* they are spaces where there is a forced all-female population. In this space where compulsory heterosexuality does not dominate perhaps there can be some alternatives. This positive benefit does not make the enforced captivity unproblematic, rather, it reflects the lack of freedom for women in the "natural" society where both men and women exist together.

Strategies of Survival

Interestingly, Pastora's change of attitude toward Perla comes after her time spent in prison where she has a lesbian experience with a cellmate. First of all Pastora tries to discourage her friend, Mary Lou, from "marrying" a butch who threatens her. With this camaraderie the women become closer and ultimately have an affair. Interestingly, in this chapter Castillo refers to Pastora as "you" whereas previously she has been referred to only in the third person or by Máximo. I believe that this change is meant to reflect the slight movement toward individual construction that is allowed without male intrusion. Castillo describes the scene between Mary Lou and Pastora which I quote at length:

> "¿Te vas a casar con ella?" you ask without looking at her, who smokes a cigarette and stares at her gym shoes.[62] She sticks the butt under her shoe and puts it out, her small hand lingering along the shoelace. Her eyes are on the foot; your eyes on her hand, the fingers playfully walking over to the rip of your own shoe She pulls at it and laughs a little. She shrugs her shoulders. "No sé."
> "And your friend, the one who's waiting for you outside?" you ask. You are aware that your voice is unsteady suddenly, awaiting her response. She feels your need to know. If Mary Lou were someone else, she would lie. But she doesn't know how to lie. "She seems so far away right now."
> Mary Lou has said this looking at you, right into your face, that kind of innocent directness that invades all your barriers. *Look at her, meet the dark, open face, and as you do, it is only inches away from your own.*
> Mary Lou's mouth is very small and thin against yours. Her dishwasher's hands are hard against your ribs and hips. You taste her with your mouth, your hands, her smell, the texture of her hair and skin.
> "And who's waiting for you out there?" Mary Lou whispers, a gruff voice in your ear, along your neck.
> "No one," you answer, your throat full, so that the words are hardly uttered, "But I won't forget you." And Mary Lou has entered you, so that you haven't had to say that. (192)

Castillo describes this relationship with Mary Lou as restorative for Pastora, strikingly opposite to how she describes Perla's. The sexual encounter with Mary Lou opens Pastora up to the joy and pain of her past and consequently heals her. Pastora is able to escape the image of the "goddess" that Máximo has created for her and that she has accepted. She starts to conceive of herself as independent of her "place" as an object within a Latino mindset and is beginning to see and accept Mary Lou's honesty (and perhaps respond with her own). As she opens herself to Mary Lou she literally rewrites her life within her culture and she is able to begin to exorcise the domination of the male specter. Castillo writes:

> *You will take Mary Lou with you. Mary Lou, who is the abandoned buildings you explored with a child's courage; rooftops jumped, fast double-dutch tournaments; black girls who pulled your red-ribboned braids; pink and white roses offered to the Virgin the month of May; Christmas pilgrimages which taught you the hymns that gave you the gift of song; urban renewal and the upheaval of your Mexican world; white city workers who relocated each family after its building was marked with an X in a circle, the next one to be torn down; your father who left, and the mother's new husband who never spoke your name or looked you in the face until you were thirteen and he tried to have you in bed; your mother, who stopped being Catholic after your confirmation and went to Protestant church meetings in a storefront every night; Abuelita who took care of you from the age of three months and taught you about the healing of the body with herbs and of the soul with your own; Mary Lou, who banished the devil of your childhood.* (193)

It is after this experience that Pastora attends Perla's wedding and realizes what she has lost. Ultimately though, perhaps because this female universe is a temporary construction, Pastora can only envision her identity in connection with a man and eventually as a mother of a male child for whom she sacrifices everything. Thus showing that the specter of male domination exists within "normal" societal conditions. Castillo describes Mary Lou and Pastora's relationship in terms of what it means for Pastora. She states that:

> the two women, Mary Lou and Pastora, stop at the moment that they come together. At the moment that Mary Lou starts to kiss her everything opens up for her. It's that old metaphor of being with a mirror, and the minute she's with a mirror everything that she's been able to escape from, through objectification with a male, comes

Strategies of Survival

> through for her. She cannot deny it anymore. where she came from, what she feels, every pain she's ever experienced, her struggles, open up through this intimate encounter with this woman (127)

I believe this is an appropriate description of the affect Mary Lou has on Pastora because Castillo contrasts it with how Pastora "forgets" herself by allowing men to turn her into an object that only exists in relation to them. After Pastora is released from prison and loses touch with Perla because of her marriage, she soon turns back to Máximo and her comfortable identity as a sexual object for men. Most devastating, however, is that fact that her acceptance of herself as an object is apparently responsible for Máximo's ability to savagely murder her.

Castillo implies that the continuance and acceptance of the patriarchal paradigm means death for the female subject. She hammers this home because the novel actually begins with Pastora's murder; however, she is nameless at this point in the text, so we are not sure who the victim is or why Máximo has killed her until we come under the spell of Máximo's ego just as Pastora does. After seeing how their relationship is related to the possibilities for male versus female subjectivity the scene in the first chapter is chilling. He watches her on his bed after they have made love and connects her to his feelings about a cat that came to his apartment. He says:

> While he thought it cliché, he saw her in the eyes of the cat, because it was with her that he discovered how seductive that animal was, indifferent and capable of attack when disturbed, so unlike the dog, unlike his own obedient animals that watched his house and his back on the street (7–8).

After the cat doesn't return for a few days he feels rejected by it; when it shows up again he feels such rage towards it that he lets his dog attack it. It escapes. It is after he looks at Pastora and calls her a "damned alley cat" (8) that he murders her.

> In one thrust his clenched fist holding the scissors from her sewing table comes down to pierce the hollow spot between the lumps of nippled flesh. Her eyes open and are on him. Her face is wild as she inhales with the thrust and exhales when he pulls the scissors out. His hands are wet and drip red, he wipes the sweat from his brow mixed with tears ¿Estás muerta ya, puta? (8–9)[63]

He will not meet her eyes, or look at her face, because "he doesn't want to die either" (9). After he looks into her eyes Pastora's spirit, or spirit force, seems to vengefully attack him: "the yellow spotted cat leaps out at him, claws dig into his brow and cheeks, catch in the delicate skin of his eyelids, and yank them with loud screeches" (9). He then apparently falls to his death, and while he falls his thoughts turn to his family of whose description begins his narration within the novel.

This scene could be read as suggesting that the entire community collapses upon itself when its primary goal is to forge and secure male identity or, that this male identity cannot survive without the complicit female object. Because we realize what this relationship ultimately means to Pastora, as we read about its beginning we realize the implications of her choices within this male-centered environment.

Beth Brant's short story "The Fifth Floor, 1967" also describes a woman who has willingly embodied the female object. However, at the beginning of the story this unnamed native woman is placed on a mental ward by her family apparently for losing interest in and connection with her role as wife, mother, and daughter. She describes herself: "I am a piece of cloth—useless, with no pattern" (70). As she narrates her story she alternates between referring to herself in the third person, when describing her life with her family, and the first person, when she describes her life in the hospital. She begins to look for herself by exploring her own body: "I feel my body, seeking a relationship with myself. I wish to know this woman" (71). Slowly, during the night, she touches herself in an autoerotic way in order to find herself. She refers to herself in the third person as a woman who becomes excited and eventually more "whole" and "real" because of her sexual excitement. She says:

> I stroke the soft place of her inner thighs with both hands. Her skin becomes warmer. She trembles with each brush of my fingers. The hair of her cunt is straight and heavy and thick. I touch the slit, the opening of her cunt, the inside of her. She is wet and open. Her clitoris pulses under my finger. I touch her there Try to find her. She is wet and open. I taste her juice off my finger. She is tart, like sweat and medicine. Both hands attempt to enter her, to go up inside her hole, to touch a place in her that will tell me who I am. I rub her clit. She spasms and comes on my hand, the syrup from her coating my fingers. I bring my hand to my mouth and suck myself to sleep. I

Strategies of Survival

have dreams about her. She looks in the mirror, and I see with her eyes. (73)

This ritual becomes her therapy, with every night making her more and more "sane" as this woman opens herself up and is willing to be sexually aroused by the female speaker. In other words, when she acknowledges her pleasure in another woman's body she becomes more whole. Of course whether one can claim this is an example of a lesbian identity being acknowledged, something that most feel goes beyond sexual experience, is arguable. It is impossible to tell whether she "becomes" a lesbian here even though she definitely finds solace and power in visualizing herself as part of a lesbian relationship. What is clear here is that her role, as defined by heterosexual norms, is losing its grip upon her life seemingly because, as in *Sapogonia*, she has developed her own identity in an enforced all-female environment.

She claims when she is released from the hospital that she still has not "found me—yet" but that this finding will only be possible with the "other woman." She decides that

> I am taking the woman with me. I am smuggling her out. She will go with me as my secret. During these six weeks her face has begun to take on my features. My face has begun to take on lines, and my skin is toughening. Her hair has one thread of silver. My hair is getting darker and thinner. . . .My breasts feel everything. Inside her is blood, muscle, electric pulses, and rage. Her fingers send currents through mine.
>
> I am taking the woman home with me. It is our secret. She keeps me alive. (75)

I wouldn't argue here that the woman clearly articulates herself as a lesbian, nor does she refuse the label, but again what is clear is that Brant describes her behavior as representative of the attainment of individuality and self. I also argue that the hidden desire for another woman, or even the ability to see herself as sexually independent of her husband, was interpreted as a sign of her mental instability when in fact it keeps her whole within her male dominant household. One wonders what would happen if this woman directly articulated a lesbian identity—surely the family that needs to see her as mother, wife, and daughter would need to reject her as these are roles that she consciously or unconsciously rejects. Because Brant leaves some confusion here she focuses on how the family has defined the unnamed woman as having "lost herself." Clearly Brant shows two opposing reasons: the family thinks its because she finds no meaning in her prescribed roles, whereas the woman apparently sees herself lost without a sexual connection to another woman.

Religion is also a hostile force towards the articulation of lesbianism for the woman of color, and some authors focus on its power as well because to some degree it is an extension of compulsory heterosexuality. Clearly different cultural traditions contain different religions and different views governing religion and therefore these writers don't treat "religion" as a monolith. However, they do confront its capacity to silence them.

Much of Ann Allen Shockley's novel *Say Jesus and Come to Me* illustrates Reverend Myrtle Black's own coming to terms with both her lesbianism and her religious self. Indeed, it is fascinating that Shockley chose to create Myrtle as a minister, seemingly a role that would make her an "enemy" to lesbian identity. Truly, then, she is a tormented soul as she must speak doctrine and hide behind it simultaneously. For most of the novel she must hide her lesbianism because she knows that the Black church will not her accept her otherwise. She feels that because she has such a strong connection with the Black community "she had to conceal her sexuality. Religion and race mattered first to her" (133). In other words, she is forced to separate out facets of herself and live some publicly while others must be kept hidden. She knows the parts of her community that she would have to reject in order to name herself as a Black lesbian and she simply cannot do it. She maintains her silence partially for reasons related to the safety of family as well as for economic ones: she could not continue to be a minister as an "out" lesbian. Shockley here focuses on Myrtle's pain as understandably closeted because of the homophobia within the Black community.

Myrtle chooses to work within "white" circles in order to achieve some feeling of connection to her lesbianism. She is outraged by the white lesbians whom she works with, however, reacting to the sort of privilege that Castillo describes. Further, it is noteworthy that many lesbians of color describe white lesbians as free to claim their lesbian identity; probably because the opposite is true for them. Shockley describes Myrtle's meeting with Rita, a white lesbian:

> It wasn't an overly difficult thing for Rita to affirm her sexual preference. She was white, self-sufficient, and had an organization behind her.
> "Are there many black lesbians around here?" Rita pumped Myrtle.
> "I suppose there are lesbians everywhere. It is a matter of who is in and out of the closets." Again, a Judas to her own. She felt Rita's eyes burning on her, heating the frustration already within her, the conflicts, the deception of masking. But no one had asked; therefore, she hadn't denied. There was comfort in this. (135)

Myrtle is one who cannot reject these elements of confinement and so must pass as a "straight" Black woman in order to succeed in her community. However, by doing this she slowly unravels her own soul and, to borrow Audre Lorde's phrase, wastes her "woman energy."

A different religious tradition occurs in Castillo's novel, *So Far from God*, where she focuses on a whole family and all of their relationships and experiences. The four daughters are of primary interest to Castillo although she tells the stories of other family members and acquaintances. The daughter most relevant to this discussion is Caridad. We are introduced to her early on as a young woman who goes out to bars to pick up men and have sex with them. One night, though, she is brutally mutilated. She is also miraculously restored by the prayers of her youngest sister, La Loca, and subsequently develops clairvoyance. She becomes somewhat of a recluse and ultimately begins to learn to be a faith healer, or curandera, under her teacher Doña Felicia. Here at least the spirituality is female-centered and of prime importance to the family, and to the culture; however, it still fails Caridad. This suggests that the patriarchal dominance of Christian religion still affects the culture making the power of the curandera threatening.

It is when Caridad and her teacher Doña Felicia go on a pilgrimage to Chimayo during Easter week that Caridad falls under the spell of a young woman. Caridad is stunned by her beauty and continually stares at her; the woman seems to be looking back but she cannot tell. Doña Felicia thinks perhaps the young woman knows Caridad but Caridad's feelings are quite different from just surprise over recognition. Castillo describes Caridad's feelings thusly:

All the while, Caridad could do nothing but think of the woman on
the wall. Maybe she had sunstroke and had just imagined her. She
was exhausted and nearly dehydrated and surely she could not have
experienced what she felt throughout her entire body just from the
sight of a woman! But as soon as they were outside, coming around
from the back of the church, she saw the woman in question, more
real than before, still on the wall. Moreover, the woman on the wall
was looking over her shoulders in Caridad's direction! (76)

After seeing this woman and being affected so deeply by her,
Caridad, while on her way to take a mineral bath, gets lost and ends up
spending a year alone in a cave in the mountains during which she
never stops thinking of the Woman-on-the-wall. She ultimately does
come down from the mountain and to the mineral baths where she
meets the woman. All Caridad can do is cry in her arms. This is all the
information that Castillo gives about this relationship. Caridad comes
back home saying nothing about her experiences, and she also becomes
very skilled at interpreting dreams and seeing visions. Her sister, Fe,
constantly says that her disappearance and subsequent abilities are due
to her having lost her heart.

Interestingly, it is Caridad's ability to love another woman that
brings her visions into clarity and usefulness. Judy Grahn's well known
work concerning homosexuality and spirituality gives insight into this
connection between spiritual power and homosexuality. She writes
extensively about Gay myth, tradition, and history and discusses
shamanism, spirituality, ritual transvestitism, and gay offices to name a
few of her topics. It's not unusual then that Castillo would use two
women's love as the springboard for a strengthening spirituality. Grahn
reveals a larger cultural tradition when she writes that

> Tribal people make use of ceremonial homosexual behavior, so in
> such cultures an identification of a person as Gay, in the sense that
> industrial society means it, is actually irrelevant. Healing, shamanism,
> divination, or special access to the spirit worlds may be the qualities
> by which a person is known, and the sex rites she or he follows are
> simply connected to the office. (118)

In comparison to the way lesbian feeling sustains her and brings
about her spiritual development is the destructive quality that a man's
obsession for Caridad has on the women's relationship. This man,

Strategies of Survival

Francisco el Penitente, follows Caridad while she simultaneously follows the woman she loves—Esmeralda. The consequences of Francisco's obsession are confusing but apparently Caridad has a vision about Esmeralda's death which Esmeralda also feels when she sees Francisco watching them. Esmeralda then takes off running, Caridad chases after her, and they both jump off the mesa and disappear. They seem to enter into legend while doing this, or perhaps they uncover a tradition that has been hidden from them. Castillo writes:

> Esmeralda was flying, flying off the mesa like a broken-winged moth and holding tight to her hand was Caridad, more kite than woman billowing through midair.
>
> *Tsichtinako was calling!* Esmeralda's grandmother holding tight to her little grandson's hand heard and nodded. The Pueblo tour guide heard, cocking her ear as if trying to make out the words. The priest at the church, who happened to be performing baptisms that morning, ran out and put his hands to his temples. Two or three dogs began to bark. The Acoma people heard it and knew it was the voice of the Invisible One who had nourished the first two humans, who were also both female, although no one had heard it in a long time and some had never heard it before. But all still knew who It was.
>
> Just the spirit deity Tsichtinako calling loudly with a voice like wind, guiding the two women back, not out toward the sun's rays or up to the clouds but down, deep within the soft, moist dark earth where Esmeralda and Caridad would be safe and live forever. (211)

Clearly here the tradition of lesbianism and its connection to spirituality has been buried and hidden, even from within Caridad's mind, and the deities can only lament its passing and preserve the lovers' spirits. It seems that the women travel back into the past before Christian mythology as they fall off the mesa, and it is only then that they can be transformed into legend and myth safe from Western reinterpretation. In the present there is no room for the love between these two women to exist; the destructiveness of Francisco as compulsory heterosexual threat is quite poignant here.

Castillo provocatively shows that there is no place for a same sex, same race couple in the actual world. And yet if the lesbian of color is able to even conceive of herself as such, then she must fight for her existence and face more serious consequences than this battle, depending on how she chooses to live with her identity. One of the consequences for this woman is to live either identified as a lesbian (generally seen as a white-identified label) or to pass as a "straight" person of color.

Consequently it seems understandable that in many of the texts the lesbians of color have white lovers. In some arenas this choice is a subtle mode of passing and it also seems to emphasize the mythology that all lesbians are white, because lesbianism is seen as a white "disease," and because lesbian identity has been defined by white women as I have argued within Chapter One. Also, with a white lover the lesbian of color has at least the possibility of some entrance into a "safe" community because she can be accepted through foregrounding her lesbian identity. Although, there are definite problems that come hand in hand with this entry.

Perhaps the most crucial problem with these relationships is that some lesbians of color internalize white dictates of beauty and/or their own culture's distrust of lesbians of color and so see white women as the only available and desirable love objects. Because, as Barbara Christian points out, being a lesbian of color is at times putting one's self in harm's way and therefore "lesbians that did show themselves had to be tough and were defined by white standards of beauty" (*Black Feminist* 197). As Christian describes it, though, this choice of whiteness as desirable has deeply felt consequences for the lesbian of color "For racism was as ingrained in the lesbian community as it was in society at large" (*Black Feminist* 197–8).

A perfect example of this alienation, occurring even within an intimate relationship, exists in Audre Lorde's relationship in *Zami* with a white woman named Muriel. Lorde shows the problem inherent in imagining their identities in concert when Muriel ardently claims that "we're all niggers, all equal in our outsiderhood" (203) and Lorde "hated to hear her say it" (203).[64] Clearly here Lorde has not internalized Muriel's ignorance but she is deeply affected by it as well as by Muriel's privileged position in being able to say it.

On the other hand, if the lesbian of color overcomes this alienation and chooses to articulate herself as a lesbian of color, and not in isolation within the white community, then the hostilities from her own culture must somehow be negotiated. One way that this can be accomplished is for her to reject her culture in its entirety or in selected parts. Either choice leads to danger from those hostile forces outside her own culture. For example, this is what one woman, "Anu," articulates in an interview:

> What I would like to stress the most is that women of colour, lesbians of colour, have essentially, a smaller community of people that we can expect support from, so to us it is a big risk to jeopardize that community. For if all that we have left is the lesbian community, then we are in big trouble. No matter how much they would like to believe otherwise, the lesbian community is still a representation of the larger society, infected with the same sorts of diseases: racism, classism. ("Lesbians of Color" 166)

In her text *Loving in the War Years*, Cherríe Moraga describes her own personal need to reject elements within her culture that threaten to disavow her existence as a lesbian. Her need to move away from Chicano culture in order to resist the limiting sex roles was crucial. Critic Leslie Bow states that Moraga's "process of revelation necessitates separation from family, culture, and sanctioned sex roles in order to claim a 'right to passion'" and that because of these limitations "she must first turn away from her family and therefore her culture" (1). Moraga herself describes this process in relation to her different identities:

> I did not move away from other Chicanos because I did not love my people. I gradually became anglocized because I thought it was the only option available to me toward gaining autonomy as a person without being sexually stigmatized. . . . This primarily meant resisting sex roles as much as I could safely manage and this was far easier in an anglo context than in a Chicano one. (99)

Moraga makes it clear that it was her light skin that made this freedom of movement possible, and she also implies that whiteness is inherently a marker of privilege for those articulating a lesbian identity. She also clearly states that the stronger one's family is the easier it is for a Chicana to live in a predominantly anglo society. However, as Bow states "For Moraga, Chicana culture is [also] associated with Catholic guilt in sexual pleasure" (2). So it seems that the only option is if the Chicana lesbian leaves the safety of the family, because as Moraga states "lesbianism, in any form, ... challenges the very foundation of la familia" (111). So then how does the lesbian of color protect herself?

If the lesbian of color critiques her own community not only does she give up part of the safety from anglo dominance that she has if she stays safely within it, she can also earn constant distrust from her people. Moraga recollects her own movement outside of the Chicano community:

> I grew white Fought to free myself from my cultures' claim on me. It seemed I had to step outside my familia to see what we as a people were doing suffering. This is my politics. This is my writing. For as much as the two have eventually brought me back to my familia, there is no fooling myself that it is my education, my "consciousness" that separated me from them. That forced me to leave home. This is what has made me the outsider so many Chicanos—very near to me in circumstance—fear. (ii-iii)

It is intriguing that the only choice Moraga envisioned for herself was to be a repressed Chicana or a free white girl: either/or. At this point in her text she saw no other possibility for herself, therefore, her choices for survival as a lesbian of color were slim.

Carla Trujillo sees a similar vision of Chicana lesbian existence in her essay "Chicana Lesbians: Fear and Loathing in the Chicano Community"; however, she does see some positive aspects in this rejection of community. She writes that the main task of the Chicana is to re-envision her sexuality as not dependent on a Chicano. This apparently small task, though, is a rejection of her own culture; a culture that valorizes the macho, the male. Trujillo states that "Chicana lesbians are perceived as a greater threat to the Chicano community because their existence disrupts the established order of male dominance, and raises the consciousness of many Chicana women regarding their own independence and control" (186). She also states the consequences that she feels are of most importance: "The effort to consciously reclaim our sexual selves forces Chicanas to either confront their own sexuality or, in refusing, castigate lesbians as *vendidas* to the race, blasphemers to the church, atrocities against nature, or some combination" (187). These consequences are clearly devastating and similar to those described previously by Audre Lorde that turn sister against sister for the perception of saving the community stability.

Ana Castillo also discusses some of the consequences of "coming out" for Latinas. She again points out that to claim a lesbian identity is inherently to challenge family cohesion and Latino culture. She states simply that "As a mexicana, whenever you decide to rebel against your family, the status quo, you are going to get punished. How you're going to get punished we can only guess, in a million ways, but that you will get punished, that's very real and it's very hard to conscienticize women and say 'take that risk'" (Navarro 123). She also discusses the very real economic factors involved in taking such a risk. Castillo feels that a white lesbian in some ways has the luxury of coming out to her family because the rest of her world can remain intact if she wishes; she can still keep the job and the economic security. She argues that the Latina, and any other woman of color, has to work five times as hard as a white woman at whatever she is doing in order to survive and the extra burden is sometimes impossible to even consider. She states that

> In a homophobic world, "coming out," or establishing a relationship that is seen by and large by a religion and then by law as perverted, is taking away everything, it's suicidal. If you're barely surviving, and then you're going to take the risk to lose the respect, and the love, and the sense of place that you have with your own family, you have nothing. (Navarro 122)

This experience of absolute loss is dramatized in Gloria Naylor's novel *The Women of Brewster Place*. As I mentioned in Chapter Two of this project Naylor's chapter "The Two" contains the stories of a Black lesbian couple—Lorraine and Theresa—who experience their lesbianism in very different ways. Barbara Smith finds it poignant and disturbing that Naylor describes these two women as completely isolated. She finds them a hopeless couple in a hopeless situation; she is disappointed that "both Lesbian characters are ultimately victims" ("The Truth" 698). Smith feels that because the women are complete opposites they have no way to support each other and so must be destroyed when they come up against the homophobic community. For example, Lorraine attempts to pass and does not feel that she is any different from anyone else. In other words, she is able to deny that her community puts limitations upon her because she has the outward appearance that the community accepts: restrained femininity.

Theresa, on the other hand, dresses in a sexy way and does not mind getting in people's faces even though she doesn't advertise her lesbianism. Lorraine has all the markers of assimilation into the heterosexual community while Theresa is marked for alienation—even in skin color. Smith concludes that

> What feels disturbing and inauthentic to me is how utterly hopeless Naylor's view of Lesbian existence is. Lorraine and Theresa are classically unhappy homosexuals of the type who populated white literature during a much earlier era, when the only options for the "deviant" were isolation, loneliness, mental illness, suicide, or death. (702)

Even though it is understandable that Smith does not find that the two women offer positive constructions of lesbians of color, she does not examine what might cause Naylor to represent them this way. They are confronted with a highly vicious homophobic community and respond in the way they feel will help them survive. I believe that Naylor offers a critique of the Black community within this chapter and not of Black lesbians. Even though Smith feels that the hopelessness that Naylor describes is inauthentic, in many ways it is actually representative of the feelings many lesbian writers discuss.[65] They are both pragmatic in this view; they wish to keep their jobs as well as the peace in their home.

Naylor describes the reactions to the two women when they move into the housing complex as very different because of the differing external markers that the two display. The description is a very interesting exploration of the consequences of narrowly prescribed female roles:

> the women of Brewster had readily accepted the lighter, skinny one. There wasn't much threat in her timid mincing walk and the slightly protruding teeth she seemed so eager to show everyone in her bell-like good mornings and evenings. Breaths were held a little longer in the direction of the short dark one—too pretty, and too much behind. And she insisted on wearing those thin Qiana dresses that the summer breeze molded against the maddening rhythm of the twenty pounds of rounded flesh that she swung steadily down the street. Through slitted eyes, the women watched their men watching her pass, knowing the bastards were praying for a wind. But since she seemed oblivious to whether these supplications went answered, their sighs settled around her shoulders too. Nice girls. (130)

When someone notices that the women are uninterested in men's opinions but rather in one another, and assume that they are "that way," their opinions drastically change. This forces Lorraine to present herself as an "out" lesbian within her community, and she must deal with this identity within herself, which is something that she has actively run from.

She describes to Theresa the view she has of herself as a Black lesbian:

> "I have accepted it!" Lorraine shouted "I've accepted it all my life, and it's nothing I'm ashamed of. I lost a father because I refused to be ashamed of it—but it doesn't make me any *different* from anyone else in the world."
> "It makes you damned different!"
> "No!" (165)

When Theresa pushes her, she begins to realize that because the world is "owned" by heterosexuals, and so is driven by compulsory heterosexuality, her identity does put her in some jeopardy. Naylor disturbingly portrays this jeopardy by having her walk out of their apartment on her way to a party, within the gay community, because "If I can't walk out of this house without you tonight, there'll be nothing left in me to love you. And I'm trying, Theresa; I'm trying so hard to hold on to that" (167) and losing her mind because of being brutally raped by a group of young men solely because they know she's a Black lesbian.

The story suggests that when one Black woman attempts to define herself within her community, even silently, she seemingly must be erased in order to validate male dominance and the power of the family. Interestingly, Lorraine takes the path through the alley, where the boys are hiding, because she wants to talk to her adopted father, Ben, who offers her a positive connection to a family. A relationship with him is the way that she can have her "father's" approval which she desperately wants. It is Ben, this figure of connection, whom she in turn murders, showing that she is a direct threat to the father's power.

Naylor directly shows a nightmare vision of a lesbian's effect on the Black family: she must be "shown her place" as victimized female by young males, and as a result she kills the patriarch. Because Lorraine's rape and loss of sanity causes such powerful psychic trauma throughout the community it seems that Naylor is being critical of the community's behavior toward Lorraine. And yet, no one outwardly mourns her or seeks vengeance on the perpetrators; in fact, the women all repress knowledge of the blatant victimization Lorraine has suffered apparently because it has the power to destroy the neighborhood's fantasy of unity. If they were to feel any empathy with what has happened to her, and stand up against the male dominance of the community, it is difficult to believe that the unity would remain at Brewster Place. Thus, Lorraine can only symbolically haunt them. Far from being inauthentic, Naylor's vision of Black lesbian existence powerfully demonstrates the consequences of its articulation within a community that desires to erase her.

It is also disturbing that even some literary critics deny the reality represented by Lorraine's story to varying extents. They seem to distance the brutality that Lorraine faced and was destroyed by in order to make a sweeping statement about the novel's women. Kathryn Palumbo finds that Naylor uses "female imagery" in order to construct a new archetype of heroic (read straight) women. She finds, though, that the lesbians are the "personification of female separation in the world of Brewster Place" (6). After describing the scene presenting Lorraine's assault she finds the heroic elements in "the common dreams [that] possess the women with a heritage and kinship. This is a history and family which are not part of the men's story. It is purely female" (7). Palumbo has neglected to discuss, however, that the dreams were brought on by Lorraine's suffering and that the other women dream of her and yet repress direct awareness of it. Also clearly, they do not include her or Theresa in their heritage and kinship.

Maxine L. Montgomery also has some disturbing lapses in her discussion of the novel. She finds that Lorraine's end is symbolic of "the suppressed conflicts underlying the women's troubled lives" (10). And after she discusses the ending of the novel, asking whether the dream of the block party is real or not, she states that each of the women in the book:

> draws upon ancient, transforming rituals from the black folk past and, like the ebony phoenix, finds a rare kind of survival power, thereby violating the decrees of those who are in positions of power and authority (11).

Clearly, though, Lorraine is not transformed nor does she metaphorically rise from the alley; it is because she has taken steps to survive as a lesbian (she attempts to connect with the larger lesbian community to end the isolation lamented by Smith) that she is murdered. These misreadings of the importance of the simple fact that Lorraine is murdered because she is a Black lesbian have the effect of another attempt at her erasure. These critics elevate the need to imagine a coherent community over a recognition of what lesbians face.

Thus, while critics often seem to negate the dangers facing lesbians of color, many writers actually insist upon them because the dangers constitute a very powerful context present in their lives. Paula Gunn Allen also writes of a woman, in her novel *The Woman Who Owned the Shadows*, who suffers a nervous breakdown because of her inability to directly articulate her lesbian identity and connect this identity with her community. In fact her inability to do so at all, and then to do so in conjunction with her native culture, causes her to try to find stability throughout the narrative. It is implied that the punishment that she and her childhood friend Elena receive for falling in love with each other is what separates her from her harmony with native culture and her family. She must reject her native identity and her family in order to allow herself to grow as a lesbian. She joins an all white therapy group, works with a white psychiatrist, marries a Japanese man and befriends a white woman; all attempts at finding wholeness outside her culture but all leading to emptiness. She tells her white friend Teresa her problem:

> Thinking, I'm not even sitting here Someone else is. Then who am I here. Who is she across the tablecloth from me. The panic rising in her lashing her in waves over the length of her body. Because they have taken my body. They have taken my mind. . . .Because I don't live here in me. Because I have nowhere to go. Because I can't get out of here. Because you can't hear me, can't understand the danger I'm in. Because it is so real to me here . . .because they have stolen my name (134).

This separation is at the heart of Ephanie's struggle. Because she feels she has been forced to leave her family to find wholeness she becomes defined by white norms. Gunn Allen describes how Ephanie's white friends see her: "They talked a lot about Indians. About massacres and victims and Sand Creek and Wounded Knee. They snorted and shrugged, railed and analyzed. They treated her like she was the wooden Indian outside the trader's store" (136). She becomes increasingly distant from herself because of these external forces of definition, which she continually internalizes. Finally, she decides to hang herself. As she calmly prepares to do so she repeats to herself: "The only good Indian's a dead Indian. Die savage die. Lice. Indians are lice. Vermin. Gotta be exterminated. Terminated. They're all alike. Sly. Cunning. Vicious. Nits breed lice. Y'all come out of there with your hands up" (162-3). Again, it is clear that the consequences that she suffers in order to begin to even allow herself to think of herself as a lesbian of color threaten to kill her.

Patrice Leung also focuses on the dangers that she encounters while trying to envision herself as a Chinese lesbian. In her autobiographical essay "On Iconography" Leung discusses her own need to reject her parents' Chinese immigrant culture in order to survive as a lesbian. Because of her immigrant background her culture becomes a combination of middle class American and Chinese values. Because of this conflict she does not know how to define herself. She describes her first connection to her lesbian identity:

> I have fucked mostly white women. It occurred to me the other day while I was brooding about life, that each of these women was the fulfillment of my Marcia Brady fantasy.
>
> Marcia Brady, of course, was the eldest of the three Aryan vixens on "The Brady Bunch", a show I watched with religious abandonment every Friday at 8 pm precisely, on ABC.
>
> My physical yearning for Marcia Brady was the realization of my parents' dream for me (108)

Along with this icon of middle class white America came the Chinese value of passivity in women: "But I was not, under any circumstances, to make waves; to make a spectacle of myself; to do anything that would anger the gracious white hosts who had allowed us into their country" (108). The author incorporates her family's desire to succeed in America within herself and so she wishes to become "invisibly" middle class, white, and heterosexual.

She eventually becomes detached from herself as a lesbian of color and can only love and find beauty in white women. Even though her family is Chinese, the strong desire of the new immigrant culture to erase difference has emerged dangerously in the "internalized idiocy of [the author's] erotic patterns" (109). Her need to live as a lesbian, necessarily outside her own family and within a predominantly white community, causes her to "lose" her racial identity. There seem to be

Strategies of Survival 131

no options here; her "home" culture has no room for her as a lesbian and the internalization of white lesbian identity has turned her against herself.

C. Allyson Lee writes even more powerfully about her need to reject her family's plan for her life as well as about the confusion that her life as a Chinese woman and as a lesbian create. The immigrant mentality also comes to play here as the author's father both valorized American values and chastised her for losing her Chineseness. She describes that he:

> He kept telling me that I should be playing with Chinese kids—there were none in our neighborhood. He chastised me for not being able to speak Chinese—by the time I entered Grade One public school, I was fluent in both English and Chinese, but my parents, worried that I may not develop good English skills, stopped conversing with me in Chinese. And my father warned me ominously, "You'd better marry a Chinese. If you marry a white, we'll cut you out of our will." All of this succeeded in driving me away from my roots, leading me to believe that if I acted white enough, i.e. not chatter noisily in Chinese and not hang around in groups, I would actually not look Chinese. (115–6)

Because the author is female, her father's desire that she connect to traditional Chinese culture requires that she carry other burdens besides perceived ostracization. Her father had the

> expectation that I grow up to be a "nice Chinese girl". This meant that I should be a ladylike, submissive, obedient, morally impeccable puppet who would spend the rest of her life deferring to and selflessly appeasing her husband. He wanted me to become all that was against my nature, and so I rebelled with a fury, rejecting and denying everything remotely associated with Chinese culture. (116)

After her affirmation of her lesbian identity, she realizes that she can never be what her father's Chinese traditions force her to be: heterosexual. She states simply that "Becoming a lesbian challenged everything in my upbringing and confirmed the fact that I was not a nice, ladylike pamperer of men" (116). Again the desire to claim her life as a lesbian forces the lesbian of color to reject her racial identification. By having relationships primarily with white women, much of her own attitude towards herself as Chinese is challenged because of the attitudes shown by her lovers. She writes:

> Years later, white woman lovers came into my life, teasing me and calling me a "fake" Chinese because, after all, I did not even speak the language. This helped to bring back the old feelings of sinophobia again, and it did not occur to me then that certain white people would seek me out and be attracted to me because of my ethnic background. . . .It would be much later that I would coin the phrase "Asianophile", my own description of such women. (117)

Finding solace in the white lesbian community is only temporary, as Lee becomes an object on different grounds—and in her view an object of perverse attention. The racism of her lovers pervades her perception of her own identity as hollow and exotic jeopardizing her affinity with herself as a lesbian of color. This effect is in startling contrast to Brant's vision of the healing powers of desire between lesbians of color that she illustrates in "The Fifth Floor, 1967". Here, the unnamed woman literally loves herself into existence as a lesbian while Lee is loved by other women into confusion. This shows the negative power that ignoring/denying one's own ethnic/racial community can have on individual lesbians of color.

In Karin Aguilar-San Juan's essay "Exploding Myths, Creating Consciousness: Some First Steps Toward Pan-Asian Unity," she describes the consequences that she suffers in various arenas of her life because of her identity as a Filipina lesbian. She echoes the thoughts of other lesbians of color who discuss the risk of separating from one's family and culture when she states that:

> For the most part we . . choose not to talk about our sexuality, that choice is not made freely but under duress; we risk losing our jobs, our homes, our children, our friends, our family. For those of us who are Asian, losing connections to our family represents one of our greatest fears, since in this white society our cultural identity depends precisely on family links. Some of us are forced to conclude that coming out is simply not worth the price. (191)

She also describes a more personal image of the consequences of rejecting her culture to create a space for herself. When invited to a friend's grandmother's home for a traditional Filipino meal she knows that the grandmother does not realize that all of the guests are gay or lesbian and they all must pretend to be straight and therefore acceptable to the hostess. She describes the way that all of the guests behaved:

> like dutiful Asian children who know when it's better to acquiesce to the demands of our parents (no matter how oppressive to our sense of self), once we entered the house, we arranged ourselves strategically around the living room—boy, girl, boy, girl. Looking back, passing for "straight" can be easy, but it's a game that always leaves a bitter taste. (191-2)

Aguilar-San Juan describes this behavior as having to choose between being gay or being Asian, realizing that for most people they are mutually exclusive. Obviously implied is that being a lesbian is only possible in white company and being a Filipina means being straight. To be a lesbian of color again means either temporarily passing as straight in the ethnic community, or rejecting both communities and remaining in total isolation. This passing is not empowering because it does not raise critical attention to itself as performance; instead, because it is not transformative, it is limited as role-play. It is not a choice for these agents, rather they are forced into it in order to exist within their cultures.

Christine Wong articulates the impossible situation of the either/or of rejecting one's community or passing within the larger white community in her short play entitled *Yellow Queer*. The speaker, the "yellow queer," describes the limits to her ability to pass based on her physical characteristics: "So, I tried being White, But my skin was too dark. Then I tried being Red But my eyes were too slanted. So I tried being Black But this time my skin was too light. And, I tried being Brown But my nose was too flat" (53). Of particular interest here is that the speaker wishes to be any other race than what she is, showing her simple hatred for who she is as taught to her by her own racial/ethnic community, as well as by the dominant white society. After the speaker joins the women's movement and at least has an identity in being an exotic "other" ("they had to like me because I was the only one they had" (53)), she soon realizes that she has internalized all of the discourses that require her to erase her identity and as a result she is left completely bankrupt. She states that:

> It's fun being a Yellow Queer. I can play White and everyone pretends that I am. It's a thin line where one half is playing White and the other half is who I really am. but I know Which Side I'm on. I think Well, maybe not. Actually, I'm not too sure I can tell the difference. I don't know if "playing White" is part of being A Yellow Queer And all this playing has left me really confused. I think I've been fucked over! (53)

Wong not only articulates the racism in the women's movement and the hatred and denial of Asian lesbians but the pitfalls in passing and performing identities without changing the external defining forces.

Much is being written about lesbian identity and the type of subversive potential it has to denaturalize sexuality and gender constructions. However, most of these ideas have not included an account of race/ethnicity, and so it remains only theorizing without any accompanying liberatory practice. The unconscious or conscious inability of the dominant critical discourses to fully account for people of color, and all the contexts that they inhabit, shows that they leave the well dry of options to identify as a lesbian of color. Perhaps it is still only the privileged who have the ability to change their external circumstances, and indeed the circumstances of the world, because of their ability to be otherwise visually neutral in the larger community. The texts that I have explored here posit that the struggle with identity is not an internal one, not just a choice or a matter of courage, but an external one. The multiple communities that the lesbian of color exists in, and is constructed by, are actively intrusive upon her subjectivity and attempt to erase her in the name of preexisting conceptions of race or ethnicity, no matter how she names herself. Because most of preexisting theory fails to account for these parameters, these women must depend on themselves, and each other, to conceive of and develop theories that are inclusive enough to incorporate their multiplicities. Clearly certain individual women have been articulating these ideas for some time, but they have not been recognized for it by the dominant voices within the academy.

CHAPTER FOUR

The Path To Survival: Rewriting Cultural Traditions and Creating Living Theories[66]

After looking at the ways lesbians of color are limited by theoretical paradigms and multiple communities, it seems that any possibility for their existence is minimal. Since I have, until this point, focused on representations of women who fail to survive, the existence of the lesbian of color might seem impossible. Indeed, most of the existing textual representations of lesbians of color focus on them as closeted, alienated, silenced, or murdered. However, there are some depictions of lesbians of color who can survive as such and articulate their identities within their "home" communities. Given all of the circumstances that I have been enumerating, it is important here to discuss the strategies that lesbians of color use to survive. Obviously they must negotiate the minefields that they inhabit in order to successfully name themselves. This chapter will focus on texts that exemplify how lesbians of color can survive within the communities that wish to destroy them and will also explore the strategies they employ in order to do so. The authors I will look at here create this space by re-envisioning and rewriting their cultural traditions, weaving articulations of lesbian identity into the very fabric.

It is worthwhile first to investigate some identity theories that might account for the limitations lesbians of color face in order to see if they might provide some useful strategies. These theorists recognize that there are externally constructed limitations placed on all subjects.

Of particular concern though is to explore how these analyses assist lesbians of color in negotiating these limitations.

A useful place to begin is with the work of Kath Weston who critiques Butler's assumption that any agent can have a free moving subjectivity when she claims that the ability to perform is indeed limited by society. Weston writes that:

> there is no such thing as the "free" play of signification. In a material world, bodies are not passively inscribed by signs; they are inscribed by people who select items of material culture from a restricted range of options and arrange them according to imaginations that are shaped by historical development (13–14).

Weston proceeds to describe "the" lesbian looking within her closet confronting some very real limitations to performance. Yet, again this unnamed "lesbian" is neutral in other identity categories—she is white.[67] So, even when adding Weston's provocative thoughts into the mix there is no analysis of the dynamics that race and ethnicity add to these performances. Because "color" is not easily visually manipulated, thereby making the acts less fluid, does this conflict point to an unreconcilable difference between acting and being?

Julia Creet argues for the affirmative in her essay "Anxieties of Identity: Coming Out and Coming Undone" where she critiques Butler's elaborations on lesbian identity. She states in contrast to Butler that:

> I do not "play my lesbianism as a role." It is "psychically entrenched play," as Butler points out, but, one must insist, physically and historically entrenched play also. Identity as fantasmatic and parodic can work to both display and displace the operations of power. But even fantasies have historical contexts, and parodies can wreck [sic] permanent havoc on the body. (196)

This affirmation comes from a white lesbian who does not have to negotiate racial communities. When the havoc that is wreaked is not only homophobic but simultaneously racist and sexist then the violence is even more insidious because choice becomes irrelevant. Because most people of color are visually signified (the term certainly implies it) then changes in behavior in order to parody have little deconstructive power. I suppose one could parody racist constructions of blackness or

Asianness, for example, but after the performance one still goes home with that blackness and Asianness, to be externally defined by a white supremacist society. Clearly not even these critics, who oppose Butler's lack of consideration of external realities, provide an adequate framework with which to consider lesbians of color. The power of white supremacy, that I have discussed previously, still seems to overwhelm any chance that lesbians of color have of creating paths to survival.

Therefore in order to articulate a theory that accounts for lesbians of color, this white supremacy must be negotiated; because the white theories of identity that I have discussed reflect the privilege inherent in white supremacy they become of little use to lesbians of color. I find the most straightforward of all responses to the dominance of "white" neutrality is that exemplified by Gloria Anzaldúa's use of labels. She describes her negotiations of categories anecdotally:

> When asked what I am, I never say I'm a woman. I say I am a Chicana, a mestiza, a *mexicana*, or I am a woman-of-color—which is different from "woman" (woman always means whitewoman)... Similarly, for me a woman-of-color is not just a "woman", she carries the markings of her race, she is a gendered racial being—not just a gendered being. ("Bridge" 221)

Here, Anzaldúa clearly shows the inherent connection between gender and racial identities for women of color, and she could add sexuality within the mix as well. This need for specificity in labeling oneself could be seen as further entanglements for women of color to negotiate; however, I believe that Anzaldúa's point here is to differentiate herself from the white supremacist tendency to conflate "womanhood." She also points to the very important differentiation between women's experiences, demanding that identity theories be of pragmatic use. She states that "nonintellectual, working-class women-of-color do not have the luxury of thinking of such semantic and theoretical nuances, much less exempting themselves from the category 'woman'" ("Bridge" 221). She implies that if one intends to develop a theory that is actively strategic, it must be useful and not just a luxury limited to a privileged few.

Sagri Dhairyam also challenges the view that privileged theories are merely luxuries. She takes Butler's oversights to task when she claims that Butler's status as a white academic allows her to produce a theory that seems to challenge, but actually *reinforces* traditional philosophical exercises. For example, Dhairyam states that:

> More disturbing, in privileging the parodic aspects of sexuality through drag, she implies that, unlike sexuality, other identities of race or class have more at stake in foundationalist identity politics and are therefore less able to mobilize subversive drag. Identities that cannot sustain themselves through history triumph in her formulations because of the very differences that tear them apart against the "regulatory fictions" of essence that are sustained over time. But to safeguard the openness of the signifier in an anxiety for a future of radical democracy is also to overwrite the all-too-material forces of a present that would erase dissident identity. (29–30)

Obviously a deeper consideration of racial and ethnic identity must be made in order to make a theory of performance of more use for lesbians of color. Sagri Dhairyam critiques the white assumption of neutrality evident in the lack of a consideration of racial/ethnic identity within Queer theory. She states:

> even as we acknowledge that the cultural boundaries defining straightness are suspect acts that keep an implicit lesbianism at bay and define the parameters for its manifestations, we gloss over our internalized fantasy of the lesbian who not only plays herself through our bodies, a fantasy not only sexed queerly but raced white. (26)

Dhairyam uses this "we" in an ironic fashion, questioning the whole of Queer theory as a purely white pursuit. She also alludes to the consequences of this "internalized fantasy" for queer women of color: "the" lesbian is always white, therefore women of color question where they fit into the scheme, if at all.[68] She also critiques the typical position that seems to originate for the sake of convenience: a disregard for racial identity in order to claim the "truth" of a gendered experience. She writes that:

> "Queer theory" comes increasingly to be reckoned with as critical discourse, but concomitantly writes a queer whiteness over raced queerness; it domesticates race in its elaboration of sexual difference. In order to confront the dual implications of an other who is always

> already internal to straight as well as to white subjectivity, I raise the problematic of racial difference through the lens of lesbian identity. This is not to subsume race into sexuality or to render their oppressions homologous, but rather to force whiteness to confront its investments in heterosexuality, masculinity, and literacy. (26–7)

She considers the position that the lesbian of color has within a white supremacist society and finds Butler's theory not only lacking but in part complicitous with the consequences of the invisibility of whiteness:

> When skin color and physical traits italicize the continued threats that racial identity runs without any concomitant imperative for self-conscious positionality, the performative act of identity voices itself through the body. The visible stigma of race is endlessly produced through discourses that effect the boundaries for white culture. The marked, raced body is repeatedly discovered and re-enacted through a matrix of imperiled whiteness for which any taint of color—black, brown, red, or yellow—signifies biological and genetic as well cultural contamination. (43)

She believes that because whiteness is still taken, primarily uncritically, as the neutral, then all of the risks of identifying as a self are taken on by people of color. Surely, the texts that I have discussed thus far support this assertion. Dhairyam ultimately claims that:

> Hardly a matter of critical self-negotiation, identities that are both raced and sexed enact effectively embodied realities that are necessarily purblind to the extent of the risks they run, the exclusions they perpetrate—in order to continue to exist at all. (43)

Obviously Dhairyam believes that whatever strategies lesbians of color use to exist they are not critically developed or implemented in relation to clearly understood risks.

Whereas I agree with Dhairyam's articulation of the limitations of Butler's theory specifically for a racially/ethnically marked lesbian subject, I do not agree with the idea that these subjects do not create subversive theories of their own in order to carve out existence both within texts and reality. The rest of this chapter is focused on the dynamics surrounding the lesbian of color in the position of theorist, as well as the transformative theories they articulate in order to survive.

As I have already pointed out, one such identified theorist, Gloria Anzaldúa, has articulated her theory of a "mestiza consciousness" which allows the lesbian of color to exist in a context that continually wishes to ignore or destroy her. I argue that this is an articulated theory of being, of identity, that has multiplicitous (sex, gender, race, etc.) identifiers at its heart. Anzaldúa does not "add on" race to an identity theory that speaks from a white perspective, but rather she has developed her theory from the perspective of a lesbian of color and therefore has accounted for numerous constructions of self and varied, sometimes contradictory, identifications.

Anzaldúa's discussion of mestiza consciousness comes primarily from her text *Borderlands/La Frontera: The New Mestiza*. I have already discussed the foundations of Anzaldúa's theory in my introduction, therefore I will focus here on its connection to performance theory and how it might be a meaningful theory not just for biological mestizas, women of Mexican Indian and European parentage, but metaphoric/cultural mestizas as well.[69] Anzaldúa is clearly concerned with the biological mestiza—the woman who is a combination of India, Angla, and Mexicana—but she also opens the door for a broader view of this consciousness. In order to truly live on the borderlands, and to thereby obliterate the possibility of a center, the inclusiveness that she constantly speaks of must be applied to the figure that she constructs. Indeed she describes the border psychology playing out in numerous communities. She states that:

> The struggle is inner: Chicano, *indio*, American Indian, *mojado, mexicano*, immigrant Latino, Anglo in power, working class Anglo, Black, Asian,—our psyches resemble the bordertowns and are populated by the same people. (*Borderlands* 87)

Clearly Anzaldúa is allowing for the possibility of other embodiments of this paradoxical identity. Also important to her is that there must be attention paid to the connections between theory and material reality in order to create the possibility of real transformation. She states that:

> The struggle [for "border" people] has always been inner, and is played out in the outer terrains. Awareness of our situation must

The Path to Survival

> come before inner changes, which in turn come before changes in society. Nothing happens in the "real" world unless it first happens in the images in our heads. (*Borderlands* 87)

These perspectives are deeply connected within experience and contexts and therefore can be more easily connected to lesbians of all colors. Of key importance here, which differentiates Anzaldúa from the other theorists mentioned, is that she envisions reality and abstraction as existing on equal planes, joined together in order for an individual to conceive of the processes involved in their own transformation (which will ultimately have wider affect). In my view this is of prime importance because it shifts the focus off of the "race for theory," to use Christian's phrase, and onto the individual's own use of the theory, as well as the larger political consequences of these uses.

The mestiza can be connected directly to Butler's idea, based on Foucault's genealogies, that "natural" gender identities are constructed over time by interactions of subjects with discourses speaking compulsory heterosexuality along with other forces. In the same way Anzaldúa implies that the concept of a "pure" race (and therefore the solidity of racial identity) is an effect of a white supremacist agenda. This agenda has led to the need for those who are of mixed race to attempt to separate out portions of themselves in order to fit within that paradigm; one must claim one or the other of the self. Instead, Anzaldúa describes an identity that does not attempt to separate out portions of self (woman, lesbian, white, lower class, Mexican Indian, etc.) in isolation, but that sees the point of overlap among these contradictory identities as the border of all and the connection between all. She describes this place as:

> That focal point or fulcrum, that juncture where the mestiza stands, is where phenomena tend to collide. It is where the possibility of uniting all that is separate occurs. This assembly is not one where severed or separated pieces merely come together. Nor is it a balancing of opposing powers. In attempting to work out a synthesis, the self has added a third element which is greater than the sum of its severed parts. That third element is a new consciousness—a mestiza consciousness—and though it is a source of intense pain, its energy comes from continual creative motion that keeps breaking down the unitary aspect of each new paradigm. (79–80)

Anzaldúa connects this conscious energy with creativity which in her case is realized with writing. Again she emphasizes the need to connect both abstract and concrete conceptions of, and uses for, a new consciousness. One of the most important acts in her view of personal and political realities is speaking/writing one's existence. She writes that for her the writer's blocks that she experiences "are related to my cultural identity. The painful periods of confusion that I suffer from are symptomatic of a larger creative process: cultural shifts. The stress of living with cultural ambiguity both compels me to write and blocks me" (*Borderlands* 74). This mestiza consciousness is both a spark of creativity and a block that threatens to destroy itself and her with it: but this is the growth state. "And once again" Anzaldúa writes, "I recognize that the internal tension of oppositions can propel (if it doesn't tear apart) the mestiza writer" (74).

She also feels that the writing itself is a mode of performing identity—both directly and indirectly. The work lives without her by its side to give it context and so it is interpreted again and again. She says that "My 'stories' are acts encapsulated in time, 'enacted' every time they are spoken aloud or read silently. I like to think of them as performances and not as inert and 'dead' objects. Instead, the work has an identity" (67). This textual existence is important to consider when theorizing identity and performance because it is a unique performance that escapes the visual. However, it entails rethinking the object, the written page, or work of art, not as "dead" as is typical of the Western tradition but in the Aztec way she describes: there is no "split [of] the artistic from the functional, the sacred from the secular, art from everyday life." (66)

Another connection to Butler is Anzaldúa's own notion of performing identities; however, her discussion is centered on a performance of race rather than gender. Here she describes how the mestiza connects to the external forces that wish to see her in categorized sections. She writes:

> The new *mestiza* copes by developing a tolerance for contradictions, a tolerance for ambiguity. She learns to be an Indian in Mexican culture, to be Mexican from an Anglo point of view. She learns to juggle cultures. She has a plural personality, she operates in a pluralistic mode—nothing is thrust out, the good the bad and the ugly, nothing rejected, nothing abandoned. Not only does she sustain contradictions, she turns the ambivalence into something else. (79)

This section can be read as showing how her identity is constructed based on how others view her or on how she chooses to present herself to others. In Anzaldúa's example of how she is defined externally, the outsiders define her negatively in comparison to themselves. She, though, chooses to allow this negative judgment in order to allow space for the ambiguity of the racial/ethnic identity that she embodies.

Obviously there is an amount of agency involved to operate in this "pluralistic mode," and therefore I suggest, and this is a key point, that choosing to *perform* pluralism within one's cultural tradition can be a useful strategy for the lesbian of color. It is one that potentially allows some the freedom of movement that Butler describes while incorporating the understanding of real contexts and racial theory that Anzaldúa describes.

This is exactly what some of the lesbians writers that I have discussed have their fictional characters do and what the authors themselves desire to do in order to successfully articulate their chosen identities while remaining within their communities. This combination forces them to rewrite their cultural traditions in order to make room for these identities. "Performing la mestiza," then, amounts to a choice to identify and play out the paradox of embodying a oneness that should not be able to exist based on the existing "rules," thereby challenging many articulated theories of identity.

Happily, as of late, Anzaldúa's ideas have been entering debates focusing on lesbian identity. Unfortunately, I do not think the real power of her ideas has yet been realized. Indeed, they have more often than not been dismissed as utopian or reduced to solely lesbian (read white lesbian) purposes. I find this an important illumination of the academy's desire to dismiss ideas that have as their foundation a questioning of why the academy (and other institutions) tries to dismiss these same ideas. For example, Judith Raiskin in her "Inverts and Hybrids: Lesbian Rewritings of Sexual and Racial Identities," outlines Anzaldúa's theory and then concludes that it is:

> ultimately utopian. It is a vision that, while grounded in modernist longings for salvation, does not locate that salvation in a desire for coherence, simplicity, or stasis. Anzaldúa uses the tools of postmodern deconstruction to offer a new dream that in its slipperiness, its nonmateriality, can sustain us when the old fictions of

identity or their dismantling threaten our psychological survival (163).

It seems that any time one optimistically considers the possibilities of the future one is in jeopardy of being accused of "spin[ning] for us a dream of cosmic interconnectedness" (167). Perhaps this critique is in response to Anzaldúa's use of the mythic. I don't find her incorporation of myth as necessarily relegating her ideas to a different realm; rather, I believe she discusses how the mythic invades the "real" within Aztec/Mexican/Chicano history and culture to illustrate a point. This connection is also another instance of overlap and connection which breaks down exclusive dichotomies and categories. Raiskin proceeds here apparently assuming that Anzaldúa's strategy has no connection to material reality; actually Anzaldúa is much more embedded in material nature than other theorists who have not been dismissed in this way. One wonders if her status as Chicana has put her in that second tier of thinkers whose ideas seem specific and pertinent to only a small audience and a narrow, less relevant reality.[70]

In my view another misreading of Anzaldúa occurs in Annamarie Jagose's *Lesbian Utopics*, more specifically in the chapter entitled "Slash and Suture: The Border's Figuration of Colonialism, Homophobia, and Phallocentrism in *Borderlands/La Frontera: The New Mestiza*." She argues that Anzaldúa's text actually reinscribes that which it critiques—the existence of difference. Jagose posits that:

> Nevertheless, and despite her insistence on the double function, the slash and the suture, of the border; Anzaldúa's final utopic projection attempts to install the *mestiza* beyond distinction and demarcation, as the harbinger of a global miscegenation and hybridization which eliminates forever the possibility of difference and separation. In this sense, *Borderlands* replicates the mechanisms of defense that it critiques. In order to reclaim the border as a utopic site, *Borderlands* must disavow the border's difference from itself. This disavowal is an instance of the taxonomic closure which, for *Borderlands*, is properly symptomatic of prohibitive power Ironically, then, this nostalgia for the *mestiza* as the site of a utopic intermixture, hybridization, and confluence merely inverts the privileging, in the discourses of colonialism, homophobia and phallocentrism, of the slash of the border as the site of taxonomic closure. (138)

Again, I would not agree that the borderlands is indeed a utopian site nor that the mestiza is primarily an image of utopic "breeding" to erase difference. In fact, Anzaldúa does not ignore the existence of difference; she, as a mestiza lesbian, lives with difference constantly—both internally and externally derived. The point of mestiza consciousness is not to erase difference and see only confluence and combination but rather to deal with the inevitability of the psychic disturbances that categorizations of difference (this or that, either/or) bring. I feel that Jagose is incorrect in her conclusion that "Finally, *Borderlands* fixes the border as only the site of indistinguishability and not also distinction; of confluence and not also divergence" (153). Mestiza consciousness, which inhabits the borderlands, inherently exists within both difference and sameness and that is precisely what makes this consciousness a mestiza one.[71] I do not think that Anzaldúa sees la mestiza as completely separate from these elements but as actually embodying them and "in a state of perpetual transition" (*Borderlands* 78).

Shane Phelan in her book *Getting Specific: Postmodern Lesbian Politics* discusses Anzaldúa in a different way. She discusses Anzaldúa's theory as one that has many possibilities for active social change. Phelan states that:

> Anzaldúa's concept of the "new mestiza" illuminates a view of multiple oppression as the site of a new consciousness, a consciousness with a heightened appreciation of ambiguity and multiplicity. The effect of interlocking systems of power is to prevent a secure singular identity This is not a weakness, but is a strength; only such a dislocation can provoke the awareness of possibilities and the tolerance of ambiguity that she sees as requirements for real social change (57).

Phelan agrees that social change is possible through the refusal of dualisms that limit social exchange. Definitely a different perspective than the one that limits Anzaldúa to merely a utopic fantasy.

Unfortunately, from my perspective, Phelan seems only interested in how the mestiza is useful for white feminists. She clearly distances herself from the move of appropriation and discerningly articulates the problems that it would cause:

> Appropriating *mestizaje* does not serve to build alliances; it serves to convince mestizas that white women don't get it, that white women are blind to their own privilege and oblivious to the force of history. Our alliances cannot be built by grafting ourselves onto others' identities (72).

This move by Phelan shows some acknowledgment of privilege in that she does not find it useful to equate herself with a racial mestiza for fear that she will not build an alliance but rather create a barrier of silence. She doesn't wish, then, to steal the life experience of this woman but rather to consider the consciousness that she embodies in order to put it into practice as a theory of acceptance and alliance building. While I see no problem in Phelan's interest in considering the usefulness of this theory for white women's lives, and Anzaldúa herself clearly sees little problem with acknowledging metaphorical mestizas including white women, I still find it difficult to see lesbians of color erased from the discussion that should focus on them.

I don't intend to totally dismiss the validity of any of these critical responses to, or uses of, Anzaldúa's theory. Nor do I intend to simply valorize her above all other theorists. However, I find fault with the critics I have discussed for continuing the erasure of lesbians of color in general and especially as theorists. When white academics are the only critics described as the important theorists, then they will continually ignore or limit the value of the theories that women of color produce. I believe that the existence of this fact is proven because if these women's ideas were already meaningfully incorporated into the academy the academy itself would not exist as it does (Yarbro-Bejarano "Expanding" 124–33; Anzaldúa "Haciendo" xv-xxvii; Uttal 42–5)

Women of color have generally been seen solely as "creative" writers and not as producers of theory because their theory tends to be presented differently than the critical theory of white academics. This trend exists in many discourse communities not just within discursive issues concerned with identity theory. Therefore the writers that I have investigated have primarily not been viewed as theorizing about their own identities but as telling stories only about and from their authentic and authorized experiences. The fact that these women continue to be erased proliferates the illusion that there need be no consideration of intersecting identities and theories and that the white perspective can "stand" as the monolithic "always already" neutral perspective.

Lesbians of color, on the other hand, write from a continually changing perspective, one that is constantly in jeopardy of being both explosive and ignored. Why do these women risk losing their "authentic" voices by not attempting to reify an identity specific to them?

Clearly a political agenda is behind the forces attempting to silence them which asks with astonishment: why not organize and speak in a simpler mode, by connecting with a single identity model, to have a more powerful political impact? As I have argued throughout, lesbians of color adopt the strategies they do because to separate out elements of the self is impossible if these women are to ever conceive of themselves as whole. Therefore they do not have the luxury of attempting to become free-floating signifiers (to deny any fixed identity) because they already embody this disruption by their very nature. It might also be politically expedient to isolate elements of identity, and therefore to disavow certain elements, in order to organize under a singular label, but it is also deadly. It has been necessary to risk obscurity rather than to buy into the paradigm of hierarchical identity that continues to have the power within academic discourse and society.[72]

Not many women have been able to negotiate these dangers completely enough to articulate a successful self. This is evident in that the number of texts I shall discuss here, that illustrate a successful articulation of identity through a revisioning of culture, is much smaller than in previous chapters.[73] Some of the texts that I have already discussed do have moments of success but do not illustrate a notion of *enduring* identity construction. Only the following texts have accomplished a process of negotiating identities that leads to a *sustained* revision of boundaries.[74]

Carla Trujillo summarizes the seemingly simple but in fact incredibly dangerous thinking that is necessary for this revision. She writes of a student of hers who suddenly realized that being a Chicana lesbian meant that "Not only do you have to learn to love your own vagina, but someone else's too" (187). This is a tall order in Trujillo's mind because it means rewriting the whole of Chicano cultural tradition that would inherently disallow the possibility of this "loving." Still, in order to speak her survival the lesbian of color must enact this literal and metaphoric loving of vaginas.

I start this examination with Cherríe Moraga's fictional and non-fictional text *Loving in the War Years*. By doing this I don't intend to equate her own personal words with the fictional characters that follow; I do, though, wish to convey the power and magnitude in how she describes how she began to fashion herself as a Chicana lesbian within the Chicano community. Therefore, I freely discuss both non-fiction and poetry here, and connect her ideas with the close-readings that follow.

Moraga strongly connects her love for Chicanas with her feminist politics, and with her own negotiation of her identities as a light-skinned middle class English educated Chicana. After reckoning the forces lined up against her and by using her experiences "loving in the war years" she connects her identity to the origination of political change within her community. The change she describes necessitates a cultural change in tradition and ideology:

> a political commitment to women must involve, by definition, a political commitment to lesbians as well. To refuse to allow the Chicana lesbian the right to the free expression of her own sexuality, and her politicization of it, is in the deepest sense to deny one's self the right to the same. (139)

So, Moraga calls the political Chicano community to recognize a seemingly simple fact and in doing so calls that same community into question. I believe that she accomplishes this best through her poetry about her own mother, as within it, she weaves together lesbian desire with the recognition of the central importance of her mother (and by extension la Virgen and the myth of "la madre") as well as her political alliance with working class Chicanas. Moraga writes that:

> For you, mamá, I have unclothed myself before a woman
> have laid wide the space between my thighs
> straining open the strings held there
> taut and ready to fight.
>
> Stretching my legs and imagination so open
> to feel my whole body cradled
> by the movement of her mouth, the mouth
> of her thighs rising and falling, her arms
> her kiss, all the parts of her open
> like lips moving, taking me into loving.

> I remember this common skin, mamá
> oiled by work and worry.
> Hers is a used body like yours
> one that carries the same scent
> and silence I call it home. (140)

Through this physical, political, creative, and revisionist act Moraga is able to "*El regreso a mi pueblo. A la Mujer Mestiza*" (140)[75]

Another author who has written both personal narrative and fictional narrative on this subject is Paula Gunn Allen. Much of her work can be said to highlight the importance of Native American women for the benefit of both Native and white societies, if not an actual rewriting of cultures specifically for Native American lesbians.[76] However, in her novel *The Woman Who Owned the Shadows* she accomplishes this cultural revision through her main character, Ephanie, who has been falling apart from the opening pages. Her search is for wholeness; for a livable identity that blends all of the worlds in which she exists: white, Native, feminist, lesbian, traditional, and cosmopolitan. After confronting all of the hostilities that wish to eradicate her, she is finally able to connect her identity to that of the woman within the tales her people tell, within her own cultural traditions.

Throughout the text, Gunn Allen has continually played these traditional stories off of Ephanie's own story and Ephanie eventually becomes aware of this connection. Gunn Allen shows the direct connection between Ephanie's search for identity and an articulation of a useful theory for lesbians of color. In other words, her use of storytelling is a device both for Ephanie's search and to serve a larger need for identity theory.

The story of "The Woman Who Fell from the Sky" is connected to Ephanie's own remembrance of a fall she took. The woman in the story is forced by her dead father to marry a man, a magician, whom she does not know. The woman obeys her husband and eventually gains a power of sexual self-sufficiency of which her husband is afraid. Her power is symbolized by a flowering tree which impregnates her with its blossom. After the sorcerer has become irrelevant through her power, he also becomes ill; he is certain his wife is to blame so he gets rid of her by encouraging her to leap through a hole in the ground left by the uprooted flowering tree. The woman's fall causes the creation of the earth.

This story is followed by Ephanie's own fall under the heading "A Lot Changed After She Fell." It begins with Ephanie attempting to understand the meaning of the other woman's story. She thinks:

> Was it the sorcerer-chief's jealousy, his fear that betrayed her? Or was it her own arrogance, her daring, leading her to leap into the abyss from which there was no return? Ephanie wondered about that, turning the question over and over in her mind. In her mind laying the question against many memories, against the history, against the tales, against the myths. Against her own life. Hours she pondered, slowly growing stronger, more clear, as the light in the room turned to shadows, to twilight, to dark. Still she sat, re membering. (195-6)

This remembering brings Ephanie's recollection of her fall from an apple tree. Although her friend Elena cautioned her, she was encouraged by her cousin Stephen, fell and ended up in the hospital. Afterwards her behavior changed from being an adventurous "tomboy" to a cautious "woman" who accepts the tenets of Catholic femaleness. Instead of being free-spirited she becomes invested in an image:

> Instead highheels and lipstick. That she suddenly craved, intently. Instead full skirted dresses that she'd scorned only weeks before. Instead sitting demure on a chair, voice quiet, head down. Instead gazing in the mirror, mooning over lacey slips and petticoats. Curling endlessly her stubborn hair. To train it. To tame it. Her. Voice, hands, hair, trained and tamed and safe. (203)

Not only does she embrace a very "femme" image but also a straight white middle class one that denies her Native self. For example,

> After she fell the sun went out. . . .She sang long plaintive songs of love, of romance, dreamed of leaving Guadalupe for someplace else. Dreamed of being tall and pretty and dated. Adored. Mated. Housed in some pretty house somewhere far from the dusty mesas of her childhood, somewhere that people lived in safe places and had lawns and plenty of water and spoke in soft voices. Like her mother, like the nuns, had told her about. Like the books had said. Someplace green and soft. Someplace nice. With vacuum cleaners and carpets and drapes. with sofas instead of couches, refrigerators instead of iceboxes, shopping centers instead of general trading stores. (203)

The Path to Survival

As she considers these two stories she realizes the place that her fall has had in her life simply because she had applied the traditional interpretation of the first story to her own life. Also clearly the Christian myth of the Fall has intruded upon her consciousness as well. She falls from the apple tree and becomes the punished sinful woman: a vulnerable possession who must be shut away and made harmless. She can only conceive of these traditional stories in a way that erases any possibility for a different existence than the one she describes in the above quote, and because of that misreading she begins her downward spiral. She thinks:

> "I never realized what had happened." And now she knew. That what had begun had never been completed. Because she fell she had turned her back on herself. Had misunderstood thoroughly the significance of the event. Had not even seen that she had been another sort of person before she fell. "I abandoned myself," she said. "I left me. . . ." Elena and I, we were going to do brave things in our lives. And we were going to do them together (204)

She realizes that she had blamed Elena for her fall instead of Stephen and had therefore abandoned everything Elena represented: her loving of women. Annette Van Dyke relates this western feminization as connected directly to Ephanie's mixed race status. She states that

> As a part Guadalupe woman, Ephanie is caught in the erosion of the traditional place of honor and respect in which a Guadalupe woman is held by her tribe. In the non-Indian world she must deal with both the patriarchal stereotypes of Indians and of women. She is surrounded by forces that work to destroy whatever link she has to the traditional culture in which women were central figures (19).

As Allen herself states in an interview, "[Ephanie] keeps expecting men to do her life for her, because she got feminized in the western way instead of the tribal way. She made a terrible mistake and she paid for it until she understood that she had power in her own right" (103).

After this revelation Ephanie has a vision of a traditional woman who has the symbols of the Spider. The spirit woman connects both the tradition of loving women with Native stories and culture for Ephanie; something Ephanie thought was not possible: that the love of women created the universe and that identities need not be concrete to be whole.

> She understood the combinations and recombinations that had so puzzled her, the One and then the Two, the two and then the three, the three becoming the four, the four splitting, becoming two and two, the three of the beginning becoming the three-in-one. One mother, twin sons; two, mothers, two sons; one mother, two sons. Each. First there was Sussistinaku, Thinking Woman, then there was She and two more: Uretsete and Naotsete. Then Uretsete became known as the father, Utset, because Naotsete became pregnant and a mother. . . .and so the combinations went on, forming dissolving, doubling, splitting, sometimes one sometimes two, sometimes three, sometimes four, then again two, again one. All of the stories formed those patterns, laid down long before time, so far. (207–08)

The spirit woman enlists her to tell the stories to save her own people. She links the creation of story to the existence of Native lesbians and to the cultural power they hold.

She ultimately calls upon the tradition of the Native lesbian as prophetess and healer. She shows the centrality of a female tradition within Native culture and stories and tells Ephanie to embrace it in order to save Native peoples. Ephanie then ultimately sees the rewriting of the tales she had heard and misinterpreted and remembers an erased and hidden tradition, which Allen and other Native lesbians are recovering, and which would include her:

> And she dreamed. About the women who had lived, long ago, hame haa. Who had lived near caves, near streams. Who had known magic far beyond the simple charms and spells the moderns knew. Who were the Spider. The Spider Medicine Society. The women, who created, the women who directed people upon their true paths. The women who healed. The women who sang.
>
> And she understood. For those women, so long lost to her, who she had longed and wept for, unknowing, were the double women, the women who never married, who held power like the Clanuncle, like the power of the priests, the medicine men. Who were not mothers, but who were sisters, born of the same mind, the same spirit. They called each other sister. They were called Grandmother by those

who called on them for aid, for knowledge, for comfort, for care. (211)

By rewriting her knowledge of her own people's traditions, by way of a spirit woman, she realizes that the universe was not only created and fostered by women who have the power to be whatever is needed for the sake of survival, but also that to be a Native lesbian is to be on the pulse of the creative tradition and the survival of the race. The doubleness is what caused Ephanie's confusion; and her own people's attempts to erase her. She thinks her fall is a source of punishment when indeed it is a source of creation. Instead, then, of being a blasphemy, a potentially destructive force within the community, she is the source of power and the upholder of tradition.

Beth Brant also writes provocatively of how she, as a Native lesbian, fulfills this role that Allen dramatizes in this novel. She sees Native lesbian writers as starting a new tradition that is a continuance of the old. She writes that

> We write not only for ourselves but also for our communities, for our People, for the young ones who are looking for the gay and lesbian path, for our Elders who were shamed or mythologized for the rocks and trees, for the wingeds and four-leggeds and the animals who swim, for the warriors and resisters who kept the faith. For Creator. For our mothers, fathers, grandmothers, and grandfathers who gave us our Indian blood and the belief system that courses through that blood. (946-7)

Like Gunn Allen, Brant is describing a Native lesbian existence that incorporates both the importance of writing and a revisioning of cultural traditions that make this woman a natural and integral member of her "home" community. Not only her immediate community but of a historical lineage as well.

It is particularly interesting to me that Tom King, a reviewer of this novel, is disgusted with Allen's "simplicity" in having Ephanie "moralistically" talk about herself as an Indian who is not stereotypical. He is also disappointed in the conclusion of the novel which he sees as being too convenient after all of Ephanie's turmoil (he also implies that Allen is stealing material from Scott Momaday to create the images). He sees the ending as a "fairy [tale] where everyone lives happily ever after" (King 264). What he sees as a "fairy tale" is this lesbian's successful connection of her identity with her Native traditions. Perhaps in many ways it is a fantasy, as most of the texts I have explored make clear; however, King does not make this comment with attention paid to this context. He means simply that her work is oversimplified in its vision and concludes that "Allen may possess a talent that will come into its own place in its own time" (264).

Allen creates a complex story of a Native American lesbian's existence and struggle to find wholeness within the midst of numerous fragmentations. She theorizes that the Native lesbian's assuming her position as healer and storyteller is central to the continuation of her race; she has the perspective of the "double woman" who can see the spirit world and the world to come. If this position were to be accepted by the larger Native communities it would cause a rewriting of both culture and gender construction in order to account for her.

Beth Brant rewrites the lesbian into Native American culture and family within her collection of short fiction *Mohawk Trail*. For example in her story "A Simple Act," she connects groups of Native women who are making gourds into tools for life and family cohesion with the act of two women loving each other. She starts the story by describing the women with the gourds:

> A gourd is a hollowed-out shell, used as a utensil. I imagine women together, sitting outside the tipis and lodges, carving and scooping. Creating bowls for food. Spoons for drinking water. A simple act—requiring lifetimes to learn. At times the pods were dried and rattles made to amuse babies. Or noisemakers, to call the spirits in sorrow and celebration. (87)

She then begins a story about two girls, one a Russian immigrant and the other an American Indian. The speaker describes their connection: "We were children from another planet. We were girls from an undiscovered country. We were alien beings in families that were "different." Different among the different" (88). They are different because they fall in love and then are discovered by their parents and separated. The speaker looking back at this childhood and her relationship with Sandra, the Russian immigrant, connects what could have been between them with the gourds. She therefore connects the simple and profound act of Native women continuing life with two women's love for each other. The Native female speaker describes her imagined relationship with Sandra:

> We have a basket filled with gourds. Our basket is woven from sweetgrass, and the scent stirs up the air and lights on our skin.... Desire shapes us. Desire to touch with our hands, our eyes, our mouths, our minds. I bend over you, kissing the hollow of your throat, your pulse leaping under my lips. We touch. Dancers wearing shells of turtles, feathers of eagles, bones of our people. We touch. (90)

Brant here clearly connects this lesbian desire with the continuity of Native American life and tradition thereby creating a new space where both culture and lesbianism survive and nurture each other. Lesbian sexuality is directly connected to the survival of her people both physically and spiritually. The love between women is connected to all of the things that the gourds represent: family cohesion and survival. Within this framework, then, lesbian desire is a kind of talisman to keep culture alive, though Brant reinterprets this talisman's power to necessitate the existence and understanding of lesbianism as central to everyone's progression.

Another revision of Native culture is Brant's story entitled "Coyote Learns a New Trick." The coyote figure is generally seen as a trickster within Native American Literature and Brant gives this figure a particular twist within her story. Coyote here is a mother who decides to go out in drag to play a joke on everyone. She dresses as a human male, as opposed to a male coyote, and believes that she is convincing in her performance. She is encouraged in the "truth" of her appearance when she runs across the very feminine Fox whom she thinks she can fool easily. It is obvious that Fox sees through Coyote's disguise yet she plays along flirting with Coyote. Coyote ultimately propositions Fox planning to reveal her joke at the best moment.

Brant writes:

> Lying on Fox's pallet, having her body next to hers, Coyote thought maybe she'd wait a bit before playing the trick. Besides, it was fun to be rolling around with a red-haired female. And man oh man, she really could kiss. That tongue of hers sure knows a trick or two. And boy oh boy, that sure feels good, her paw on my back, rubbing and petting. And wow, I never knew foxes could do such things, moving her legs like that, pulling me down on top of her like that. And she makes such pretty noises, moaning like that. And her paw feels real

good, unzipping my pants. And oh oh, she's going to find out the trick and then what'll I do? (34)

Fox, sensing Coyote's uneasiness at being discovered soon says "Coyote! Why don't you take that ridiculous stuffing out of your pants ... And let me untie that binder so we can get down to *serious* business" (34–5). Brant then continues to conclude the tale: "So Coyote took off her clothes, laid on top of Fox, her leg moving between Fox's open limbs. She panted and moved and panted some more and told herself that foxes were clever after all" (34–5). Brant here has a wonderful time having a Coyote story that shows the existence of lesbian desire and sex within a Native American tradition and as a natural part of life.

Another example of this cultural revision occurs within the work of Audre Lorde. Much of Lorde's life was spent speaking about the realities of the lives of Black lesbians and how their lives relate to the Black community as a whole. Nowhere is this more apparent than in her "biomythography" *Zami: A New Spelling of My Name* where she writes about the process of coming out as a Black lesbian and more importantly learning to live with this identity.[77] Because of all the societies that Lorde exists in and passes through, she has a heightened sense of the performative aspects of not only roles within the straight world, but racial identities, and roles within lesbian circles as well. Because she exists in so many communities where some part of her identity must be hidden she has a heightened awareness of her own performances and so sees them within the constructed communities she interacts with. She sees the performative within butch and femme lesbian circles, as well as within straight circles between husbands and wives, and also within race relations. She ultimately derives a new idea of identity that makes sense of her multiplicitous experience of self. She writes:

> In a paradoxical sense, once I accepted my position as different from the larger society as well as from any single sub-society—Black or gay—I felt I didn't have to try so hard. To be accepted. To look femme. To be straight. To look straight. To be proper. To look "nice." To be liked. To be loved. To be approved. What I didn't realize was how much harder I had to try merely to stay alive, or rather, to stay human (181)

This description of the refusal to submit to an identity that is sectioned and categorized is similar to that of Anzaldúa's la mestiza and Lorde clearly does not see it as utopian but rather as strategic and necessary for survival. Clearly there are differences between the two women's view of categories and survival tactics; however, I am interested here in how they resonate with one another. Lorde is obviously rewriting identity here to accommodate her own experiences within her social contexts.

It is within Lorde's story of her relationship with Kitty, which is short for Afrekete, that her rewriting of her community's tradition occurs. Afrekete is a goddess that Lorde continually referred to throughout her writing and it is fitting that is through a woman with this name that Lorde would connect her lesbianism and her heritage.[78] Lorde describes their lovemaking's connection to a plethora of exotic fruits that the women must buy from the West Indian markets. It becomes a ritual to them to buy the fruit, bring it home, and then incorporate it into their lovemaking. It's an interesting connection between Afrekete and the fruit: the fruit from Lorde's mother's homeland is a bridge to the love of a specific woman (named Kitty) and all women (the goddess). She describes the phrase "I got this [the fruit] under the bridge" as symbolic of a connection between home and lesbian love. Lorde states about this phrase that it was "an adequate explanation that whatever it was had come from as far back and as close to home—that is to say, as authentic—as was possible" (249). It is after Lorde describes this relationship that she ends her book with a tribute to all the women in her life and her connection with her mother's heritage; she intentionally connects these two things as being interdependent. This desire to build bridges between females is reminiscent of Adrienne Rich; however, I don't think that Lorde is claiming all of these women as lesbians but rather that she is toppling a male-centered tradition of genealogies by listing all of the influential women in her life.

Lorde then incorporates herself into the family, by toppling any sense of the mother being responsible for her "perversion" by the way she was raised, and rather celebrating her lesbianism as a family inheritance—a treasure. As Barbara Christian claims "Society has tended to blame the mother for the daughter's lesbianism. Lorde sees her mother as her starting point, but she turns the analysis on its head" (199). Indeed, one critic claims that "In her lovemaking with Kitty, Lorde comes full circle; by reclaiming her mythological roots, she reconnects with her matrilineal heritage" (Keating 26). Lorde ends the book with: "Once *home* was a long way off, a place I had never been to but knew out of my mother's mouth. I only discovered its latitudes when Carriacou was no longer my home. There it is said that the desire to lie with other women is a drive from the mother's blood" (256).

AnaLouise Keating describes the importance of Lorde's revisions in terms of women's relationship to patriarchy. She sees the importance of *Zami* as a testament to the "power words give women to redefine themselves and their world" (20) in adding to the work done on women's use of language. She focuses on Lorde's use of Afrekete as a replacement of Judeo-Christian myth in order to validate her female experiences. She also sees Lorde's claiming a Black African goddess as the representation of female spirituality as an important expansion on the work done by Mary Daly and Carol Christ for example. The final element of importance to Keating is the connection of Afrekete to Lorde as poet, trickster, and communicator. Keating believes that with this claiming Lorde "affirms her identity as a Black woman warrior poet" (28). The final affirmation then is Lorde's taking over of Afrekete's identity and "renam[ing] herself and becom[ing] the Black goddess" (29). She ultimately then sees Lorde as making bridges to all of womankind through her revisionism:

> Recognizing the sacredness of her own female power, Lorde defines herself and all women—physically, emotionally, and spiritually—as divine Her revisionist mythmaking offers women of all races an image of ancient female wisdom and strength which empowers them to put their differences into words and create networks connecting them to other women. (31)

While arguably all of these are important consequences to Lorde's revisionism, Keating underestimates the power of Lorde's making Afrekete a flesh and blood lover. This is a relationship that is connected to her community and is accepted by the family. Lorde describes that after she and Kitty would come down off of the roof where they had made love they would come "into the sweltering midnight of a west Harlem summer" that was filled with children and "mothers and fathers" (252–3). She laments that Harlem is not Winneba or Annamabu and yet has consolation in that "It was onto 113th Street that we descended after our meeting with the Midsummer Eve's Moon, but the mothers and fathers smiled at us greeting as we strolled down to

Eighth Avenue, hand in hand" (253). This "family" accepts the women as Black lesbians within their community as just another element of the summer evening along with their irritable children, insomnia, the heat, and their jobs. So, this goddess not only does all of the things that Keating describes but also allows Lorde an entrance into her community as a Black lesbian.

As Jewelle Gomez writes:

> Zami takes place in the bosom of the Black community which Black Lesbians recognize as the place of their beginnings. It reveals how Black Lesbians can and do maintain a connection to their culture and families in order to survive. Even when the connection is more spiritual than physical, it is a key part of the sub-text. (119)

Lorde then rewrites her community's traditions in order to successfully perform her Black lesbian identity, because simple performance is not transformative for her. Lorde makes it clear that performance within a clearly understood context can be.

Ann Allen Shockley's novel *Say Jesus and Come to Me* also contains a Black lesbian's process of accepting her own identity and ultimately rewriting her community's religious tradition in order to survive as a minister. Shockley then directly confronts a cultural limitation for lesbians within the African-American community: the church. Throughout her novel the main character Myrtle, a lesbian minister, has been hiding her lesbian identity in order to keep her place within the church and remain respected within the community, as discussed in previous chapters. She has realized that this separation is killing her, is draining the life force from her. Within her mind she actively connects her lesbian desire with God's love, and even seduces members of the church during sermons, but she fears describing herself as a lesbian within the confines of her social contexts.

However, when she falls in love with Travis and wishes to live as an out lesbian she finally decides to connect her ministry with her lesbian self. She tells Travis that "When you leave, I am going to deliver the most important sermon of my life" (277) in which she is going to reveal her lesbian identity. She uses scripture to support an acceptance of homosexuality as natural and as equally loved by God. Shockley illustrates that in order for Myrtle to pave the way for Black lesbian existence within her community she must reinterpret and rewrite Judeo-Christian tenets. Only then can she challenge the nature of sexuality and gender in order for her to successfully endure as a part of her community. She announces that:

> "I am one of those people who imprisoned herself. I *locked* my tongue in silence and carried the weight within my heart. But this morning, I decided to *free-e* myself before you. *To walk in the light!* For in freeing myself, I hope to give courage to others like me to be free-e-e *themselves*, too!"
>
> Descending slowly down from the pulpit, Myrtle held herself erect before her congregation. *"Look at me,"* she beseeched. "I am of the same flesh and blood as *you* I am still the same minister who gave you spiritual guidance and solace in the past. I have been your leader in the church, as well as the streets. Standing here before you declaring unashamedly who and what I am—a lesbian—I feel cleansed, washed in the blood of the lamb, baptized anew in the sight of our wonderful savior, Jesus Christ—and *you!* (281)

She asks her congregation to accept her and they do, which shows that by weaving herself into the traditions and beliefs of her culture, instead of completely stepping outside of them, she gains acceptance as a Black lesbian.

It is after this successful presentation of her new self that she and Travis can go "home" together. Myrtle has then successfully negotiated the limits of the black church by rewriting the lesbian's importance within it; she says that because "gays are the most rejected by the church" (281) she indicts it as in conflict with God. The home that this black lesbian couple can go to then is within the church. By rewriting their "home" culture these Black lesbians can be accepted as such. If they were to subvert the limits to their identities by attempting to perform a racial identity other than blackness, and therefore transcend the Black community's boundaries, they could exist only in performance and not in reality. By actually rewriting their own culture, they transform that which limits them thereby changing reality so they can exist as they chose within their own community.

I suggest here that all of these women are metaphoric/cultural mestizas. They occupy a space of paradox, of embodying the impossible and thus making the existence of the lesbian of color possible. Anzaldúa develops her vision of mestiza consciousness in a way that is relevant to many more lesbians of color in her essay

The Path to Survival

"Bridge, Drawbridge, Sandbar or Island: Lesbians-of-Color Hacienda Alianzas." She states that:

> Being a mestiza queer person, una de las otras ("one of the others") is having and living in a lot of worlds, some of which overlap. One is immersed in all the worlds at the same time while also traversing from one to the other. The mestiza queer is mobile, constantly on the move, a traveler, *callejera*, a *cortacalles*. Moving at the blink of an eye, from one space, one world to another, each world with its own peculiar and distinct inhabitants, not comfortable in anyone of them, none of them "home," yet none of them "not home" either. (217–8)

The women with whom I have dealt within this project clearly suffer from this "alienness" and "homelessness" and therefore the new mestiza consciousness is at work within different people and different communities.

With this kind of generalized language Anzaldúa, I believe, is opening up the possibility for the existence of metaphoric mestizas (while still keeping the cultural specificity of the term intact and important). In an interview Paula Gunn Allen describes this same kind of mestiza experience of being fragmented and under attack. She claims that to survive one "ha[s] to incorporate [all the parts of oneself]. I think that's where you get into alienation, thinking that you cannot have the whole bulk, that you *have* to choose" (103). She further finds that this externally constructed necessity to choose is in fact a weapon in the continuing colonization process. Clearly this idea of incorporating the paradoxical within one's subjectivity is central to the enduring survival of lesbians of color.

The authors that I have focused on in this chapter have been able to overcome the separation brought about through external construction, by retaining the parts and rewriting its contents. This success comes in a number of ways depending on the individual context. For example, in some cases they rewrite traditional stories, or redefine religious tenets; they refocus traditions within the community's self construction to reaffirm their place within it. Some authors create lesbian subjects who perform lesbian identity as a connection between those "outside" and those "inside" to destabilize these separations. They anticipate dissent and recontextualize it in order to shine the light on the traditional places of lesbians within their own cultures (as healers, goddesses, etc.).

Ultimately they rework the very limits that have been built within their own communities in order to create a space to survive as simultaneously sexually and racially defined subjects.

As is clear from the previous discussion within this chapter there are only a few texts that illustrate a successful revisioning process. Consequently, in order to illuminate these successful instances and to make them most useful, I advocate what Anzaldúa refers to as "a symbolic behavior performance made concrete by involving body and emotions with political theories and strategies, rituals that will connect the conscious and the unconscious" ("Bridge" 229). She makes this statement to show how lesbians of different colors can build alliances between their communities, but it definitely is a poignant and relevant prescription to describe a theory of lesbian identity that has as yet been missing. I believe Anzaldúa's desire to include "ritual" as well as the unconscious is similar to Butler's focus on the use of repetition. In other words, both critics are advocating individually deployed behavioral strategies. I believe one major difference between them is that while Butler sees this repetition as an external phenomena, as if one walks onto a stage, performs, and can walk off again unharmed, Anzaldúa insists on a change in one's internal psychology.

Anzaldúa constantly refers to states of being, perspectives on life, but she does not discuss how exactly one might uses these states and perspectives as strategies for survival. I suggest here that this consciousness needs to be focused into a strategy, or strategies, of survival that can be deployed by individual agents in order to negotiate their identities.

This need is perhaps best exemplified within moments in *Zami* wherein Audre Lorde discusses her experiences of feeling a fluid racial identity (something difficult to obtain in America as a dark-skinned Black) but is not to mobilize its power. When she lived in Mexico, as racial consciousness was very different, people did not see her as black but as Cuban—in other words, definitely one of "them" (Latina) but still unique.[79] In a different cultural context her dark skin signified a self she had not expected. She also describes such a moment of confusion when she goes back to the United States. She says good-bye to two men she had befriended at a diner: Sol, an older Jewish man, and Jimmy, a working class Puerto Rican man. When she explains that she is leaving the neighborhood to work elsewhere because she has received a fellowship for Negro students Sol exclaims "Oh? I didn't know you was cullud!" (183) Lorde goes on to say that:

> I went around telling that story for a while, although a lot of my friends couldn't see why I thought it was funny. But this is all about how very difficult it is at times for people to see who or what they are looking at, particularly when they don't want to. Or maybe it does take one to know one (183).

With these moments Lorde questions the stability of racial categories by showing her (apparently) static self as interpreted differently in different cultural contexts. She ultimately sees racial identity as culturally determined.

Lorde here also sees the humor in the moment of confusion but is also temporarily mourning the loss of a stable racial self, as she cannot clearly signify what she wants to whom she wants. On the other hand, while in Mexico she describes being in a sea of brown faces and "being noticed, and accepted without being known" (154) as an occasion for opportunity, freedom, and boldness. She feels she has greater access to the "real" Mexico. Obviously her own attitude towards the slipperiness of racial identity is dependent upon the effect it has on others. She does not, however, attempt to engage in making herself "slippery" intentionally. Again, like Anzaldúa, she describes a mode of being, a state of self, but not how to use it strategically.

These examples are illustrative of the first steps towards using a theory as a strategy in the hostile atmosphere that the lesbian of color finds herself in. However, in order for her to endure within her community she must intentionally put the theory into practice in order to affect more lasting change.

The task then is to do just that. It calls for *performing* the paradox, the slipperiness that has recurred among these women's narratives—"performing la mestiza." In order to escape the limitations, and best utilize the dynamic nature of identity, one can subversively perform racial and sexual identities through cultural positioning. If one attempts this without the knowledge of history or cultural tradition, one is simply parodying stereotypes in public and returning to life as usual afterwards. This does not have any lasting subversive potential and can actually reinforce the safety that whites find in these performances. Because the lesbian of color has a tenuous place within her own community, she can knock the traditions on their heels—the Coyote can be rewritten to serve her own purposes and illuminate not only lesbian desire but Native tradition as well. I believe that by pointing out the paradoxes while continuing to embody them is what has the potential to change the recognized site of cultural power as existing within traditions and identities that are "stable" and "natural."

A consideration of Michel Foucault's study *The History of Sexuality* is helpful to illuminate the cultural power that resides in the interpretations of performed selves. Foucault states that:

> Indeed, it is in discourse that power and knowledge are joined together. And for this very reason, we must conceive discourse as a series of discontinuous segments whose tactical function is neither uniform nor stable. To be more precise, we must not imagine a world of discourse divided between accepted discourse and excluded discourse, or between the dominant discourse and the dominated one; but as a multiplicity of discursive elements that can come into play in various strategies. (100)

By analyzing the interpretations, offered by the dominant society, of all the differing categories that make up the self, one can see its agenda. In other words, it is easy to question who stands to benefit from the notion that, for example, certain sexualities are "natural" while others are "perverse." It is the heterosexual agenda, the "Straight Mind" in Monique Wittig's words, that must prove to itself that it is the first, the truth, the right way to be. Because heterosexuals fear the instability of identity that comes with an acceptance of the homosexual, they label the homosexual as a threat to their power and sanctity; really it is the heterosexual who wields the power of interpretation over sexuality and gender identity. The homosexual is not the threat to the "natural;" it is the heterosexual who both denies and wields this same power of determining naturalness. In other words, power and resistance are intertwined and the critique of the power of homosexuality really demonstrates what Foucault terms "a more devious and discreet form of power" (11) within heterosexuality. And this power is that heterosexuality is situated as that which is under attack, that which must resist external threat in order to remain "pure." In actuality, heterosexual-centered theory resists a recognition of the diverse subjectivity that queer theory illuminates. This sometimes heated dialogue depends on the status quo to keep these discourses in oppositional stances. As Diana Fuss and Judith Butler argue, there has to be a closet to be an "outside." (Fuss Introduction 1–8; Butler

The Path to Survival

"Imitation" 15-18) Real resistance then requires a realization of this amalgamation.

This connection between power and resistance is true of all identity categories, not just sexuality. For example, the external agenda that Lorde describes in *Zami*, from the examples above, dictates what her blackness means—the politics become central to racial identity as well as sexual identity. La mestiza brings into focus the fact that racial/ethnic categories are not naturally occurring but rather are imposed from both within and without various communities. This kind of conscious performing of identity also calls for an attention to its culturally imposed limitations as well. Instead of assuming that this is possible for all women at all times, it calls for the "sandbar" mentality that Anzaldúa describes. The person who functions as a sandbar, instead of a bridge for example, constantly shifts from touching both sides of paradox, to disengaging all together, to touching one and not the other (224).

Therefore, the subversive performance of la mestiza is one strategy that lesbians of color can use to negotiate the varying identities that are forced upon them. This performance isn't a slippery evasion of all culturally imposed limitations on identity, or an escape from one's heritage and "home" community, but rather a manipulation of these external contexts that revises past interpretations and, indeed, reclaims the past.

However, let me reiterate that it also sheds light on all identity constructions and identity-based studies. This is not just a case of "adding" minorities to present identity theory, which has been the predominate gesture thus far and has left these theories unchanged. Instead this theory forces a recognition of the politics of white identity theory and the limitations that exist for its subjects as well. In other words, with a recognition of the value of incorporating ethnic/racial identities into any theoretical discussion comes a new view of all theoretically gendered sexual subjects.

Conclusion

The first aim of this book has been to avoid merely "adding on" minorities to a theory that positions itself as universal because this practice works against understanding how the "major" and the "minor" are interrelated and affected. Rather, a consideration of these texts shows the limitations within the construction of the identity of any subject regardless of minority status. It also shows the limits of identity categories (and the theories based upon them) that focus on "one" state of being implying that individual identities can exist, and be discussed, in a vacuum. This project has intended to do what Yvonne Yarbro-Bejarano calls expanding the categories of "race" and "sexuality" (124–35) in order to account for lesbians of color and to also change the way we, as academics, view identity-based studies.

As I have already posited and as Yarbro-Bejarano asserts:

> The rigid separation of these [identity] categories reveals that people generally resist acknowledging that they experience racial and cultural identity inseparably from gender and sexual constructions of the self. The emphasis on gender alone or sexual identity alone reaffirms white dominance just as the exclusive emphasis on race and culture reaffirms male and heterosexual dominance. ("Expanding" 127)

She calls for a recognition of these facts in order to rework the goals of Lesbian and Gay Studies. I found that the work of lesbians of color strongly illustrates this need as well because their existence and identity construction have generally not been considered within current theoretical parameters. Also important is the certainty that not only are these identity categories interrelated but genre categories are interrelated as well. Women of color, and others, have been mixing genre conventions for quite some time in order to articulate their ideas, generally leading to a dismissal of the work because of its inability to be categorized. The rethinking of categories, then, must also extend to an expansion of the understanding and acceptance of genre as well in order to see lesbians of color as agents within this discussion. Again Yarbro-Bejarano advocates that:

> a consideration of the cultural construction of white sexuality would enrich analyses of the representation of desire and contribute to the destabilization of the separate categories of race and sexuality. In this regard, we must emphasize the contribution of lesbians of color to this theoretical project of categorical expansion . . . because lesbians of color have provided a significant piece of the theoretical groundwork that could and should serve as the foundation of lesbian and gay studies. ("Expanding" 130)

Of course as Yarbro-Bejarano suggests, and I state directly, these women's ideas don't just apply to lesbian and gay studies, but to all identity categories because they disrupt easy dualisms and tidy categories of self.

I have intended not just to "read" some primary texts, by or about lesbians of color, "through" a theoretical framework, but to enlist these texts in a creation of a theoretical framework. They have not been considered here as solely existing within the creative realm but also as legitimate and important theoretical constructions. I feel that these texts demand the application of a special sort of methodology, one that forces the critic to interact with them in a way that causes her to be "read" by its theory just as she reads it with hers. This forces the critic to foreground cultural materiality and perhaps conceive of what Anzaldúa and Moraga call a "theory in the flesh" (*This Bridge* 23).

So even though most of the lesbians of color I've considered exist within *textual* societies and not the sort of society and history that Kath Weston speaks of when she sees performance theory neglecting "particular historical and material contexts" (17), the particular contexts do affect and limit their subject's performances. These texts illustrate that because their specific textual societies cannot accommodate the kind of subversion that Butler describes, those who attempt to perform

Conclusion

different roles freely must be erased because they attack all the power structures held in place by the performance of prescribed roles.

There is no doubt that this is a limit of agency. The societal discourses that limit gender identity necessarily want to squelch subversion and therefore erase all troublemakers. This constant threat to one's existence does make theory difficult to translate into reality: be it textual or material. This is shown well in the example of bell hooks's discussion of *Paris is Burning* as well as many of the texts that I've discussed throughout. Clearly there has been blood all through these pages; blood that performance theory does not account for. All these texts reflect how those forced into certain performances that violate their sense of identity by a culture that only values what they can approximate are often killed for showing that all identity is imitation. Indeed, Gloria Anzaldúa describes a psychic trauma when she provocatively states that "After years of wearing masks we may become just a series of roles, the constellated self limping along with its broken limbs" ("Haciendo" xv).

Clearly the lack of focus on these devastating losses that lesbians of color can suffer by attempting to cause "trouble," reflects how minimally historical, cultural, and social contexts are seen to affect individuals. After critiquing and dismissing this approach, however, I agree with Yarbro-Bejarano's call for literary critics to study whiteness as constructed through these same contexts ("Expanding" 130). Undoubtedly there are markers of privilege within this society and these markers still come with significant expectations and limitations of their own. It is important to see whiteness in this way: as a marker of race and of privilege simultaneously. This combination is obviously different from a consideration of "color" as race because color *is* linked to oppression as opposed to privilege.

As I showed earlier, within Gould's novel *A Sea-Change*, even Jessie, who lived in the "high culture" world of beautiful, white, educated, wealthy people, the gender "transgressor" is erased and transformed into something monstrous in order to have gender power: all possibility of a positive lesbian existence is denied and destroyed.

This text definitely questions the view that even white subjects have free-floating signification. Indeed, and this is my point here, this myth is only possible when whiteness is ignored as a social construction. This questioning of varying lesbian identities does not mean, of course, that there are no differences between white lesbians and lesbians of color and that one can conflate lesbian identity into one, static entity.[80] Clearly this entire project has argued that there are differences between and among these women and an exploration of these differences is crucial for many reasons.

Not only does this project call for further studies of whiteness as a construction, but it also suggests that because lesbians of color undermine the usefulness of present ethnic studies (that use "strategic essentialism" and do not include whiteness) that a further dialogue amongst the critics who position themselves from the theoretical perspectives of essentialism, constructionism, and authenticity is needed so that political power can remain possible. Again, I have argued that some lesbians of color have been able to succeed within this dialogue but have given up some political power because of the external definitions of their work. I do believe, though, that it is crucial for lesbians of color to remain actively engaged in the battle by both writing and thinking in their own ways and by mobilizing politically important language in order to transform the academy and society.[81]

Because performing identities hinges on both essentialism and constructionism, as I have suggested, the whole concept of authenticity (which is so central to people of color and gays and lesbians, etc. within the academy) is placed in question. This paradox exists because performance focuses on *constructing* a self, whereas attempting to "identify" with a culturally and/or biologically formed community implies an acceptance of the (to varying degrees) essential nature of that community. In order to exist successfully, lesbians of color must negotiate this, and other, paradoxes. Authenticity has been used to validate the experiences and the voices of people of color, and, indeed, whole canons and fields of study have been developed through it. But clearly it is challenged if identity is performable to any extent; it seems, then, that it could not simultaneously be essential. However, because I suggest that lesbians of color must perform *within* their "home" communities, an element of essential identity remains in their performances. At the same time, individual elements of authenticity are questioned and at times discarded. Thus, these lesbians illustrate the connection between essentialism and constructionism and both undermine and manipulate the markers of authenticity.[82] In my view this figure, better than any other, represents the paradox of constructing an identity by performing it, and so brings the debate of polarizing essentialism and constructionism to a head. Anzaldúa clearly

Conclusion

recognizes that limitations within the "counterstance" approach when she states that

> Because the counterstance stems from a problem with authority—outer as well as inner—it's a step towards liberation from cultural domination. But it is not a way of life At some point, on our way to a new consciousness, we will have to leave the opposite bank (*Borderlands* 78).

Of key importance to me here is how she describes the political usefulness of the counterstance, but that for people of color it is ultimately limited because it locks us into a "duel of oppressor and oppressed" (*Borderlands* 78) never to *transform* but simply to be categorized.[83]

Also Kath Weston speaks about the importance of essentialism and constructionism as related to lesbians of color. First, she describes the experience related to her by a Black lesbian at Prom Nite. Weston states that "every time [the Black lesbian] asked a white woman to dance, she might be choosing a partner who would type her as butch simply because she was black. Presentations are negotiated not only in the act but also in contexts that shape interpretation" (16). Essentialism is clearly questioned within this interaction as Weston implies a difficulty in determining whose definition of the Black lesbian is "true." Also of interest are the dynamics between what contexts are being deployed or negotiated within this moment. Weston also describes a constructionist view of racial/ethnic identity which is related to performance as she discusses the possibilities within a hypothetical lesbian's wardrobe. She states that:

> the commodification of clothing and accessories in the United States yields artifacts that are not only gendered but also infused with nuances of race, age, and class. If not every lesbian is prepared to become a biker, voguer, *chola*, prom queen, or video vamp, she can at least assume the trappings. (12)

Weston does not describe to what degree one might "become" these people. For example, could a white woman "be" a chola as easily as a Mexican woman?

The other "trappings" that must be included are visible racial and ethnic markers. To go back to previously stated examples, within *Zami*

Audre Lorde can move easier in Mexico where her brown skin was interpreted differently when she was in the majority versus when she was a minority in the United States. On the other end of the spectrum, Cherríe Moraga had the ability to reject privileges available to her because of her fair skin. Her experience with her Chicana identity was choosing to be identified as a Chicana rather than being immediately recognized as such. There is a world of difference within these examples that also should be considered when one considers the limits of performance within this context.

Weston again implies the other danger in seeing race and ethnicity as something to be "worn" by anyone. Yes, anyone can dress in the cultural markers of a certain race or ethnic group but to do so is to be caught up within an entire web of cultures and histories. She warns that:

> anyone may be able to adopt a prefabricated version of *chola* femme or bulldagger butch, but the act itself will implicate you in a legacy of race relations whose violence depends upon this ability to recreate and then appropriate the "Other." (17)

This relates most vividly to white lesbians but is appropriately used in relation to any person outside of the specific group. I am not, however, endorsing a view of lesbians of color as the quintessential (tres)passers of outside communities because my point is not how they might best deceive but how they can transform their own "home" communities through performance.

The lesbian of color can create her own identity through the very performance of herself within her own community. She negotiates both essentialism and constructionism within this performance; each is always playing against the other. She is never completely static and so can never be easily categorized and limited and judged by the criteria of authenticity. This allows her the most freedom possible to construct an identity within an already defined space. She performs the metaphor of *la mestiza* as a way to claim an ethnic identity while not being entangled within all of the limitations that such a claim engenders.

Anzaldúa's description of mask building is also useful in order to illuminate this kind of identity construction. She states that:

> we . . . strip off the *máscaras* others have imposed on us, see through the disguises we hide behind and drop our *personas* so that we may

> become subjects in our own discourses. We rip out the stitches . . . and remake anew both inner and outer faces. . . . We begin to acquire the agency of making our own *caras*. "Making faces" is my metaphor for constructing one's identity. ("Haciendo" xvi)

However, instead of seeing all masks as negative and externally imposed I believe that playing with these constructed masks, toppling them, disturbing their assumed meanings, and accepting and rewriting the traditions that define them as more powerful than stripping them off and uncovering one "truth."

Performing la mestiza is claiming a performative identity: racial/ethnic, female, lesbian, and so on. Even though most of the textual representations that I have discussed are not of "true" mestizas, in the biological sense, they all exhibit the kind of mestiza consciousness that Anzaldúa describes. They all can be seen as metaphoric mestizas (or culturally originated); however, my point here is not to *insist* on the complete domination of this metaphor on all lesbians of color. It also does not mean that the culture and history behind the definition of la mestiza should be ignored, rather, it means that, following Anzaldúa's lead, a recognition of the consciousness that la mestiza so aptly embodies, exists in other places and in other states. The important framework that the mestiza provides is a way to combine all the contradictory elements that threaten to limit the lesbian of color in order for her to exist as a whole individual in the way that she chooses. These choices are not monolithic but ever changing. They must change if the lesbian of color is to survive because her external environments constantly change. Therefore, I find that this metaphor is a useful one both to describe lesbians of color and to articulate how they construct their identities. I do not find this paradigm necessarily utopian; yes, it can be appropriated by white feminists, for example, to dismiss themselves of their own privilege so that all women can join in mythological unity. Yet, Anzaldúa does not include this kind of falseness within her concept of mestiza consciousness; the difficulty of truly accepting her theory comes with its brutal honesty. She calls one to accept oneself, for example, as victim *and* oppressor at once (the amalgamation which the mestiza embodies). The hard edge of Anzaldúa comes when she describes the future as a place only mestizas will inhabit. Yes, she hopes for "healing" and "peace" and even the end of "rape, of violence, of war" (*Borderlands* 80) But ultimately she believes that "*En unas pocas centurias*, the future will belong to the mestiza" (80). Thus, only the mestiza will survive and perhaps the dominant culture will be "writ[ten] off altogether as a lost cause" (79).

The acceptance and deployment of paradox is the crucial element within a performance of mestiza consciousness. I have outlined the paradoxes, the limitations, that exist for these subjects. I have outlined the theoretical discourses that frame her identity, and have discussed how and why she is primarily absent from them. I have also illustrated the many hostilities that are focused on her at all times from the larger white society, and most importantly from her own culturally specific location. These external frameworks are active forces within her consciousness and cannot simply be ignored. I have discussed some of the strategies these subjects employ in order to negotiate these many hostilities. And finally this consideration of lesbians of color has questioned the elements of identity theory as it presently exists.

This method of configuring identity goes beyond, and yet still includes, essentialism; it also goes beyond, and yet includes, constructionism. As Minnie Bruce Pratt points out:

> The African-American woman eating sushi at the next table may be a woman lovely in her bones, gestures, tone of voice, but this does not mean that her genitals are female. If the handsome Filipino man in the upstairs apartment is straight-appearing, this does not mean his erotic preference is the "opposite sex." The white woman next to you at the doctor's office may have been born male, and have a complex history of hormones and surgery. Or she may have been born female and have a different but equally complex history of hormones and surgery. The person on the subway who you perceive as a white man in a business suit may have been born female, may consider herself a butch lesbian, or may identify himself as a gay man. The *M* and the *F* on the questionnaire are useless. (22)

This list of possibilities and complexities of sex and gender identity could easily be applied to lesbians of color, though as I have argued throughout there are also possibilities and complexities of racial and ethnic identity—perhaps the Filipino woman has a long history of surgeries to "make" her white. I don't agree that the questionnaire that Pratt refers to is totally useless. It is useless in its attempt to solidify a singular identity, but it might *allow* a subject a space to claim identities. The negotiations are endless and yet the choosing does not drain the "truth" out of each identity because it is performed through a web of

Conclusion

cultural specificities that interpret it. The "truth" comes with the individual's motivations and intentions; these choices are not whimsical nor free from consequences. For the lesbian of color they can be life and death decisions; and yet the option to choose gives her the language to negotiate.

Notes

1 See numerous works including *This Bridge Called My Back: Writings by Radical Women of Color,* Barbara Smith's "Racism and Women's Studies" from the volume *All the Women are White, All the Blacks are Men, But Some of Us are Brave,* Lynet Uttal's "Inclusion Without Influence. The Continuing Tokenism of Women of Color", and Chela Sandoval's "Feminism and Racism: A Report on the 1981 National Women's Studies Association Conference."

2. zami is a complex Carribean word denoting a woman-identified woman and/or sexual (or other) women's bonds. Elwin states " Women made zami or your zami was your closest friend. Whether the word was used as a noun or a verb, it was understood that a zami was intimate with other women or with another woman." (10) See also Audre Lorde's biomythography *Zami: A New Spelling of My Name.*

3. See for example the introduction and numerous pieces within *This Bridge Called My Back: Writings by Radical Women of Color* for historical perspective.

4. This ignorance of difference can be seen, for example, in the early work of Gilbert and Gubar such as *The Madwoman in the Attic* (1979), in Shosana Felman's "Women and Madness: The Critical Phallacy," (1975) Elaine Showalter's *A Literature of Their Own* (1977), and the French feminists including: Hélène Cixous's "The Laugh of the Medusa," (1975) and Luce Irigaray's "The Sex Which is Not One" (1977). Of course there were political reasons for this inflation of "woman" but also there existed (and exists) an inability to account for the realities of difference. This view of the female self as binary has continued within feminist discourse with many white feminists still using the royal "we" as well as many feminists of color addressing only women of their own groups (implying that only the racial/ethnic element of self is worth foregrounding). This is even reflected in the contents and arrangement

177

of the text *Feminisms* for example. For the most part, the contents are arranged by subjects such as "class" and "ethnicity" and those who speak within these groups are placed only within those subjects. It's only the more established African-American critics who "escape" the ethnicity section. To me, the implication here is that these facets of self can be categorized and so limited. This restricted view of the female self has been detrimental to feminist theory specifically in its inability to meaningfully account for difference.

5. I don't intend to posit that there is only one "lesbian of color" by my use of this language. However, at the same time I do believe there are connections, in how they are viewed and constructed, among all the women who can be described this way. Therefore in order to account for the specificity of their experiences as well as their commonalities I will vary my use of the singular and the plural noun to hopefully reflect this complexity.

6. Clearly any conception of certain identities as primary or secondary is flawed. But when one deals with white subjects it seems easier to employ because of the perceived neutrality of whiteness. Therefore, when one deals with white lesbians it appears that one can focus on lesbianism in a vacuum apart from other signifiers.

7. I am being reductivist here because of course it is difficult to label one group of ideas as equating to "feminist theory"; however, I am referring to the group of ideas that is generally seen to equate to these theories. To outline all of the currents and complexities here is beyond the scope of this project.

8. I wish to make clear that I use racial/ethnic and "of color" interchangably to describe the lesbian subject because they are generally seen as synonymous. However, I am very aware of the possibility of the assumption that I'm implying whiteness is not a race. I do believe it is; however, for simplicity's sake I have used the categories as they are generally understood. The study of whiteness, though, is beyond the scope of this project.

9. Throughout this book I will make a distinction between "role-play" and "performance" where role-play is non-transformative gender play and the performance of gender, in Butlerian terms, as potentially transformative.

10. It becomes difficult to determine what type of texts are appropriate for this discussion. It is easy to be confused by the problem that I discussed above about attempting to find, or create, an "authentic" subject to explore within an "appropriate" text. I study both texts written by "out" lesbians of color that include lesbians of color as characters, non fiction written by "out" lesbians, and texts written by women of color (who are straight or who don't identify themselves as lesbians) in which there are lesbians of color as characters. Therefore, I do explore this subject position represented through authors, characters, and literary devices I focus on the elements within each text that are

relevant and identify when the author is discussing a construction within a work of fiction or poetry and when the author is discussing her own self construction, or when I'm concerned with a character's life. I find the blending of elements here relevant to this project because it shows how these subjects must negotiate even genre to articulate themselves. For simplicity's sake though I do refer to the gamut of perspectives (author, narrator, character) in one breath even though I'm aware of the major differences among them. Each text is discussed independently and it is within these discussions that the individual perspective is made clear and relevant.

11. I am defining this articulation of self as the moment when the female subject considers herself to be a lesbian of color and can behave and exists as she chooses. This is directly opposed to her not being aware of the possibility of defining herself as a lesbian or to not being tolerated as she defines herself in the communities she inhabits.

12. Clearly there have been other articulations of a multiple self within history. For example W.E.B. Dubois articulated in 1903 that Blacks have a strange experience of "double-consciousness, this sense of always looking at one's self through the eyes of others, of measuring one's soul by the tape of a world that looks on in amused contempt and pity. One ever feels his twoness,—an American, a Negro; two souls, two thoughts, two unreconciled strivings; two warring ideals in one dark body, whose dogged strength alone keeps him from being torn asunder" (29). There have been other models such as King-Kok Cheung's "hybrid," Chela Sandoval's "oppositional consciousness," and María Lugones's "world traveling" to name just a few. I do not mean to imply that Anzaldúa is the one and only voice in this arena. But I do find hers most useful because she discusses the multiplicities of identity within many different contexts including: language, history, mythology, gender, etc. She also simultaneously focuses on the specificity of actual mestizas and the metaphor of la mestiza.

13. I consider a queer critic to be an academic critic who is interested in exploring queer theory. I personally consider the adjective queer to identify a more outspoken and politically strategic stance in both theory and literature, as well as activism, and this is how I use it here. I also use this description as applying to an individual, within the academy, who is not necessarily defined by sexuality but to any critic who is willing to be defined by the parameters of queer theory, who advocates and employs its political goals, and who is aware of and attentive to its history, ideology, and tradition. I am aware of the problematic nature of this use of language; however, I wish to push the envelope of identity politics here and encourage a new politics within the academy where those who have a privilege to choose to be defined by labels

can peacefully work alongside those who may be defined by their identity. There may never exist a peace but I will risk that in order to open up this debate further. This personal ideology also extends to other identity theories such as feminist and racial/ethnic.

14. See Cherríe Moraga's "La Guera" within her *Loving in the War Years* for a more in depth discussion of the politics of skin color within a hispanic community.

15. This position can be read as a misuse of the privilege of movement by those who do not have it and even though I'm aware of this possibility, I think that the need to challenge categories is more important.

16. See for example numerous works by bell hooks including *Feminist Theory: From Margin to Center* (1984) and *Talking Back: Thinking Feminist/Thinking Black* (1989), Paula Gunn Allen's *The Sacred Hoop: Recovering the Feminine in Native American Traditions* (1986), Barbara Christian's *Black Feminist Criticism: The Development of a Tradition* (1985), Chandra Talpade Mohanty's edited volume *Third World Women and the Politics of Feminism* (1991), Audre Lorde's *Sister Outsider* (1984) and many others.

17. I think it of value to note here that Frankenberg's book is very much tied to the academic perspective. She does not pay much attention to the meanings of whiteness outside of the academic environment. Clearly, this creates limitations for her project's usefulness.

18. Further, this seems to be the reason the white academy has allowed certain marginalized texts and persons inside the canon only if they remain defined by how unlike the white canon and academy they are If these writers/theorists remain satisfied with a long set of descriptors "Black, gay, feminist, Chicana," etc. and do not claim to be writing "theory" or "literature" (meaning white theory or literature) then they will survive within those boundaries. Until we decide that African American theory belongs in a "theory" course/text not just in an African American theory course/text then the constraints of theory based on identity will remain.

19. It is worth noting here that this claim is not unlike many of the claims of critics of ethnic studies who posit that this power of disruption is also a characteristic of their identities. This can definitely be seen as reflective of Fuss's discussion of "outsiderhood" wherein she implies that those who have been "othered" share a similar contextual experience which should be explored.

20. For example, arguably the theories and criticism of Black women are more developed than, for example, those of Native American women. I suggest it is an issue of time: the longer the theories exist the more developed they will become. There are quite a few different theories about Black identity and many

literary studies based on them; the same cannot be said of Native American identity. It seems necessary to any political theory that the first step is to proclaim one's existence, usually meaning articulating an orthodoxical stance on one's identity. This orthodoxy, while strengthening the group politically, weakens and ultimately limits the theory.

21. I don't intend to valorize the African-American community over any other ethnic community by this remark. Clearly all communities of color have suffered oppressions and have spoken out about them and because of them. My only point here is that the timing of this activism in the United States has allowed the words and ideas of African-Americans more time to be discussed and debated within and without the Black community.

22. See for example Baker's discussions of multiculturalism within the MLA Newsletter *Profession*, as well as Gates's discussion of gay Black men in the volume *Fear of a Queer Planet*.

23. I do believe that there are complex factors that account for this fact within the academic community. Clearly it is in reaction to academic political discourses regarding the status of African-American literatures and theories, yet it still exists.

24. *Home Girls: A Black Feminist Anthology* is an obvious exception here as is Barbara Smith's "Toward a Black Feminist Criticism" wherein she reads Sula as a lesbian text

25. Note that many African American critics have discussed the differences within the community between men and women, differences of class and education and differences in skin color and other outside appearances. But generally Black identity is implied as more consistent than any of the other "ethnic" identities. I am basing this generalization on a comparison between anthologies wherein the editors try to account for who is included in their volumes. It is within this microcosm that there is the most direct definition of ethnic and racial identities. See such anthologies as *Narrative Chance: Postmodern Discourse on Native American Indian Literatures*, *The Black Woman: An Anthology*, *Spider Woman's Granddaughters: Traditional Tales and Contemporary Writing by Native American Women*, *Cuentos: Stories by Latinas*, *Breaking Boundaries: Latina Writings and Critical Readings*, *Charlie Chan is Dead: An Anthology of Contemporary Asian American Fiction*, and *Home Girls: A Black Feminist Anthology*.

26. I do not mean to suggest here that all Blacks are always visually distinguishable either, the monkey wrench in the categorical machine is of course the "Black" person with light skin. Also important to note is that not all Black Americans are "free" of ethnicity. Categories become confused when one is dark-skinned but not racially identified as Black, or one is racially Black and

ethnically Latino for example. However, white Americans generally "see" Blacks as more visually distinguishable than other peoples of color and thus they are more frequently assigned the marker of race.

27. Clearly any time more than one Latina feminist writes an essay from a feminist perspective one could argue that a "Latina feminism" is being created. I don't mean to be privy to the moment that a few individual voices "add up" to a movement, but what I am acknowledging as representative of "Latina feminism" would be a history similar to that of Black feminist criticism. It would be a moment where a critic or critics claim the need for it, develop its elements, and are recognized by the larger theoretical community.

28. Another text concerned with Latino/a literature is Cordelia Candelaria's *Chicano Poetry* (1986); however, she is concerned with literary history and not with identity theory. She also clearly sees Chicano writing as inherently tied to its political and cultural beginnings but not as clearly as does Saldívar. Teresa Mckenna's *Migrant Song* (1997) is a recent volume that does not focus on identy, but does again posit the political beginnings of Chicano literature. She does not develop the issue of identity but rather the connection between the Chicano process of creativity and migration. See the Preafce to this volume for additional texts published since the completion of this project.

29. For example, Ana Castillo has been criticized for not being "Chicano" enough because she does not write in protest of white oppression. Many times she writes about the lives of Chicanas and consequently ruffles some feathers within her own community. This situation has existed in other identity marked aesthetics such as the Harlem Renaissance where it is well known that Zora Neale Hurston was dismissed by many male authors for not writing about white oppression. Barbara Christian also points to the tendency of urban blacks being representative of "one way" of being black other writers were criticized "as not being black enough" ("The Race" 341). Clearly this is one danger of having a "list" of characteristics that an "x" identified person must follow in order to be authentically "x."

30. Note that the later *The Big Aiiieeeee!* (1991) sticks to this same definition but only anthologizes Chinese and Japanese Americans.

31. In King-Kok Cheung's Articulate Silences (1993) she is critical of the editors of *Aiiieeeee!* for their attempt to "reclaim" an Asian Heroic tradition and thereby canonize a certain kind of Asian text and subject: "In their attempt to advocate a 'masculine' language, for instance, the editors of *Aiiieeeee!* valorize such novels as Louis Chu's *Eat a Bowl of Tea* and John Okada's *No-No Boy*, both of which are written in vociferous styles" (9). She also critiques these same male editors who also compiled *The Big Aiiieeeee!* in a far more devastating way. She writes "I am especially uneasy about the hard-line

distinction Frank Chin draws .. between the 'fake' and the 'real' Asian American Literature ... In his concern for cultural purity, he ignores one of the most defining characteristics of Asian American Literature and Ethnic American Literature generally: hybridity" (19). Certainly Cheung could be seen as speaking an empowering hybridity very similar to that of the editors of *Cuentos* claiming their mestiza identity.

32. Perhaps the clearest definition is given within the text *Making Waves: An Anthology of Writings by and About Asian American Women* (1989): the editors distinguish between familiar Asians and those who are non familiar. Chinese, Filipina, Japanese, and Korean Americans are grouped in the first category and South Asians in the latter. To define the non familiar they state: "By South Asian women, we mean those whose roots extend to India, Pakistan, Bangladesh, and the other countries in that area. The term Southeast Asian refers to women from the Indochinese Peninsula—Vietnam, Cambodia, Laos— as well as women from Burma and Thailand" (ix-x). Interestingly this discussion takes the common sense approach of including peoples from the continent of Asia; and still there is the very important category of nationality which again apparently differentiates as well as defines the Asian subject.

33. I don't intend to conflate all of Christian's words to apply equally to all women of color, since she herself is an African-American critic and she makes some comments specific to that field, but because she opens this essay to make general statements about many groups I find it appropriate to borrow her useful ideas here.

34. This concept has come up many times and has taken many different forms: from the notion that someone is white washed and therefore inauthentic for behaving in a "non Indian" way to deciding arbitrarily what fraction of Indian blood equals a "real" Indian versus a "fake." In the realm of literature Louise Erdrich, a very popular American Indian author, has been dismissed by some for not being "Indian enough" because of her fraction of blood. It's interesting to consider whether the reason here is the fraction or the fact that she has been accepted by a mainstream readership which could make her easily labeled as white washed or a "sell out."

35. Also at play here is the recurring problem for writers of color of the white academy forcing the one to represent the many. Acceptance by the white community has many positive and negative consequences for the individual author as I have illustrated, for example, with the case of Gates and Baker.

36. There is also some discussion of language within the American Indian tradition.

37. This is not meant as a degradation of Vizneor's volume. Perhaps it is reflective of critics outside the American Indian community who wish to see

"real" discussions of Indianness by Indians and who determine this text to accomplish this.

38. I don't intend here to posit that there is "one" ethnic/racial theory or "one" lesbian theory that account for "two" critical perspectives. Thus, I am using this generalization here for the sake of simplicity.

39. This fact has nothing to do with the validity of the theories but rather that lesbian theory is dominated by more privileged white speakers as compared to racial/ethnic theory. I think, however, that this fact can be used to the benefit of lesbians of color as they might transform the field before it gets completely entangled in many of the problems that white feminism has, which has made it of minimal use to non-white subjects.

40. An interesting note here is that whenever I have discussed this position I have received the most negative remarks from white scholars rather than scholars of color. For example, when I discuss the idea that if an author connects primarily with her American Indian identity then she has every right to claim it, I am met with exasperated gasps proclaiming that chaos would ensue if we could all decide which categories we belong in. I am aware of this problem and find that the confusion and the discomfort that ensue are actually helpful in conceptualizing racial/ethnic identities because it illustrates how strongly we are invested in them.

41. It is of course arguable that this opening allows white people to claim the status of oppression for their own benefit outside of accurate historical contexts. However, I suggest that it is necessary to base these choices on real life experience not whim. This standard, of course, does not always enforce "truth-telling" within all claims but I believe this will always be impossible to ensure and the obsession with "purity" on all levels is one that benefits whiteness not people of color.

42. See for example my quote from the editors of *Aiiieeeee!* from earlier in this chapter.

43. See for example, Frederick Douglass's *Narrative of the Life* and Harriet Jacobs/Linda Brent's *Incidents in the Life of a Slave Girl*.

44. See Henry Louis Gates's "The Blackness of Blackness. A Critique of the Sign and the Signifying Monkey" in his *Black Literature and Literary Theory* for a discussion of his theory of Signifying based on oral tradition.

45. Bogus's essay is a study of the Queen B as a positive figure. She springboards from Judy Grahn's discussion of the historical figure, Queen Boudica, from whom the names Queen Bulldagger or Bulldyker are apparently derived. Bogus takes the label and description of Queen B to be another evolution of this name. Grahn states that "Queen Boudica's name could very well have been a title rather than an individual queen's name: bulldike and

bulldagger may mean bul-slayer-priestess. As high priestess of her people, perhaps the queen performed the ceremonial killing of the bull (who was also the god) on the sacred altar-embankment, or dyke. . . .If Boudica is in fact a title, meaning sacred Bull- or Cow-slayer, or sacred Bull-slaying-altar, she would have been vested with the power of the people transferred through her from the dying bull" (139). In any case, Grahn's main point is that this figure is a powerful one in history.

46. I do find it quite disturbing that Lorde has been used as the token Black/person of color who is "allowed" into otherwise white collections. I believe it is because *Zami* is such a complex and yet clear text that it lends itself to being made to "stand" for difference. For example, in Munt's text *New Lesbian Criticism* there are only two essays that discuss a nonwhite author/text and they both cover *Zami*. This is also true of Wolfe and Penelope's *Sexual Practice, Textual Theory*—*Zami* is the only text by a nonwhite author discussed. However, I do not think that this blindness is cause to dismiss Lorde but rather to question why she has become a token and to read *Zami* in a different way than it has been before.

47. See, for example, Gomez's "A Cultural Legacy Denied and Discovered: Black Lesbians in Fiction by Women."and Shockley's "The Black Lesbian in American Literature: An Overview".

48. SDiane Bogus outlines some of the disagreements regarding Shockley. Shockley was originally not recognized as contributing to lesbian fiction because she herself is not a lesbian Although Shockley's first relevant book was published in 1974, Gloria Wade-Gayles claimed that Black lesbians were not written about from 1946–1976 (18). This statement leads Bogus to deduce that only Black lesbians are accepted as authentic writers of Black lesbian experience: "Some do not even recognize the import of that 'first' published black lesbian portrait drawn by a black woman" (277). She writes that "the belief that only black lesbian feminists can speak the truth about their lives denies the contribution of the nonlesbian Shockley who seemingly lacks the political credentials of a black lesbian writer" (277). Jewelle Gomez believes that Shockley's lesbians lack credibility and authenticity and Bogus counters with the statement that Gomez could not even have discussed these issues before 1974. Ultimately Bogus decides that "Shockley's 'daring' portraiture excited such reactionary critical response in the fields of Afro-American and women's studies that it may not be an overestimation to credit Shockley with literally provoking the critical dialogue about the black lesbian character by her 1979 essay 'The Black Lesbian in American Literature'" (276).

49. For simplicity's sake when referring to the group I will use the term Latina to refer to women from Mexico, Central or South America and Puerto

Rico. When discussing writers individually I will refer to their specific identity claim such as: Chicana or Puerto Riqueña. In this way I hope to maintain simplicity as well as an awareness of the complexity of this group of women.

50. See Frankenberg's *White Women, Race Matters: The Social Construction of Whiteness* for her discussion of white feminists' romanticization of things that they see as authentic "culture" that are usually associated with poverty and the consequences of this sentimentalism on white women's treatment of women of color.

51. See for example her essay "La Macha: Toward a Beautiful Whole Self" from *Chicana Lesbians. The Girls Our Mothers Warned Us About* where she discusses this issue at length.

52. Some of the legislation focused on Asian laborers include: The Gentlemen's Agreement of 1907 that limited Japanese and Korean immigrants, the 1917 act focused on immigrants from India, the Chinese Exclusion Act of 1882, and that of 1924 when the 1882 law applied to immigrant laborers from all of mainland Asia. No Asian could be naturalized as a citizen from 1924 through 1943 and in 1943 immigration was limited to a quota system per country. Ultimately, in 1965 the nationally specific legislation was abolished however the quota system remained. (Mazumdar 4)

53. See Sucheta Mazumdar's "General Introduction: A Woman-Centered Perspective on Asian American History," in *Making Waves: An Anthology of Writings By and About Asian American Women* for a more in-depth study of the various histories of immigration and the consequences for Asian American women.

54. Possibly it is the perceived silence/acceptance of Asian Americans by the wider society that accounts for the editors of *Aiiieeeee!* and *The Big Aiiieeeee!* choosing their selections based on whether they contained language which is outspoken and forthright. It is the predominance of "masculine" language in these volumes that causes King-Kok Cheung to critique their vision of Asian-American literature.

55. Maxine Hong Kingston's classic *The Woman Warrior* also describes a similar ideology with the "No Name Woman." The No Name woman is the speaker's aunt who was compelled to suicide by her village and family because she had a baby by someone other than her husband. As a response to this woman's behavior the villagers destroy the family home and possessions. The speaker's mother uses this story of the forgotten shameful aunt to warn the speaker about herself as a sexual being because she has started menstruating. The mother warns the daughter not to mention this story of her father's sister because "He denies her. Now that you have started to menstruate, what happened to her could happen to you. Don't humiliate us. You wouldn't like to

be forgotten as if you had never been born. The villagers are watchful." (5) Kingston's story focuses on the behavior of a heterosexual woman as unacceptable because she apparently has chosen to be sexually independent. One wonders about the extent of the punishment to be levied on women who desire each other outside of the heterosexual norms.

56. The history of the Chicano people could be seen along these same lines as they were in fact created by the 1848 Treaty of Guadalupe Hidalgo which surrendered Mexican territory to the United States. Indeed, many people went to sleep in Mexico and woke up the next morning in a different country with a very different status.

57. See Paula Gunn Allen's "Whose Dream is This Anyway? Remythologizing and Self-definition in Contemporary American Indian Fiction" in her *Sacred Hoop* for a concise discussion of "the dying savage" theme in American literature.

58. I do not intend to argue either that racial or ethnic identity is somehow more central than any other facet of identity. It is mentioned here because it is central to this project. I do agree with Butler's assertion that just uncovering different possibilities of identity is ultimately useless because one theory cannot hope to account for them all. As she states: "The theories of feminist identity that elaborate predicates of color, sexuality, ethnicity, class, and able-bodiness invariably close with an embarrassed 'etc.' at the end of the list. Through this horizontal trajectory of adjectives, these positions strive to encompass a situated subject, but invariably fail to be complete" (143). However, I feel that rather than dismissing these adjectives as unimportant one must articulate a theory that accounts for a multiplicitous identity.

59. Anzaldúa describes this Goddess thusly: "She has no head. In its place two spurts of blood gush up, transfiguring into enormous twin rattlesnakes facing each other, which symbolize the earth-bound character of human life. She has no hands. In their place are two more serpents in the form of eagle-like claws, which are repeated at her feet: claws which symbolize the digging of graves into the earth as well as the sky-bound eagle, the masculine force. Hanging from her neck is a necklace of open hands alternating with human hearts. The hands symbolize the act of giving life; the hearts, the pain of Mother Earth giving birth to all her children, as well as the pain that humans suffer throughout life in their hard struggle for existence. The hearts also represent the taking of life through sacrifice to the gods in exchange for their preservation of the world. In the center of the collar hangs a human skull with living eyes in its sockets. Another identical skull is attached to her belt. These symbolize life and death together as parts of one process." (47) Also important is the fact that "Simultaneously, depending on the person, she represents:

duality in life, a synthesis of duality, and a third perspective—something more than mere duality or synthesis of duality"(46). Clearly this description of the goddess's terrifying power gives some insight into all that Pastora represents for Máximo and helps the reader understand the depth of their love/hate relationship.

60. It is not only clear that female subjectivity is under attack here but also female physical existence. Castillo's novel is circular and begins with Máximo brutally murdering Pastora by stabbing her with a phallic pair of scissors. Since he kills her because of his need to remain a "strong" male, and she has acted complicitly in this, it is implied that she was partially responsible for her own death. This deadly connection is made frighteningly clear at the beginning of the novel and so it looms over Pastora's every decision and action for the remainder of the story.

61. Even though I borrow Adrienne Rich's phrase here I do not find her lesbian continuum overly helpful when defining lesbian identity and don't accept it as relevant to imagining lesbian selves. Throughout this book I have used examples of lesbian identity from work that is clearly defined as about lesbian life. When I focus on "possible" articulations of lesbian identity I use examples where women have intense sexual and/or emotional feelings for one another but who don't see themselves as "lesbians."

62. Pastora asks here "Are you going to marry her?" to which she answers "I don't know."

63. Máximo asks here, "are you dead yet, whore?"

64. This is an excellent illustration of Butler's theory of an "affirmative" appropriation of a slur which ocurrs in her *Bodies That Matter*. But because it is done by a white woman who is unaware of her own privileged position, and of her own power to "violate" it actually has distructive power rather than affirmative. Because Butler does not clarify who can appropriate oppressive language it also illustrates the failure of such attempts in many situations facing the lesbian of color. Butler does not discuss this dimension or contextualize this kind of appropriation.

65. In actuality what Smith seems to object to is having this example of Black lesbian existence be representative of all Black lesbian existence. Certainly, it is not. However, because of the small number of representations of Black lesbians it might seem like every one must be positive because every one carries such weight. Also the success of Naylor's novel itself makes this portrait of Black subjects highlighted as representational. It seems that because of the tenuousness of the Black lesbian's existence, the aesthetic is necessarily united to the political.

Notes

66. It is worth noting here that I do not include Asian-Americans within this chapter, simply because I, unfortunately, could not find any text that represented "successful" Asian-American lesbian identity as constructed within the parameters that I have outlined in this book.

67. Weston does occasionally refer to specific lesbians of color within her essay; she also does acknowledge that gender roles are "suffused with aspects of class, race, age, and sexual desire" (17). However, there is no discussion of this suffusion nor does she include these elements within her overall theorizing.

68. One possible scenario is a hatred of self and the belief that "whiteness" is beauty and anything less is not as valuable or beautiful. For example Kaushalya Bannerji writes that "I know of no more corrosive abuse than racism. Under its tentacles, we have been abused sexually, exploited economically, and we have been forced to internalize our colonizers' value systems and aesthetics. . . .Much of the experience of racism is constructed through gender. As a child and adolescent, I not only yearned to be a white girl, I also saw white femaleness through white men's eyes. Indeed, the first women to whom I was attracted reflected the white male gaze that I had obediently eroticized. Conversely, I found nothing sensual about my own body nor the bodies of black and Indian girls around me" (61).

69. I will develop this difference throughout this and the next chapter; however, I just want to clarify the meaning that I am assigning to these labels at this point. I consider a metaphorical mestiza to be a subject whose identity can be described as an embodiment of paradox. In the case of lesbians of color I find that the use of the mestiza metaphor is appropriate, as is the description of their mestiza-ness originating in their negotiation of the conflict between specific cultural ideologies and their lesbian identity. Therefore, when I refer to lesbians of color throughout I equate the metaphoric and cultural use of "mestiza" as in equal opposition to "biological" mestiza.

70. This assertion also seems laughable to me as a mestiza because of my daily dealing with the contradictions that Anzaldúa describes. People are constantly bombarding one with the desire to separate oneself for their convenience: female, white, Latina, middle class, professional, mother, teacher, student, etc. The only way that I can function as a whole individual is to resist this "either/or" or the "divide and conquer" mentality to use Audre Lorde's terms. For me the material reality authorizes the theory in this case. Perhaps for someone not so defined this seems an impossible task and therefore a utopian vision.

71. Because the mestiza is a woman who is the progeny of a Mexican Indian woman and a European (Spanish) male, a conquered people and a conquering one, a rape victim and a perpetrator, the serpent and the eagle of

Mexican mythology—the combination is a joining of opposites of combatants. The result is psychic chaos for ensuing generations. I don't believe that Anzaldúa is attempting to implement an eradication of difference by breeding but rather she is discussing a new way of dealing with difference internally and externally, and viewing the consequences of that new mestiza consciousness with hope.

72. Even in the creation of this project I have been counseled by certain colleagues not to use "monolithic" labels such as "of color" or "lesbian" because it negatively limits the scope of the project. Even though I see the validity of this sentiment the fact remains that people need to see a title and understand what it means about the writing's contents. If I were to forgo a title or have a title a paragraph long with explanatory comments to match I would lose my audience quickly! This is, in some ways, the kind of choice these women have to deal with. Will they be published if they present their texts in a way that represents this paradoxical self that is so difficult to understand? Clearly, many women have not been. In an interview, Paula Gunn Allen describes her experiences with publishing her work: "the people who are in the small press world, or in the big-press-but-liberal-radical world want a certain kind of Indian, just as much as Harper and Row does, just as much as Random House does or anyone else does. They want a 'sellable' Indian. That's what the big ones are after What the little ones are after is a 'pathetic' Indian, an Indian they can relate to, put back in the damn grave, and say, 'well it's been nice talking to you. I've gotten my goodies. I've used you in my speech. I've used your bodies to make my point'" (16).

73. The reader might wonder why I have not included Alice Walker's *The Color Purple* within this discussion, as it is a canonized novel that has some intimacy between two women. It is simply because whereas I do think that the relationship between Shug and Celie is a sexually powerful one, and not just a close friendship, as well as one that in some ways engages in revision, the novel does not concern itself with the true hostilites that exist for lesbians of color. Shug can be arguably seen as a revision of the Queen B figure in African American literature; the destructive woman perhaps best embodied by Eva of Jones's *Eva's Man*. Shug does not live to destroy men, although arguably she does destroy Mr. as a "man," instead she enjoys men as well as women. However, I find Walker's text too utopic in its vision of Black lesbian existence to be useful within this project's search for a meaningful theory of identity. I believe this is true because she Walker does not have her characters negotiate the hostilites of a homophobic community nor have to forge their identities within this context. Therefore, I agree with Barbara Smith who finds it to be an "optimistic...visionary tale" (703). She finds that because it is a "fable [that]

may account partially for the depiction of a Lesbian relationship unencumbered by homophobia or fear of it and entirely lacking in self-scrutiny about the implications of Lesbian identity" (703).

74. I want to mention a fascinating essay by Yvonne Yarbro-Bejarano wherein she discusses various Latina lesbians who make a space for themselves within their cultures by using elements of popular culture She argues that they use cultural icons in order to reclaim a space that dismisses them. She describes this as "working simultaneously within and against dominant cultural codes" ("The Lesbian Body" 181). She explores their methods within Latina camp shows, photographs, paintings, and stand-up comedy.

75. "I return to my pueblo. A Mestiza woman."

76. Probably most famous is her book *The Sacred Hoop: Recovering the Feminine in American Indian Traditions* as well as her essay "Who is Your Mother? Red Roots of White Feminism" neither of them is focused specifically on Native lesbians.

77. In an interview Lorde herself described this form as fiction with "elements of biography and history of myth. In other words, it's fiction built from many sources" (115). I consider the "Audre" in the text to be the author and a fictional character simultaneously.

78. Judy Grahn describes what she learned of Afrikete from Lorde. "Audre Lorde kindly took the time to tell me more about Oya and the other Orisha of the Yoruba/Macumba religion. . . . As for the trickster god Eshu, Lorde says in Yoruba ceremonies he is always danced by a woman who straps on a straw phallus and chases the other women. He is also called Elegba. Originally he was a female, Afrikete . . .Eshu/Afrikete is the rhyme god, the seventh and youngest in the old Mawulisa pantheon, Mawulisa being male/female, sun and moon. As the trickster, he/she makes connections, is communicator, linguist, and poet. Only Afrikete knows all the languages of all the gods. Afrikete always appears in guises, so it is wise to be nice to stones and bees, for instance or anything at all that might be the mischievous Afrikete" (124–5).

79. This is not to say that Mexicans have an admiration for dark colored people. Actually, it tends to be read as a marker of lower class status and of unsophistication. As Gloria Anzaldúa states "[Chicano] culture . . . defers to and prefers light-skinned gueros and denies the Black blood in our mestisaje . . . darker means being more indio or india, means poorer" ("Bridge" 226). Even though Lorde describes herself as buying "meager provisions" (clearly not acting as a tourist) she is also not impoverished either—her clear class status probably elevated her blackness in the eyes of those who asked of her heritage.

80. I disagree with Yvonne Yarbro-Bejarano's claim that "it would be a step backward to consider the experiences of lesbians and gays of color as 'different'" ("Expanding" 128). I believe that it would be a step back to consider them only as different, but I do think that gay and lesbian subjects are differently constructed as they are marked by different cultural traditions and ideologies and that it is crucial to study these contexts.

81. I believe because identity-based studies are so connected with "correct" language use and representation that an individual's choice to identify oneself, or ally oneself with, a particular group can have huge political repercussions. They can be personally damaging but they do have an impact. This belief motivates the choices I made to identify myself in the first chapter of this book.

82. Although Fuss does not discuss lesbians of color within her text, she does provide an interesting study of the interrelatedness of essentialism and constructionism in her *Essentially Speaking: Feminism, Nature, and Difference.*

83. This is also a moment where the mestiza consciousness is applied to academic fields not only individual experience. It aptly shows how a recognition of how lesbians of color construct their identities necessitates changes beyond the ones I have specifically mentioned in this text.

Bibliography

Aguilar San-Juan, Karin. "Exploding Myths, Creating Consciousness: Some First Steps Toward Pan Asian Unity." Silvera 185–92.

———. "Landmarks in Literature by Asian American Lesbians." *Signs: Journal of Women in Culture and Society* 18.4 (Summer 1993): 936–43.

Alarcón, Norma. "The Theoretical Subject(s) of *This Bridge Called My Back* and Anglo-American Feminism." Anzaldúa 356–69.

Allen, Jeffner, ed. *Lesbian Philosophies and Cultures*. SUNY ser in Feminist Philosophy. New York: State U of New York P, 1990.

Allen, Paula Gunn, ed. *Spider Woman's Granddaughters: Traditional Tales and Contemporary Writing by Native American Women*. New York: Fawcett Columbine, 1989.

———. "A *MELUS* Interview: Paula Gunn Allen." *MELUS* 10.2 (1983): 3–25.

———. Interview. Balassi 95–107.

———. Introduction. *Spider Woman's Granddaughters: Traditional Tales and Contemporary Writing by Native American Women*. New York: Fawcett Columbine, 1989. 1–25.

———. *The Sacred Hoop: Recovering the Feminine in American Indian Traditions*. 1991. Boston: Beacon, 1992.

———. *The Woman Who Owned the Shadows*. San Francisco: Spinsters/Aunt Lute, 1989.

———. "Who is Your Mother? Red Roots of White Feminism." *Sinister Wisdom* 25 (1984): 34–45.

Anzaldúa, Gloria, ed. *Making Face, Making Soul/Haciendo Caras: Creative and Critical Perspectives by Feminists of Color*. San Francisco: Aunt Lute, 1990.

———. *Borderlands/La Frontera: The New Mestiza.* San Francisco: Spinsters/Aunt Lute, 1987.

———. "Bridge, Drawbridge, Sandbar or Island: Lesbians-of-Color Hacienda Alianzas." *Bridges of Power: Women's Multicultural Alliances.* Ed. Lisa Albrecht and Rose M. Brewer. Santa Cruz, CA: New Society, 1990. 216–233.

———. "Haciendo Caras, Una Entrada." Anzaldúa xv-xxviii.

Asian Women United of California, ed. *Making Waves: An Anthology of Writings by and About Asian American Women.* Boston: Beacon, 1989.

Baker, Houston A., Jr. *Blues, Ideology, and Afro-American Literature: A Vernacular Theory.* Chicago: U of Chicago P, 1984.

Balassi, William, and John F. Crawford et al eds. *This is About Vision: Interviews with Southwestern Writers.* New America Studies in the American West ser. Albuquerque, NM: U of New Mexico P, 1990.

Bambara, Toni Cade, ed. *The Black Woman: An Anthology.* New York: Penguin, 1970.

———. Preface. Bambara 7–12.

Bannerji, Kaushalya. "No Apologies." Ratti 59–64.

Bergmann, Emilie L, and Paul Julian Smith, et al, eds. *¿Entiendes? Queer Readings, Hispanic Writings.* Q ser. Durham, NC: Duke UP, 1995.

Bogus, SDiane A. "The 'Queen B' Figure in Black Literature." Jay 275–90.

Bond, Jean Carey, and Patricia Perry. "Is the Black Male Castrated?" *The Black Woman: An Anthology.* Bambara 113–17.

Bow, Leslie. "Hole to Whole: Feminine Subversion and Subversion of the Feminine in Cherríe Moraga's *Loving in the War Years.*" *Dispositio* 16.41: 1–12.

Brant, Beth, ed. *A Gathering of Spirit: A Collection by North American Indian Women.* Ithaca, NY: Firebrand, 1988.

Brant, Beth. "A Simple Act." Brant, *Mohawk.* 87–94.

———. "Coyote Learns a New Trick." Brant, *Mohawk.* 31–36.

———. "Giveaway: Native Lesbian Writers." *Signs: Journal of Women in Culture and Society* 18.4 (Summer 1993): 944–47.

———. "Introduction: A Gathering of Spirit." Brant 8–11.

———. *Mohawk Trail.* Ithaca, NY: Firebrand, 1985.

———. "The Fifth Floor, 1967." Brant, *Mohawk.* 69–76.

Butler, Judith. *Bodies That Matter: On the Discursive Limits of "Sex."* New York: Routledge, 1993.

———. *Gender Trouble: Feminism and the Subversion of Identity.* Thinking Gender ser. New York: Routledge, 1990.

———. "Imitations and Gender Insubordination." Fuss 13–31.

Candelaria, Cordelia. *Chicano Poetry: A Critical Introduction.* Westport, CT: Greenwood, 1986.

Carby, Hazel. *Reconstructing Womanhood: The Emergence of the Afro-American Novelist.* New York: Oxford, 1987..

Castillo, Ana. *Loverboys: Stories.* New York: Norton, 1996.

———. *Peel My Love Like an Onion.* New York: Doubleday, 1999.

———. *Sapogonia.* Tempe: Bilingual Press/Editorial Bilingüal, 1990.

———. *So Far From God.* New York: Norton, 1993.

———. *The Mixquiahuala Letters.* Tempe: Bilingual Press/Editorial Bilingüal, 1986.

Castillo, Debra A. *Talking Back: Toward a Latin American Feminist Literary Criticism.* Reading Women Writing ser. Ithaca. Cornell UP, 1992.

Cheung, King-Kok. *Articulate Silences: Hisaye Yamamoto, Maxine Hong Kingston, Joy Kogawa.* Ithaca, NY: Cornell UP, 1993.

Chin, Frank, and Jeffrey Paul Chan et al eds. *Aiiieeeee!: An Anthology of Asian American Writers.* New York: Penguin, 1974.

———. Preface. Chin et al xi-xxii.

Christian, Barbara. *Black Feminist Criticism: Perspectives on Black Women Writers.* The Athene ser. New York: Pergamon, 1985.

———. "The Race for Theory." Anzaldúa 335–45.

Christian, Karen. *Show & Tell: Identity as Performance in U.S. Latina/o Fiction.* Albuqurque: U of New Mexico P, 1997.

Cixous, Hélène. "The Laugh of the Medusa." *Signs* 1.4 (1975): 875–93.

Clarke, Cheryl. "The Failure to Transform: Homophobia in the Black Community." Smith 197–208.

Combahee River Collective. "The Combahee River Collective Statement." Smith 272–82.

Cornwell, Anita. *Black Lesbian in White America.* Tallahassee, FL: NAIAD, 1983.

Creet, Julia. "Anxieties of Identity: Coming Out and Coming Undone." Dorendkamp 179–99.

De La Torre, Adela and Beatríz M. Pesquera eds. *Building with our Hands: New Directions in Chicana Studies.* Los Angeles: U of California P, 1993.

Dhairyam, Sagri. "Racing the Lesbian, Dodging White Critics." Doan 25–46.

Doan, Laura, ed. *The Lesbian Postmodern*. Between Men/Between Women ser. New York: Columbia UP, 1994.

———. Preface. Doan iv-xi.

Dorendkamp, Monica, and Richard Henke eds. *Negotiating Lesbian and Gay Subjects*. New York: Routledge, 1995.

Du Bois, W.E.B.. "Of Our Spiritual Strivings." *W.E.B. Du Bois: A Reader*. Ed. David Levering Lewis. New York: Holt, 1995. 28-33.

Elwin, Rosamund, ed. *Tongues on Fire: Caribbean Lesbian Lives and Stories*. Toronto, Canada: Women's Press, 1997.

———. "Tongues on Fire, Speakin' Zami Desire." *Tongues on Fire: Caribbean Lesbian Lives and Stories*. Ed Rosamund Elwin. Toronto, Canada: Women's Press, 1997. 7-10.

Farwell, Marilyn R. "Toward a Definition of the Lesbian Literary Imagination." *Signs* (1988): 100-18.

Felman, Shosana. "Women and Madness: The Critical Phallacy." *Diacritics* (Winter 1975): 2-10.

Ferguson, Ann. "Is There a Lesbian Culture?" Jeffner Allen 63-88.

Foucault, Michel. *The History of Sexuality: An Introduction*. Trans. Robert Hurley. 1978. New York: Vintage, 1990.

Frankenberg, Ruth. *White Women, Race Matters: The Social Construction of Whiteness*. Minneapolis: U of Minnesota P, 1993.

Fuss, Diana, ed. *Inside/Out: Lesbian Theories, Gay Theories*. New York: Routledge, 1991.

———. *Essentially Speaking: Feminism, Nature and Difference*. Boston: South End, 1989.

———. Introduction. Fuss 1-10.

García, Alma M, ed. *Chicana Feminist Thought: The Basic Historical Writings*. New York: Routledge, 1997.

Gates, Henry Louis, Jr. "The Blackness of Blackness: A Critique of the Sign and the Signifying Monkey" *Black Literature and Literary Theory*. Ed. Henry Louis Gates, Jr.. 1984. New York: Routledge, 1990. 285-321.

———. "Writing 'Race' and the Difference it Makes." *Critical Inquiry* 12.1 (Autumn): 1-20.

Geok-lin Lim, Shirley et al eds. *The Forbidden Stitch: An Asian American Women's Anthology*. Corvallis, OR: Calyx, 1989.

Geok-lin Lim, Shirley. "Feminist and Ethnic Literary Theories in Asian American Literature." *Feminist Studies* 19.3 (Fall 1993): 571-95.

Gilbert, Sandra M, and Susan Gubar. *The Madwoman in the Attic: The Woman Writer and the Nineteenth-Century Literary Imagination.* New Haven: Yale UP, 1979.

Glasgow, Joanne and Karla Jay. Introduction. Jay 1–10.

Gomez, Jewelle. "A Cultural Legacy Denied and Discovered: Black Lesbians in Fiction by Women." Smith 110–23.

Gómez, Alma and Cherríe Moraga, et al eds. *Cuentos: Stories by Latinas.* New York: Kitchen Table, Women of Color P, 1983.

———. "By Word Of Mouth." *Cuentos: Stories by Latinas.* Gómez vii-xii.

Gould, Lois. *A Sea-Change.* 1976. New York: Farrar, Straus & Giroux, 1988.

Grahn, Judy. *Another Mother Tongue: Gay Words, Gay Worlds.* 1984. Boston: Beacon, 1990.

H, Pamela. "Asian American Lesbians: An Emerging Voice in the Asian American Community." Asian Women 282–90.

Hagedorn, Jessica, ed. *Charlie Chan is Dead: An Anthology of Contemporary Asian American Fiction.* New York : Penguin, 1993.

———. Preface. Hagedorn vii-xiv.

Harris, Janice. "Gayl Jones' *Corregidora*" *Frontiers: A Journal of Women's Studies* 5.3 (1981): 1–5.

hooks, bell. *Ain't I a Woman: Black Women and Feminism.* Boston: South End, 1981.

———. *Feminist Theory: From Margin to Center.* Boston: South End, 1984.

———. "Is Paris Burning?" *Black Looks: Race and Representation.* Boston, MA: South End, 1992.

Horno-Delgado, Asunción and Eliana Ortega et al eds. *Breaking Boundaries: Latina Writings and Critical Readings.* Amherst: U of Massachusetts P, 1989.

Houston, Jeanne Wakatsuki, and James D. Houston. *Farewell to Manzanar.* Boston: Houghton, 1973.

Hull, Gloria T, and Patricia Bell Scott, et al eds. *All the Women are White, All the Blacks are Men, But Some of Us are Brave: Black Women's Studies.* New York: Feminist, 1982.

Hurtado, Aida. *The Color of Privilege: Three Blasphemies on Race and Feminism.* U of Michigan P, 1996.

Irigaray, Luce. *This Sex Which is Not One.* Trans. Catherine Porter with Carolyn Burke. Ithaca, NY: Cornell UP, 1985.

Jagose, Annamarie. *Lesbian Utopics*. New York: Routledge, 1994.
Jay, Karla, and Joanne Glasgow, eds. *Lesbian Texts and Contexts: Radical Revisions*. Feminist Crosscurrents ser. New York: New York UP, 1990.
Jones, Gayl. *Corregidora*. Black Women Writers ser. Boston: Beacon, 1975.
———. *Eva's Man*. Black Women Writers ser. Boston: Beacon, 1976.
Joyce, Joyce. "The Black Canon: Reconstructing Black American Literary Criticism." *NLH* 18.2 (Winter): 335–44.
Judit. "Border Conflict." Ramos 218–19.
Keating, AnaLouise. "Making 'our shattered faces whole': The Black Goddess and Audre Lorde's Revision of Patriarchal Myth." *Frontiers: A Journal of Women's Studies* 13.1 (1992): 20–33.
Kim, Willyce. *Eating Artichokes*. Oakland, CA: Women's Press Collective, 1972.
King, Tom. Review of *The Woman Who Owned the Shadows*, by Paula Gunn Allen. *American Indian Quarterly* 8 (Summer 1984): 261–64.
Kingston, Maxine Hong. *The Woman Warrior: Memoirs of a Girlhood Among Ghosts*. 1976. New York: Vintage, 1989.
Lai, Larissa. *When Fox is a Thousand*. Vancouver, Canada: Press Gang, 1995.
Lee, C. Allyson. "An Asian Lesbian's Struggle." Silvera 115–18.
"Lesbians of Colour: Loving and Struggling/A Conversation Between Three Lesbians of Colour." Silvera 160–8.
Leong, Russell, ed. *Asian American Sexualities: Dimensions of the Gay & Lesbian Experience*. New York: Routledge, 1996.
Leung, Patrice. "On Iconography." Silvera 108–9.
Lopez, Erika. *Flaming Iguanas: An All-Girl Road Novel Thing*. New York: Simon & Schuster, 1997.
López, Natashia. "Trying to be Dyke and Chicana." Trujillo 84.
Lorde, Audre. "I Am Your Sister: Black Women Organizing Across Sexualities." *A Burst of Light*. Ithaca, NY: Firebrand, 1988.
———. Interview. *Black Women Writers at Work*. Ed. Claudia Tate. New York: Continuum, 1983.
———. *Zami: A New Spelling of My Name*. Freedom, CA: Crossing, 1982.
Lugones, María. "Playfulness, 'World'-Travelling, and Loving Perception." Anzaldúa 390–402.
Madison, D. Soyini. Introduction. Madison 1–17.

―――, ed. *The Woman That I Am: The Literature and Culture of Contemporary Women of Color*. New York: St. Martin's P, 1994.
Mazumdar, Sucheta. "General Introduction: A Woman-Centered Perspective on Asian American History." Asian Women 1–24.
McKenna, Teresa. *Migrant Song: Politics and Process in Contemporary Chicano Literature*. Austin: U of Texas P, 1997.
Mohanty, Chandra Talpade, and Ann Russo, et al eds. *Third World Women and the Politics of Feminism*. Bloomington: Indiana UP, 1991.
Montgomery, Maxine L. "The Fathomless Dream: Gloria Naylor's Use of the Descent Motif in the *Women of Brewster Place*." *CLA Journal* 36.1 (Sept. 1992): 1–11.
Moraga, Cherríe, and Gloria Anzaldúa, eds. *This Bridge Called My Back: Writings by Radical Women of Color*. NY: Kitchen Table/Women of Color P, 1983.
―――. Introduction. Moraga xxiii-xxvi.
Moraga, Cherríe. *Loving in the War Years: lo que nunca pasó por sus labios*. Boston: South End, 1983.
Morrison, Toni. *Playing in the Dark: Whiteness and the Literary Imagination*. Cambridge, MA: Harvard UP, 1992.
Munt, Sally, ed. *New Lesbian Criticism: Literary and Cultural Readings*. Between Men/Between Women ser. New York: Columbia UP, 1992.
―――. Introduction. Munt xi-xxii.
Navarro, Marta A. "Interview with Ana Castillo." Trujillo 113–132.
Naylor, Gloria. *The Women of Brewster Place*. New York: Penguin, 1980.
Noda, Barbara. *Strawberries*. Berkeley, CA: Shameless Hussy, 1979.
Ortega, Eliana and Nancy Saporta Sternbach. "At the Threshold of the Unnamed: Latina Literary Discourse in the Eighties." Horno-Delgado 3–23.
Phelan, Shane. *Getting Specific: Postmodern Lesbian Politics*. Minneapolis: U of Minnesota P, 1994.
Pratt, Minnie Bruce. "Gender Quiz." *S/he*. Ithaca, NY: Firebrand, 1995. 11–22.
Quintana, Alvina E. *Home Girls: Chicana Literary Voices*. Philadelphia: Temple UP, 1996.
Raiskin, Judith. "Inverts and Hybrids: Lesbian Rewritings of Sexual and Racial Identities." Doan 156–72.

Ramos, Juanita, ed. *Compañeras: Latina Lesbians.* New York: Routledge, 1994.

———. Preface. Ramos xiii-xix.

Ratti, Rakesh, ed. *A Lotus of Another Color: An Unfolding of the South Asian Gay and Lesbian Experience.* Boston: Alyson, 1993.

———. Introduction. Ratti 11–20.

Rebolledo, Tey Diana. *Women Singing in the Snow: A Cultural Analysis of Chicana Literature.* Tuscon, AZ: U of Arizona P, 1995.

Rich, Adrienne. "Compulsory Heterosexuality and Lesbian Existence." *Signs* 5.4 (Summer 1980). 631–59.

Russo, Anne. "'We Cannot Live without Our Lives': White Women, Antiracism, and Feminism." Mohanty 297–313.

Saldívar, Ramon. *Chicano Narrative: The Dialectics of Difference.* Madison: U of Wisconsin P, 1990.

Sandoval, Chela. "U.S. Third World Feminism: The Theory and Method of Oppositional Consciousness in the Postmodern World." *Genders* 10 (1991): 1–24.

———. "Feminism and Racism: A Report on the 1981 National Women's Studies Association Conference." Anzaldúa 55–71.

Shockley, Ann Allen. *Say Jesus and Come to Me.* Tallahassee, FL: NAIAD, 1987.

———. "The Black Lesbian in American Literature: An Overview." Smith 83–93.

Showalter, Elaine. *A Literature of Their Own.* Princeton: Princeton UP, 1977.

Silvera, Makeda, ed. *Piece of My Heart: A Lesbian of Colour Anthology.* 1991. Toronto, Canada: Sister Vision, 1992.

———. Introduction. Silvera xiii-xix.

Smith, Barbara, ed. *Home Girls: A Black Feminist Anthology.* New York: Kitchen Table: Women of Color, 1983.

———. "The Truth That Never Hurts: Black Lesbians in Fiction in the 1980s." Warhol 690–712.

———. "Toward a Black Feminist Criticism." Hull 157–175.

Sollors, Werner. "Introduction: The Invention of Ethnicity." *The Invention of Ethnicity.* Ed. Werner Sollors. New York: Oxford UP, 1989. iv-xx.

Stanley, Sandra Kumamoto, ed. *Other Sisterhoods: Literary Theory and U.S. Women of Color.* Chicago: U of Illinois P, 1998.

Stimpson, Catherine. "Zero Degree Deviancy: The Lesbian Novel in English." *Critical Inquiry* 8.2 (Winter 1981): 363–79.

Torres, Lourdes. "The Construction of Self in U.S. Latina Autobiographies." Mohanty 271–87.

Trujillo, Carla, ed. *Chicana Lesbians: The Girls Our Mothers Warned Us About.* Berkeley, CA: Third Woman, 1991.

———. "Chicana Lesbians: Fear and Loathing in the Chicano Community." Trujillo, *Chicano Lesbians*, 186–94.

———, ed. *Living Chicana Theory.* Ser. in Chicana/Latina Studies. Berkeley, CA: Third Woman, 1998.

Tsui, Kitty. "Breaking Silence, Making Waves and Loving Ourselves: The Politics of Coming Out and Coming Home." Jeffner Allen 49–62.

———. *The Words of a Woman Who Breathes Fire.* San Francisco: Spinsters Ink, 1983.

Uttal, Lynet. "Inclusion Without Influence: The Continuing Tokenism of Women of Color." Anzaldúa 42–5.

Van Dyke, Annette. *The Search for a Woman-Centered Spirituality.* The Cuttin Edge: Lesbian Life and Literature. New York: New York UP, 1992.

Vizneor, Gerald, ed. *Narrative Chance: Postmodern Discourse on Native American Indian Literatures.* American Indian Literature and Critical Studies ser. Norman, OK: U of Oklahoma P, 1989.

Wade-Gayles, Gloria. *No Crystal Stair.* New York: Pilgrim, 1984.

Walker, Alice. "In Search of Our Mothers' Gardens." *In Search of Our Mothers' Gardens: Womanist Prose.* 1967–82. San Diego: Harvest/HBJ, 1983. 231–43.

———. *The Color Purple.* 1982. New York: Washington Square, 1983.

Warhol, Robyn R, and Diane Price Herndl, eds. *Feminisms: An Anthology of Literary Theory and Criticism.* New Brunswick, NJ: Rutgers UP, 1991.

Warner, Michael, ed. *Fear of a Queer Planet: Queer Politics and Social Theory.* Minneapolis: U of Minnesota P, 1993.

———. Introduction. Warner vii-xxxi.

Weston, Kath. "Do the Clothes Make the Woman?" *Genders* 17 (Fall 1993): 1–21.

Wilson, Anna. "Audre Lorde and the African-American Tradition: When the Family is Not Enough." Munt 75–93.

Wittig, Monique. *The Straight Mind and Other Essays.* Boston: Beacon, 1990.

Wolfe, Susan J, and Julia Penelope, eds. *Sexual Practice, Textual Theory: Lesbian Cultural Criticism.* Cambridge, MA: Blackwell, 1993.

———. "Sexual Identity/Textual Politics: Lesbian [De]Compositions." Wolfe 1–24.

Wong, Christine. "Yellow Queer." *Frontiers* 4.3 (1979): 53.

Yarbro-Bejarano, Yvonne. "Chicana Literature from a Chicana Feminist Perspective." Warhol 732–37.

———. "Expanding the Categories of Race and Sexuality in Lesbian and Gay Studies." *Professions of Desire: Lesbian and Gay Studies in Literature.* Ed. George E. Haggerty and Bonnie Zimmerman. MLA: New York, 1995. 124–35.

———. "The Lesbian Body in Latina Cultural Production." Bergmann 181–200.

———. "The Multiple Subject in the Writing of Ana Castillo." *The Americas Review* 20.1: 65–72.

Yung, Judy. *Chinese Women of America: A Pictorial History.* Seattle: U of Washington P, 1986.

Zamora, Bernice. "Notes From a Chicana 'Coed.'" Anzaldúa 131.

Zimmerman, Bonnie. *The Safe Sea of Women: Lesbian Fiction 1969–88.* Boston: Beacon, 1990. London: OnlyWomen, 1991.

———. "What Has Never Been: An Overview of Lesbian Feminist Literary Criticism." Warhol 117–37.

Index

Academy, xxvii, 134, 170;
African-American criticism and, 22–23;
area studies in, 3, 14, 15;
as definer, 31, 32, 180n.18;
hierarchies in, 143, 146;
role of "queer critic" in, 179n.13;
treatment of race and ethnicity in, 19, 183n.35;
Western philosophy in, 96;
women of color in, xii , xv;
women's texts in, 39
"A Chinese Banquet" (Tsui), 78–79
Activism, xii, 179n.13, 181n.21;
as betrayal, 61;
to claim identity, 96
Africa: informing African-American theory, 22. *See also* Gates, Henry Louis, Jr.
African-American: church, 159;
constructionism/essentialism and, 21, 181n.21;
literary criticism and theory, 20–24, 41, 99;
racial/ethnic theory, 18–20, 26, 178n.4;
women, 41–44, 99, 174. *See also* Baker, Houston A., Jr.; Bambara, Toni Cade; Black; Carby, Hazel; Christian, Barbara; Gates, Henry Louis, Jr.; hooks, bell; Morrison, Toni
Aguilar-San Juan, Karin, 96, 132–133
Alarcón, Norma, 9
Allen, Paula Gunn, 161, 107–108;
Native American history, 82, 84;
Native American/American Indian lesbian tradition, 83–84, 151–154;
Native American/American Indian Literature, 33–34;
Native American/American Indian women, 34, 81, 149;
publishing, 190n.72;
The Sacred Hoop, 33, 83;
SpiderWoman's Granddaughters. Traditional Tales and Contemporary Writing by Native American Women, 33;

The Woman Who Owned the Shadows, xxiii, 86–88, 129–130, 149–154
American Indian: history, 81–82, lesbian traditions, 83–84. *See also* Native American
Anglo. *See* White
Anzaldúa, Gloria, 137, 162, 163;
  as utopian, 143–146, 189n.70;
  Borderlands/La Frontera: The New Mestiza, xxiv-xxvii, 140–146, 170–171, 173–174;
  "Bridge, Drawbridge, Sandbar or Island: Lesbians-of-Color Hacienda Alianzas", 161, 162, 165;
  Coatlicue, 187–188n.59;
  la mestiza, xiii, xxiv-xxvii, 140–143, 145–146, 161, 173–174, 179n.12, 189–190n.70;
  Making Face, Making Soul/Haciendo Caras: Creative and Critical Perspectives by Feminists of Color, 169, 172–173;
  skin color, 191n.79;
  This Bridge Called My Back: Writings by Radical Women of Color, 168. *See also* Chicano/a; Latino/a.
Appropriation, xii;
  and power, 188n.64 ;
  of language, 91– 92, 145, 188n.64
Asia(n), xxvi, 27, 28, 29, 30, 75, 140, 182n.31, 183n.32;
  homosexuality and ,75–76, 132–133;
  immigration, 71–72, 186n.52;
  women, 73–75. *See also* Asian-American
Asian-American(s), 107, 137;
  and identity, xxvii, 33, 35, 170, 172;
  as "model minority". *See* Mazumdar, Sucheta;
  as "yellow peril". *See* Mazumdar, Sucheta;
  authenticity, 30,170, 185n.48;
  definitions of, 27–30, 71, 183n.32, 186n.54;
  history, 71–74, 186n.53;
  lesbian identity, 75, 76, 77–81, 130–134, 189n.66;
  literature, 29–31, 77–81, 133–134, 182–183n.31, 186n.54, 186n.55;
  Studies, field of, xi;
  women, 28, 74–81, 107, 186n.53, 186n.55
Aztec(s), 58, 59, 142, 144

Baker, Houston A, Jr., 19, 21, 22, 181n.22, 183n.35;
  blues criticism and, 23;
  vernacular and, 23
Bambara, Toni Cade, *The Black Woman,* 20.
Bannerji, Kaushalya, 80–81, 189n.68
Black, xxvi, 4, 7, 10, 26, 31, 75, 91, 92, 93, 94, 96, 107, 133, 136–137, 139, 140, 162, 165, 180n.16, 180n.18, 181n.21, 184n.44, 185n.46, 189n.68, 190n.73, 191n.79;
  Arts Movement, The, 19;
  Feminism, 9, 20–21, 181n.24, 182n.27;
  civil rights movement, 6, 18, 44;
  identity, 19–20, 21–22, 23, 24, 179n.12, 181n.25, 181n.26, 182n.29;
  lesbians, xiii, 23, 44–56, 60, 75,98–102, 118, 122, 125–

Index

129, 156–160, 171, 185n.47, 185n.48, 188n.65;
literature, xiii, 21, 23, 24, 44–56, 98–102, 122, 125–129, 156–160;
manhood, 42–46, 47, 51–52, 180n.22;
Power Movement, The, 45,
slavery, 19, 42;
stereotypes, xx-xxi, 20, 43–44, 56,
Studies, field of, 19–20;
women, xv, 20–21, 42–44, 96, 99, 100, 118–119, 180n.20.
See also African-American
Bogus, SDiane A., 44, 184n.45, 186n.48
"Border Conflict" (Judit), 69
Bow, Leslie, 123
Brant, Beth, 112;
A Gathering of Spirit, 32–33, 85;
lesbians, 84–86, 108, 117, 132, 153, 154–156;
Mohawk Trail, xxiv, 84–86, 116–118, 132, 154–156;
victimhood, 82
Bruja (witch), 68. *See also Sapogonia* (Castillo)
Bulldagger, 44, 172, 184n.45. *See also* Queen B/Bee
Bulldyke, 44, 184n.45
Butch, 50, 99, 100, 113, 156, 171, 172, 174. *See also* Bulldagger; Bulldyke; Dyke
Butler, Judith, ix, xxi-xxii, xxiv, xxvii, 141, 142, 143, 162, 164, 168, 178n.9, 187n.58;
Bodies That Matter, 91–95, 188n.64;
critique of, xviii-xix, 5, 89, 92–95, 136–140;

Gender Trouble, xvii-xviii, 88–89;
See also Performance theory; Gender danger

Carby, Hazel: *Reconstructing Womanhood: The Emergence of the Afro-American Woman Novelist*, 42–43, 45
Caribbean, xiii, 177n.2. *See also Zami*
Castillo, Ana, xii, xxiii, 51,
Chicana/o writing, 64, 182n.29;
lesbian identity, 65–67, 102–106, 108–116, 125;
male dominance, 65;
The Mixquihuala Letters, 65–67, 102–105, 108–110;
Sapogonia, 67–69, 104–106, 110–116, 188n.60;
So Far from God, 119–122
Castillo, Debra A., *Talking Back: Toward a Latin American Feminist Literary Criticism*, 57, 61
Catholic, 150;
church, 65;
Latinas/os, 64, 105, 114, 123
Cheung, King-Kok: *Articulate Silences*, 30–31, 182n.31, 186n.54
Chicanas, xi;
xiii, 137, 144, 172, 180n.18, 182n.29, 186n.49, 186n.51;
Feminism, 62;
identity, xxiv, xxv;
lesbians, xi, xxvi, 60–61, 63–64, 123–125, 147, 148;
literature, 62, 64–69, 70–71, 108–116, 119–125;
sexual repression, history of, 59–61; *See also* Anzaldúa, Gloria; Latina/o; *La Mestiza*;

Moraga, Cherríe; Yarbro-Bejarano, Yvonne
Chin, Frank: *Aiiieeeee!*, 182n.31
Christian, Barbara: *Black Feminist Criticism. Perspectives on Black Women Writers*, 122, 157, 180n.16;
"The Race for Theory", x, 19, 24, 31, 96, 141, 182n.29
Christian, Karen: *Show & Tell. Identity and Performance in U.S. Latina/o Fiction*, xi
Christian religion, 159;
in African American community, 44, 159;
in Latino cultures, 58, 59, 119,
in Native American cultures, 84;
myth, 121, 151, 158;
patriarchy and ,44, 119
Cixous, Hélène: "The Laugh of the Medusa", 177n 4
Clarke, Cheryl, 45–46, 54
Coatlicue, 105, 187–188n.59
Color Purple, The (Walker), 190n.73
Combahee River Collective, 6
Compulsory heterosexuality. See Heterosexual(ity); See also Rich, Adrienne
Confucianism, 73
Construction(ism), xvi, xix, xx, xxii, xxiv, xxvii, 17, 32, 92, 95, 97, 100, 113, 114, 126, 140, 147, 161, 165, 167, 171, 172, 174, 178n 10, 192n 82;
of culture, 154, 168;
of gender, 6, 7, 8–9, 35, 36, 40, 88–89, 134, 154, 167, 168;
of identity studies, 3, 34–37;
of masculinity, xxi, 106;
of race, 19–20, 21–23, 27, 34–36, 136–137, 169, 170, 172,

xxi. *See also* Identity; Essentialism; Butler, Judith; Lorde, Audre
Cornwell, Anita: *Black Lesbian in White America*, 46
Corregidora (Jones), xxiii, 53–55
Costume, xx, 49–52, 171–172. *See also* Performance, Role-play
Culture, xxii, xxiv, xxv, xxvii, 8, 17, 24, 25, 35, 39–40, 45, 88, 89, 93, 96, 122, 123, 136, 139, 147, 167, 169, 172, 174;
African, 22, 73;
African-American, 23, 56, 99, 159, 160;
American Indian, 32, 81, 129, 149, 151–153, 155;
Asian, 28, 71, 75, 76, 81, 130–131;
Asian-American, 71–73, 107, 130–131, 132–133;
Chicano/a, xi, xxiv, xxvi, 27, 60, 66, 67, 103, 104, 123–125, 144, 191n.79;
Latino/a, 25, 56, 57, 58, 59–62, 65, 71, 73, 104, 111, 112, 114, 119, 125, 142–143, 144, 173;
lesbian, 13, 40–41, 81, 161;
popular, xii, 191n.74;
romantization of, 58, 186n.50; 191n. 74;
tribal, 120

Dhairyam, Sagri, 137–139
Drag, 138, 155;
queens, 91, 92, 94, 95
Du Bois, W.E.B., and "double-consciousness", 179n.12
Dyke, 53, 92, 101, 185n.45;
López "Trying to Be a Dyke and a Chicana", 70–71;

Index

Native tradition and, 84. *See also* Queen B/Bee; Queen Boudica

Earth Mother. *See* Mother Earth
Erdrich, Louise. Native American identity and, 184n.34
Essentialism, xi, xvi, xxv, 4, 14, 34, 35, 81, 82, 170–173, 174, 192n 82;
Asian-American identity and, 30;
Black identity and, 20–24;
Latina identity and, 25–27;
Strategic, xxiii, 3, 4, 18, 21, 23, 34, 170. *See also* Construction(ism); Fuss, Diana
Ethnicity, ix, x, xi, xv, xxv, 6, 71, 97, 136, 139, 171–173, 177–178n.4, 181–182n.26;
identity and, xix, xxvi, 5, 73, 75, 89, 91, 107, 138, 143, 165, 171, 173, 174, 180n.19, 181n 25, 184n.40, 187n.58;
identity politics and, 4–5;
theory and, xvi, xxiii, xxiv, 18–36, 134, 179–180n.13, 184n.38. *See also* Race; Sollors, Werner
Eva's Man (Jones), xxiii, 44, 190n.73

Farwell, Marilyn R., 16–17
Feminist(ism), xvi, xvii, xxii, 4, 6, 24, 31, 32, 39, 88, 89, 149, 178n.7, 180n.13, 180n.18, 187n.58;
Asian-American, 81,
Black, 19, 20–21, 55, 122, 157, 181n 24, 185n.48;
Chicanas/Latinas and, xi, 27, 57, 60, 62, 148, 182n.27;
French 177n.4,
la mestiza and, xxiv, 145, 173;
lesbian, xxiv, 10–18, 40, 185n.48,
Native American, 32, 81, 149, 191n.76;
theory, white, ix, x, xv, 6, 7–11, 40, 81, 145, 173, 177n.4, 184n.39, 186n.50;
theory, of color, ix, x, xii, 6–11, 40, 177n.1, 180n.16;
See also Anzaldúa, Gloria; Butler, Judith; Fuss, Diana; hooks, bell; Moraga, Cherríe
Ferguson, Ann: *Lesbian Cultures and Theories,* 40–41
Foucault, Michel, xvii, 141; *The History of Sexuality,* 12, 164–165. *See also* Butler, Judith
Frankenberg, Ruth: *White Women, Race Matters: The Social Construction of Whiteness,* 8–9, 180n.17
Fuss, Diana, ix, *Essentially Speaking: Feminism, Nature and Difference,* 4–5, 192n.82; *Inside/Out. Lesbian Theories, Gay Theories,* 14–15, 164, 180n.19

Gates, Henry Louis, Jr., 19, 21; "signifying", 22
Gay(s), 69, 79, 85, 94, 100, 102, 133, 156, 170, 174, 180n.18, 181n.22, 192n.80,
Blacks, homophobia and, 44–45, 160;
civil rights 6, 53;
community, 49, 80, 127;
culture, Asian and, 75–76, ;
gay-girl. *See* Lesbian;
identity, 4, 14, 18, 40, 153;

myth, 120;
sexuality, Asian American and, xi,
studies, 3, 14, 15, 167, 168;
theory, 14, 107. *See also* Drag queens; Lesbian; Lorde, Audre
Gender, ix, xi, xviii, xxi, xxvii, 30, 89, 91, 134, 138, 140, 142, 154, 160, 165, 171, 178n.9, 179n.12, 189n.67;
as difference, xv;
identity, xvi, xvii, xix, xx, 41, 81, 89, 137, 141, 164, 167, 169, 174, 189n.68;
studies, ix, x, 3, 7; *See also* Butler, Judith; Gender danger
Gender trouble. *See* Butler, Judith
Gender danger, xix, xxiv, 90
Geok-lin Lim, Shirley, 107;
Asian American identity 28–29;
The Forbidden Stitch 28–29
Gomez, Jewelle, 101, 159, 185n.47, 185.48
Grandmothers: as heritage, 152, 153;
as representative of cultural difference, 79, 133;
in literature, 68, 109, 121

H, Pamela, 76, 77, 78
Hagedorn, Jessica: Asian American identity, 29–20;
Charlie Chan is Dead, 29–30
Heterosexism(ist), 62, 81, 89;
language and, 91–92. *See also* Heterosexual, Homophobia
Heterosexual(ity), 6, 14, 15–16, 29, 44, 45, 51, 53, 69, 75, 80, 83, 86, 91, 97, 101, 107, 110, 117, 126, 130, 139, 186n.55;
compulsory, xvii, 12–13, 39, 47, 61, 74, 98, 101–105, 109, 112, 118, 121, 127, 131, 141, 164, 167;
Jones's *Corregidora* and, 53–55;
privilege, xvi
Homophobia, ix, 93, 96, 107, 109, 125, 126, 136, 144, 190–191n.73,
in Black community, 44–48, 100, 118;
in Gayl Jones's writing, 53–55, 185n.47;
in Native American community, 108
Homosexual(ity), xv, xxvi, 15, 75, 126, 159, 164;
Asian-American community and, 75–77, 80;
Black community and ,44–46, 56, 101;
Chicano community and ,61;
definitions of, 11, 13;
spiritual power and, 120–122. *See also* Gay; Homophobia; Lesbian; Queer
hooks, bell: *Ain't I A Woman: Black Women and Feminism,* 9–10, 43, 180n.16;
Feminist Theory: From Margin to Center, 7;
"Is Paris Burning?", 93–95, 169;
on stereotypes, 43;
on white supremacy, 7, 9–10, 11, 93–95
Hybrid(ity), xxv, 143, 144, 179n.12. See also *La mestiza*

Identity. *See* Academy, Activism, Asian-American, Authenticity, Black, Chicanas, Construction(ism), Culture, Essentialism,

Index

Ethnicity, Gay(s), Gender, Latino/a, Lesbian Immigration, and Asian-Americans, 71–73, 74, 75, 186n.52, 186n.53

Jones, Gayl: *Corregidora*, xxiii, and homophobia, 53–55;
Eva's Man, xxiii, and Queen B, 44, 190n.73
Judit. "Border Conflict", 69

Keating, AnaLouise, 158–159
Kim, Willyce, 77–78

La Llorona, 59
La Malinche, 59–60. *See also* Virgin of Guadalupe
La madre. See Mother
La mestiza, xiii, xxiv, xxvii, 26, 58, 69, 137, 140–143, 145–146, 157, 160–161, 165, 172, 173, 174, 179n.12, 182n.31, 189n.69, 189n 70, 189–190n.71, 191n.75, 192n.83;
See also Anzaldúa, Gloria; Vasconcelos, Jose; Performing la mestiza
Latin America(n), 25, 57–58, 59, 96
Latina/o, xi, xii, xxvi, 5, 24, 25–27, 56–71, 75, 104, 112, 114, 125, 140, 162, 181n.25, 181–182n.26, 182n.28, 185–186n.49, 189n.70, 191n.74;
feminism, 9, 182n.27;
See also Chicanas
Lee, C. Allyson, 80, 131–132
Leong, Russell: *Asian American Sexualities: Dimensions of the Gay and Lesbian Experience*, xi

Lesbian, xxii, 6, 35, 39, 46, 70, 136, 171, 178n.8, 178n.10, 181n.24, 185n.48, 190n.72;
identity, xi, xvii, xviii, xxii, xxvi, 4, 11–18, 122, 134, 136, 173, 188n.61;
studies, 3, 15–16, 39, 41, 167, 168;
of color xii-xiii, xv, xvi, xviii, xix, xxii, xxiii, xxiv, xxv, xxvi, xxvii, 3, 4, 5, 10, 22, 25, 34–35, 36–37, 39–40, 70, 88–90, 91, 92, 93–94, 95, 97–98, 122, 135, 137, 140, 146, 147, 160–161, 163, 164–170, 172, 173–175, 178n.5, 179n.11, 184n.39, 188n.64, 189n.67, 189n.69, 190n.73, 192n.80, 192n.83;
theory, xvi, xxiii, xxiv, 10–18, 25, 40–41, 138–139, 144–146, 147, 184n.38;
See also American Indian, Asian-American(s), Black, Chicanas, Native American, White, Zami
Leung, Patrice: "On Iconography", 130–131
López, Natashia: "Trying to be Dyke and Chicana", 70–71
Lorde, Audre, 119, 124, 189n.70, 191n.78;
A Burst of Light, 102;
Sister Outsider, 180n.16;
Zami: A New Spelling of My Name, xxiii, xxiv, 49–53, 98–100, 122, 156–159, 162–163, 165, 171–172, 185n.46, 191n.77, 191n.79
Loving in the War Years (Moraga), xv, xxiii, 59–60, 63–64, 69–70, 84, 123–124, 147–149, 172, 180n.14

Lugones, María, 179n 12

Macho, 44, 88, 124. *See also* Black men, Latino
Madison, D. Soyini: *The Woman That I Am*, 59, 72, 73, 74
Malintzin *See La Malinche*
Marina. *See La Malinche*
Maternal symbols, 59. *See also* Matriarchs, Mother; Motherhood
Matriarchs, stereotypes of, 43–44, 56. *See also* Maternal symbols
Matrilineal. *See* Mother
Mazumdar, Sucheta, 186n.52, 186n.53;
  stereotypes, Asian-American 74–75, 76–77
Men, xx, 7, 8, 12–13, 32, 42–43, 45, 51–52, 60, 62, 63, 64, 65, 71, 73, 74, 80, 81, 94, 95, 97, 102, 162, 181n.22, 181n.25;
  in literature 47, 48, 49, 55, 65, 66, 67, 68, 101, 103, 104, 105, 110, 111, 113, 115, 119, 126, 127, 151, 152, 190n.73. *See also* Macho
Mestiza/o. See *La Mestiza*
Mexican-American. *See* Chicanas, Latina/o, Mexican/*Mexicana/o*
Mexican/*Mexicana/o*, 50, 57, 66, 108, 114, 171;
  culture, xxiv, xxvi, 59, 140, 144, 189–190n.71, 191n.79;
  identity, 59, 105, 125, 137, 141, 142, 187n 56. *See also* Chicanas;
  La Mestiza
Mexico, 57, 66, 162, 163, 172, 185n.49, 187n.56

Mixquihuala Letters, The (Castillo, Ana), 65–67, 102–105, 108–110
Mohanty, Chandra Talpade: *Third World Women and the Politics of Feminism*, 180n.16
Mohawk Trail (Brant), xxiv, 84–86, 116–118, 132, 154–156
Moraga, Cherríe: *Loving in the War Years*, xv, xxiii, 59–60, 63–64, 69–70, 84, 123–124, 147–149, 172, 180n.14;
  This Bridge Called My Back, 6, 168
Morrison, Toni. *Playing in the Dark*, 19, 24
Mother, 16, 47, 49, 59, 60, 66, 77, 78, 87, 98, 114, 150, 152, 153, 155;
  and daughter's sexuality, 78, 103, 148, 150, 157–158, 186–187n.55;
  as a role, 20, 59, 60, 74, 86, 116, 117, 189n.70;
  as connection to heritage, 158;
  Virgin Mother, the, 59, 60. *See also* Virgin of Guadalupe; Motherhood
"Mother and Daughter" (Noda), 78
Mother Earth, 59, 187n.59;
  Native women stereotyped as, 32, 85, 86
Motherhood: as a virtue 59;
  as oppressive to women 104, 106. *See also* Mother

Native American, 58;
  culture, 129, 152, 154, 163;
  history, 81–83;
  identity, 33, 180–181n.20;

Index

lesbians, 83–86, 88, 108, 117–118, 129–130, 149–156, 191n.76,
literary tradition, 33;
women, 32, 59, 81, 85, 86–88, 116–118, 149–155, 180n.20;
queers, xxvi. *See also* American Indian; Allen, Paula Gunn; Brant, Beth; Vizenor, Gerald

Naylor, Gloria: *The Women of Brewster Place,* 46–49, 51, 125–129, 188n.65

Noda, Barbara: "Mother and Daughter", 78

"Notes from a Chicana Coed" (Zamora), 62–63

"On Iconography" (Leung), 130–131

Oriental, 77;
as sexual stereotype, 73–74. *See also* Asian; Asian-American

Ortega, Eliana, 24

Paradox, 165, 170;
and identity, xxvi, 37, 80, 140, 156, 160, 161, 163, 170, 174, 190n.72;
in Latin American culture, 59;
mestiza as embodiment of, xxv, 143, 189n.69;
of Gay and Lesbian Studies, 14

Passing: as identity construction, 5, 45, 89, 92, 94, 119, 122, 125, 133–134

Penelope, Julia: "Sexual Identity/Textual Politics: Lesbian [De]Compositions", 12–13

Performance: of identity, xi, xviii–xix, xxi, xxvi, 5, 49–50, 53, 92, 100, 133, 134, 136, 137, 139, 142, 143, 156, 159, 160, 161, 170–172, 178n.9

Performance theory, xvii, xviii–xix, xxi, xxii, xxvii–xxviii, 5, 89, 91–95, 138, 140, 168, 169, 178n.9. *See also* Butler, Judith

Performing La Mestiza, xxvii, 143, 163–165, 172–177. *See also* Anzaldúa, Gloria; *La Mestiza*

Poststructuralism: and African American literature, 21, 23;
and identity, 95–96

Publishing: women of color and, xii, 31, 77, 190n.72

Queen B/Bee, 44, 190n.73. *See also* Black, stereotypes.

Queen Boudica, 184–185n.45

Queer. as insult, 92;
identity, xix, xxvi, 44, 64, 133–134, 138, 161;
theory, ix, 5, 14, 15, 138–139, 164, 179n.13

Race: and feminism, ix, x, xii, xv, 7–11, 134;
and identity, ix-x, xvi-xviii, xix, xxiv-xxvi, 5, 18, 25, 33–34, 35–36, 50–51, 71, 73, 89, 130, 138, 143, 156, 160, 162–163, 167–168, 173, 181n.25, 187n.85;
and oppression, 6, 7–10, 27, 39, 51–53, 67, 72, 74, 81, 96, 108, 122, 136, 189n.68;
and purity, xxv, 141;
blending of, 58;
theories of, xvi, xxii, xxviii, 18, 29, 34, 137–139, 143, 179n.13, 184n.38, 184n.39;

whiteness and, xvi, 8–9, 19, 169, 178n.8;
See also Construction(ism); Ethnicity
Racism. See Race
Ramos, Juanita, 60
Religion, 44, 56–57, 71, 82;
as oppressive, 59, 105, 118–122;
Macumba/Yoruba, 191n.78
Representation. See Identity, Performance
Representative (canonized), ix, x, 24, 53, 188n.65
Rich, Adrienne: "Compulsory Heterosexuality and Lesbian Existence", 11–12, 105, 157. See also Heterosexuality, compulsory
Role-play, xx, 133, 178n.9

Saldívar, Ramon: *Chicano Narrative. The Dialectics of Difference*, 27, 182n.28
Sandoval, Chela: and "oppositional consciousness", 179n.12
Sapogonia (Castillo, Ana) 67–69, 104–106, 110–116, 188n.60
Say Jesus and Come to Me (Shockely), 55–56, 100–102, 118–119, 159–160
Sexism, 136: and language, 91–92. See also Heterosexuality; Heterosexism; Homophobia; Identity
Sexual: abuse, xx, 6, 42–43, 189n 68;
behavior defining identity, 11–12, 13, 35, 68, 74, 109, 113, 115,
bonds, 108, 111, 118, 177n.2;
feelings, 13, 80, 106, 110, 123–124, 188n.61, 189n.67;
oppression, 6, 8, 13, 41, 59–60, 67, 74, 84, 104, 123, 132
Sexuality: and power, 16, 44, 63, 68, 101, 149, 155;
as healing, 116–117;
as identity, xvi, xviii, 11–12, 13, 15–17, 34, 41, 54, 61, 99, 119, 134, 137–138, 148, 160, 162–164, 165, 167, 168, 179n.13, 187n.58;
as shameful, 56, 118, 186n.55;
See also Gender; Homosexual; Heterosexual; Identity
Shockley, Ann Allen: controversy about, 185n.48;
"The Black Lesbian in American Literature: An Overview", 44–45;
Say Jesus and Come to Me, 55–56, 100–102, 118–119, 159–160
Silvera, Makeda: *Piece of My Heart: A Lesbian of Colour Anthology*, 39–40
Smith, Barbara, 22;
critique of *The Color Purple* 190n.73;
"The Truth That Never Hurts: Black Lesbians in Fiction in the 1980s", 125–126, 129, 188n.65;
"Toward a Black Feminist Criticism", 20–21
So Far From God (Castillo, Ana), 119–122
Social construction. See Constructionism
Sollors, Werner: *The Invention of Ethnicity*, 35–36
Sternbach, Nancy Saporta, 24

Index

Strategic essentialism. *See* Essentialism

Tokenism, of women of color, xvii, xxvii;
in Feminism, x; 177n 1;
of Audre Lorde, 49, 185n.46
Tonantzin. *See* Virgin of Guadalupe
Torres, Lourdes: "The Construction of Self in U.S. Latina Autobiographies", 95–96
Trujillo, Carla: "Chicana Lesbians. Fear and Loathing in the Chicano Community", 60–61, 124–, 147
"Trying to Be a Dyke and a Chicana" (López), 70–71
Tsui, Kitty, 96;
"A Chinese Banquet", 78–79;
"Breaking Silence, Making Waves and Loving Ourselves: The Politics of Coming Out and Coming Home", 79–80

Vasconcelas, Jose, "una raza mestiza", xxv
Violence, 173;
history of racial, 18–19, 172;
against lesbians of color, 40, 47–49, 136;
of male dominance, 105–106;
male, xxi. *See also* Homophobia;
Sexual abuse
Virgin Mary, the. *See* Virgin of Guadalupe
Virgin of Guadalupe, the, 57, 59;
as Latina symbol, 59–60, 148. *See also* Mother;
La malinche

Vizneor, Gerald: *Narrative Chance. Postmodern Discourse on Native American Indian Literature*, 34, 183n.36, 183–184n.37

Walker, Alice, "In Search of Our Mother's Gardens", 20;
The Color Purple, 190n.73
Warhol, Robyn R.: *Feminisms*, ix, x
White, xxvi, 19–20, 21, 22, 23, 25, 26, 27, 31, 33, 40, 59, 70, 77, 82, 96, 118, 129, 133, 149, 150, 169, 174;
as a race, xvi, xxv, 5, 19, 28, 70, 136, 178n.8, 184n.41;
beauty, 52, 80–81, 122, 130–132, 180n 18, 189n.68;
disease, homosexuality as, 76, 102, 112;
patriarchy, 6, 29, 43, 52, 106, 111–112;
privilege, 6, 7–11, 167, 169–170, 184n.39, 188n.64;
sexuality, 168
White supremacy, ix, xv, xvi, xxi, 7–9, 24, 27, 29, 30, 35, 81, 92–95, 137, 139, 189n.68. *See also* Racism
White women: and feminism, x, 6, 7–11, 81, 85, 137, 144–146, 173, 177–178n.4, 186n.50;
and identity theory, xvi, xix-xxi, 8–11, 14, 34–35, 39–41, 49, 59, 70, 133, 136, 137–139, 140, 165, 173, 178n.6, 184n.39, 185n.46;
and performance, 92–95, 134, 163;
as opposite of Black women, 42,

lesbians and oppression of lesbians of color, 50–51, 52, 85–86, 118–119, 122, 132, 143, 170, 172
Witch. *See bruja*
Wittig, Monique: *The Straight Mind*, 164
Wolfe, Susan J: "Sexual Identity/Textual Politics: Lesbian [De]Compositions", 12–13
Woman Who Owned the Shadows, The (Allen), xxiii, 86–88, 129–130, 149–154
Women. *See* Academy; African-American; Asian; Asian-American; American Indian; Black; Chicanas; Feminist; Gender; Latina/o; Lesbian; Maternal symbols Native-American; Sexism; White women.
Women of Brewster Place, The (Naylor), 46–49, 51, 125–129, 188n.65
Women's movement (second wave), xv, 6–7, 8, 32, 70, 85, 133, 134
Women's Studies, 15, 19, 185n.48
Wong, Christine. *Yellow Queer*, 133–134

Yarbro-Bejarano, Yvonne: "Chicana Literature from a Chicana Feminist Perspective", 62;
"Expanding the Categories of Race and Sexuality in Lesbian and Gay Studies", xvi, xviii, xxvii-xxviii, 146, 167–168, 192n.80;
"The Lesbian Body in Latina Cultural Production", 191n.74;
"The Multiple Subject in the Writing of Ana Castillo", 96, 104, 105–106
Yellow Queer (Wong), 133–134

Zami, xiii, xxiv, 49–53, 98–100, 122, 156–159, 162–163, 165, 171–172, 177n.2, 185n.46, 191n.77, 191n.79
Zami: A New Spelling of My Name (Lorde), xiii, xxiv, 49–53, 98–100, 122, 156–159, 162–163, 165, 171–172, 185n.46, 191n.77, 191n.79
Zamora, Bernice: "Notes from a Chicana Coed", 62–63
Zimmerman, Bonnie: *The Safe Sea of Women: Lesbian Fiction 1969–88*, 10;
"What Has Never Been. An Overview of Lesbian Feminist Literary Criticism", 10, 11